The Merchant Prince
of Black Chicago

The Merchant Prince
of Black Chicago

Anthony Overton and the Building
of a Financial Empire

ROBERT E. WEEMS JR.

**UNIVERSITY OF
ILLINOIS PRESS**
Urbana, Chicago, and Springfield

Publication of this book was supported by funding from
the Department of History at Wichita State University.

Library of Congress Cataloging-in-Publication Data
Names: Weems, Robert E., 1951– author.
Title: The merchant prince of Black Chicago : Anthony
    Overton and the building of a financial empire /
    Robert E. Weems Jr. .
Description: Urbana : University of Illinois Press, [2020]
    | Includes bibliographical references and index.
Identifiers: LCCN 2019032957 (print) | LCCN
    2019032958 (ebook) | ISBN 9780252043062 (cloth) |
    ISBN 9780252084935 (paperback) |
    ISBN 9780252051920 (ebook)
Subjects: LCSH: Overton, Anthony, –1946. | African
    American businesspeople—Illinois—Chicago—
    Biography. | African American capitalists and
    financiers—Illinois—Chicago—Biography. |
    African American business enterprises—History—
    20th century.
Classification: LCC HC102.5.O88 W44 2020 (print) |
    LCC HC102.5.O88 (ebook) | DDC 338.092 [B]—dc23
LC record available at https://lccn.loc.gov/2019032957
LC ebook record available at https://lccn.loc.gov
    /2019032958

This book is lovingly dedicated to the memory of Dolores J. Weems, my mom and #1 fan.

Contents

Acknowledgments   ix

Introduction   1

1. Anthony Overton's Early Life: Myth versus Reality   11

2. A Star Is Born: Initial Years in Chicago   45

3. The *Half-Century Magazine*: 1916–1925   62

4. Business Titan: The Douglass National Bank and the Victory Life Insurance Company   79

5. What Goes Up Must Come Down: The Impact of the Great Depression   118

Epilogue: Final Years and Legacy   143

Appendix A: North Carolina Mutual Life Insurance Company   163

Appendix B: Atlanta Life Insurance Company   164

Appendix C: Liberty Life Insurance Company   165

Appendix D: Victory Life Insurance Company   166

Notes   167

Selected Bibliography   193

Index   201

Acknowledgments

This biography of the African American businessman Anthony Overton could not have been produced without the assistance and support of a wide variety of institutions and individuals. First, I want to thank my former employer, the University of Missouri–Columbia, and the University of Missouri Research Board, for providing the financial support to conduct my initial research on Anthony Overton. This funding allowed me to gather information related to Anthony Overton's first forty-seven years of life on research trips to Monroe, Louisiana; Topeka, Kansas; Oklahoma City/Kingfisher, Oklahoma; and Kansas City, Missouri. The following local libraries and repositories were especially helpful: Ouachita Parish [Louisiana] Public Library, Special Collections; University of Louisiana–Monroe Library, Special Collections; Kansas Historical Society; University Archives, Mabee Library, Washburn University; Topeka & Shawnee County Public Library, Special Collections; Oklahoma Historical Society; Kingfisher Memorial Library, Special Collections; Kansas City, Missouri Public Library, Special Collections. In addition, funds from the University of Missouri Research Board underwrote a research trip to Harvard University's Baker Library, where I examined pertinent historic Dun & Bradstreet reports. Finally, in terms of my research related to Anthony Overton's formative years, I want to thank Letha Johnson and Deborah L. Dandridge, archivists at the University of Kansas, for their assistance in helping me establish the contours of his aborted matriculation there in the 1880s.

Anthony Overton's 1911 move to Chicago proved to be an extremely profitable decision. During his subsequent years in the Windy City, he evolved from a moderately successful entrepreneur into a literal tycoon. My receipt of a 2010 Summer Fellowship from the Black Metropolis Research Consortium (BMRC), based at the University of Chicago, provided me the opportunity to do in-depth research in the city where Anthony Overton truly made his mark as a businessman. As a BMRC Fellow, I was able to collect data from the following repositories: Regenstein Library, University of Chicago, Special Collections; Vivian Harsh Collection, Carter G. Woodson Regional Library; National Archives; Chicago History Museum (Claude A. Barnett Papers); and the Christopher R. Reed Collection at Roosevelt University. Not only did I have the opportunity to consult Christopher Reed's papers, but he also graciously granted me his own time. Reed, who served as a consultant to the BMRC, is regarded as this generation's leading historian of black Chicago. His ongoing encouragement and support have been much appreciated. Two other colleagues associated with my experience with the BMRC that I want to acknowledge are historian Adam Green of the University of Chicago and Tamar Evangelista-Dougherty, who served as the Black Metropolis Research Consortium's archivist consultant. Tamar helped me understand that it is not unusual for companies to destroy their records when they cease operations. Finally, I want to acknowledge the assistance of Bea Julian, the former archivist at the BMRC partner DuSable Museum of African American History. Through her intercession, the Papers of Olive Diggs (Diggs was the editor of the Overton-controlled *Chicago Bee* newspaper), were subsequently made available to me.

I also want to thank my current employer, Wichita State University, and particularly the College of Liberal Arts & Sciences (LAS). Besides helping to underwrite research trips to Lawrence, Kansas, Chicago, the Louisiana State Archives in Baton Rouge, and the Library of Congress, LAS also hosted and promoted public lectures related to my Anthony Overton research. Developing the following four presentations: "The Making of an African American Tycoon: Anthony Overton's Business Activities, 1915–1925"; "The 'Merchant Prince of his Race': Anthony Overton's Business Conglomerate during the 1920s"; "What Goes Up, Must Come Down: Anthony Overton and the Great Depression"; and "Whatever Happened to Anthony Overton? The Final Years and Legacy of a Noteworthy African American Entrepreneur" helped me to better conceptualize the contours of this individual's life and career.

Although this biography focuses on Anthony Overton's business activities, it also discusses aspects of his personal life. My desire to tell this part of Overton's story benefited immeasurably from the openness with which his descendants met my requests for information. An extended personal interview with Sheila Overton-Levi, Anthony Overton's granddaughter, generated a wealth of information regarding this complex man. Also, Sheila helped put me in touch with other descendants of Anthony Overton: Sharon F. Patton, Sheila Green, Emily Bates, and Sandra Jones. In addition, Sharon, Emily, and Sandra shared with me priceless family pictures that are reproduced in this book (along with one from another relative, Martha Harriet Bryant). Another member of the Overton family tree, Dr. James Overton, shared information regarding Anthony Overton's family lineage. He has conducted painstaking genealogical research related to Anthony Overton's father, Anthony ("Antoine") Overton Sr. Finally, Frank Overton, the grandson of Anthony Overton's older brother, Mack Wilson Overton, shared with me pertinent information regarding his grandfather, who was also an entrepreneur.

As with many entrepreneurs, including his father, Anthony Overton's children participated in his business activities. This included sons-in-law Dr. Julian Lewis and Richard Hill Jr., Esq. In this regard, I want to extend a special thanks to Robert Branch II, who has conducted extensive research on Lewis. Over the years we have shared information about our respective projects. Also, he and Dr. James Overton are collaborating on a family history that links the black and the white Overtons. In addition, thanks are due to Ross Slacks, the executive director of the Northeast Louisiana Delta African American Museum (whom I met through Robert Branch II) for granting me permission to reproduce here an oil painting of Anthony Overton's father.

Personal interviews were not a major part of the research methodology for this biography. Nevertheless, apart from my discussions with Overton descendants and relatives, four others stand out as having provided interesting and helpful information. Tim Samuelson, the cultural historian of the City of Chicago, who in the 1980s spearheaded the subsequent renovation of the historic Overton Hygienic Manufacturing Building and the *Chicago Bee* Building. Harold Lucas, a business-minded community activist in Chicago, not only worked with Samuelson regarding the restoration of Anthony Overton's black Chicago commercial structures, but he has also worked to mobilize support for the revitalization of Chicago's entire historic Bronzeville district. Robert Howard, a member of the Black Chicago History Forum, shared information with me about the relationship between Anthony Overton and fellow black Chicago banker Jesse Binga. Centenarian Timuel Black, the griot of black Chicago, knew Anthony Overton and provided important insights about Overton and his legacy. I thank you all most sincerely for your time and assistance.

During the course of working on this biography of Anthony Overton, a number of colleagues have offered encouragement and support. Besides Christopher Reed, I want to especially thank Juliet E. K. Walker for being a longtime supporter of my work. Others who stand out in this regard include

John Sibley Butler, Jason Chambers, Clovis Semmes, Kenneth Hamilton, Jonathan Bean, and Jim Stewart. I also want to acknowledge the assistance of Chajuana Trawick, who shared with me pertinent information about Annie Turnbo-Malone, one of Anthony Overton's business competitors.

Dawn Durante, senior acquisitions editor at the University of Illinois Press, helped me craft this published version of Anthony Overton's story. The suggestions of the outside reviewers definitely enhanced the finished product.

Finally, like Anthony Overton, family plays a big part of my life. Besides my deceased mother, who this book is dedicated to, I want to thank my dad, sisters, brother-in-law, cousins, nieces, and nephews for their long-standing and ongoing love and support. Similarly, I want to thank my wife, Nisha, and daughters Morgan, Madison, and Mya for their love and inspiration.

Introduction

Anthony Overton is widely regarded as one of twentieth century's most significant African American entrepreneurs. The first businessman to win the NAACP's prestigious Spingarn Medal (in 1927); Overton, at his peak, presided over a Chicago-based financial empire that included a personal care products company (Overton Hygienic Manufacturing Company), an insurance company (Victory Life Insurance Company), a bank (Douglass National Bank), a popular periodical (the *Half-Century Magazine*) and a newspaper (*Chicago Bee*). Moreover, due to these accomplishments, he is currently cited by the Harvard University Business School's database of "American Business Leaders of the Twentieth Century" as the first African American to head a major business conglomerate.[1]

Despite Overton's impressive entrepreneurial accomplishments, he remains a mysterious figure. The most readily apparent reason for this is the unavailability of his business records and personal papers. When Overton's cornerstone enterprise, the Overton Hygienic Manufacturing Company, closed its doors in 1983, then company president Anthony Overton III (Overton's grandson) discarded company artifacts.[2] Also, in his 1967 *Black Chicago: The Making of a Negro Ghetto, 1890–1920*, Allan Spear states that Anthony Overton's unpublished memoirs were in the possession of Olive Diggs, who had served as editor of the *Chicago Bee* newspaper for several years.[3] However, a 2012 examination of Olive Diggs's papers at Chicago's DuSable Museum of African American History did not uncover this extremely relevant document.

Besides the destruction of company records (including photographs) and the apparent disappearance of Anthony Overton's memoirs, determining the contours of Anthony Overton's life, especially his formative years, has been complicated by a long-standing dissemination of misinformation. Chapter 1 surveys the myth versus the reality of Anthony Overton's pre-Chicago activities. Much of the literature—including encyclopedia entries, book chapters, newspaper articles, and obituaries—incorrectly portrays Overton as a literal young Renaissance man. According to this historiography, Anthony Overton, between his sixteenth and thirty-first birthdays (1880–95), was a teenage business prodigy in Topeka; had earned a law degree from the University of Kansas and returned to Topeka as a municipal judge; worked as a Pullman porter; and opened a variety of successful enterprises and was elected to political office in Oklahoma Territory. Moreover, Overton, himself, contributed to this distorted narrative of his teenage and young adult experiences.

A considerable amount of misinformation concerns the early life of Anthony Overton, which is not a phenomenon unique to this African American business leader. Thomas A. Bailey's April 18, 1968, presidential address to the Organization of American Historians (later expanded on and published in the *Journal of American History*), titled "The Mythmakers of American History," begins by noting that "we need only imagine how different our national history would be if countless millions of our citizens had not been brought up to believe in the manifestly destined superiority of the American people, in the supremacy of the white race, [and] in the primacy of the Nordics within the white race." Moreover, Bailey contends, "too many historical writers are the votaries of cults, which by definition are dedicated to whitewashing warts and hanging halos."[4]

While Thomas Bailey conveys his criticism of certain aspects of historical writing, he expresses caution regarding revisionist history: "we certainly cannot get at the solid timber of truth unless we first clear away the underbrush of myth and legend. But the historian who spends his life hacking at underbrush in search of shockers is misapplying his talents."[5] This admonition appears to have an ironic relevance in the context of Anthony Overton's early life. Although chapter 1 debunks the myth of Anthony Overton as a young Renaissance man, this narrative evolved as an unintended consequence of preliminary research. Historians are trained to examine surviving works on a subject to not only ascertain what has been written but also to ascertain how a new work can contribute to the literature. As has been mentioned, much of the historiography related to Anthony Overton's teenage and young adult years situates him as being successful in a variety of areas. Furthermore, because I did not know otherwise, I assumed this assessment to be true and sought to discover additional verification. Yet, as I probed deeper into this period of Anthony Overton's life, I discovered that much of what has been written is patently false. Thus, to paraphrase Thomas Bailey, I didn't search the underbrush *looking* for shockers—instead, the shockers found me.

The obvious discrepancy between what Anthony Overton (and others have) said about his early life and what I have discovered leads to the obvious question: what prompted Overton to engage in this mythmaking in the first place? Before I address this, take note that Anthony Overton is not unique in this regard. In fact, rational observation suggests there are few, if any, individuals who have *never* embellished their accomplishments to achieve their goals. As chapter 2 discusses, Anthony Overton's activities in this regard apparently commenced in earnest after he moved to Chicago. Finding himself surrounded by distinguished black Chicago businesspeople and professionals, Overton seemingly believed that enhancing his pre-Chicago activities would facilitate his acceptance by this group. Also, Overton's *contemporary accomplishments* made his pronouncements about past achievements appear credible.

Part of the ongoing nebulosity surrounding the early life of Anthony Overton involves his memoirs. Clearly, this document, which has never been found, could provide verification of whether and how Overton sought to embellish his past. In, yet, another manifestation of Anthony Overton as a mysterious and enigmatic historical figure, informed speculation suggests that the tale of Overton's memoirs may, itself, be a fabrication. As the epilogue discusses, after suffering a significant reduction in public acclaim and wealth during the Great Depression, Anthony Overton's reputation began to be rehabilitated during the early 1940s. Consequently, because of Overton's financial difficulties at the time, publishing his memoirs would have generated needed additional revenue. Also, his *Chicago Bee* newspaper, managed by Olive Diggs, could have been used as a venue to both publicize the book and to publish excerpts from Overton's memoirs to stimulate public interest. Considering Anthony Overton's documented skills as a shrewd businessman, the fact that he did not take advantage of this income opportunity suggests that he had nothing to market.

One of the tasks of a biographer is to objectively convey the complexity and nuances of the individual being studied. In the case of Anthony Overton, we see someone who sometimes exhibited contradictory behavior patterns. Notwithstanding his tendency to periodically exaggerate his early life accomplishments, Overton was not a braggart. In fact, he was widely perceived to be low-key and unassuming. As an extended obituary of Overton that appeared in the July 1947 issue of the *Journal of Negro History* notes, "Anthony Overton, after all, was a modest man. He was never extravagant and never thus indulged his family. He never lived in a fine home and never owned an automobile for his own use. He used practically all his means for the development of his enterprises and owed none of his failures to personal extravagance."[6] In retrospect, Overton's attempt to reconstruct his pre-Chicago experiences seem misguided because the struggles and frustrations he endured early in life make his later *extraordinary* success all the more compelling.

Although this examination of Anthony Overton's life could not rely on the traditional sources that scholars normally rely on to construct a biography, his prominence gave rise to a large body of scattered alternative primary and secondary sources. For example, research trips—to Monroe, Louisiana (where Overton was born and spent his first fifteen years of life); Topeka, Kansas (where Overton's family moved in 1879 as part of the "Exoduster" phenomenon); Kingfisher County, Oklahoma (where Overton and his new wife and child moved as part of the famous Land Rush of 1889); Kansas City, Kansas, and Kansas City, Missouri (where Overton actually started the Overton Hygienic Manufacturing Company) and Chicago, Illinois (where Overton moved in 1911)—were extremely helpful in constructing the contours of his life. Materials generated from these research trips were especially useful in determining the myth versus the reality of Overton's early years.

A fact-based overview of Anthony Overton's pre-Chicago experiences, also presented in chapter 1, reveals the important influence of three individuals. First and foremost, Overton's father, Anthony Overton Sr., had an enormous impact on his namesake. The elder Overton, also referred to as "Antoine," was both a successful merchant in post–Civil War Monroe, Louisiana, and a prominent Reconstruction-era Republican politician. He, no doubt, served as a model of emulation for Anthony Overton Jr. and his older brother, Mack. Second, the Philadelphia retailer John Wanamaker was an important source of inspiration to Anthony Overton Jr. The most compelling evidence in this regard is that Overton, as the apparent leader of an African American contingent participating in the 1889 Oklahoma Land Rush, convinced his compatriots to name their subsequent settlement Wanamaker. Finally, Booker T. Washington influenced the thinking of the young Anthony Overton. Overton's subsequent association with Washington's National Negro Business League (NNBL) illuminates an important dynamic of African American men's agency during the late nineteenth and early twentieth centuries. The NNBL and its precedents sought to provide ambitious black men (like Overton) the encouragement to actively seek a place in America's growing capitalist economy. Moreover, unlike the era's so-called robber barons whose commercial success came at the expense of others, Washington urged Overton and other black entrepreneurs to establish enterprises that served the needs of the broader African American community.

Anthony Overton's 1911 move to Chicago marks a major milestone and turning point. At the time, his Overton Hygienic Manufacturing Company, established in Kansas City, Missouri, in 1898, was a moderately successful enterprise. Although Overton's company began by producing baking powder, he quickly realized there was a potentially bigger market for face powder that complimented and enhanced the complexions of African American women. Thus, around 1900, he launched his pioneering High-Brown Face Powder. Moreover, within a few years, Overton expanded the High-Brown product line to include a variety of beauty preparations aimed at black female consumers.[7] Still, despite Overton Hygienic's promising start as a business entity, the ambitious young entrepreneur soon concluded that his company's growth opportunities in Kansas City were limited. Thus, Overton, like thousands of African Americans before and after him, migrated to Chicago to seek a better life and more opportunity. Among other things, Overton believed that Chicago, with its network of railroads that facilitated the distribution of products, would be an economic boon to his young business.

Chapter 2 relates that Anthony Overton moved to Chicago at an especially opportune time. During the late nineteenth century, before his arrival, Chicago's black leaders focused their attention on desegregating all areas of civic life and concurrently deemphasized the importance of race-based institutions. However, after 1900, in the wake of growing white hostility, black Chicago leaders increasingly adopted "a northern variation of the philosophy of racial solidarity and self-help that had emerged in the post-Reconstruction South and had found its greatest vogue in the teachings of Booker T. Washington."[8] Moreover, from a business standpoint, as Chicago's African American population steadily increased, it became conceivable that black Chicago could sustain a separate economic infrastructure.

In this favorable business environment, the Overton Hygienic Manufacturing Company increased its corporate viability. While Overton Hygienic records do not survive, the Library of Congress holds reports generated by Dun & Bradstreet, the preeminent business financial reporting agency, which yield pertinent fiscal data for much of the company's existence. Also, during his first years in Chicago, Anthony Overton quickly established himself as a black community leader. Still, this was a bittersweet period in his life. Within a year after moving to Chicago, his wife and business partner, Clara Gregg Overton, suddenly passed away. Moreover, the evidence also suggests that after Clara's death, Overton began to consciously embellish his past activities and accomplishments. Because his wife, the only person who knew otherwise, was now deceased, this facilitated Overton's reinvention of his pre-Chicago career. Finally, after Clara's death, Overton began to more fully incorporate his son (Everett) and his three daughters (Eva, Mabel, and Frances) into company operations. This culminated in the successful 1915 opening of a branch office staffed entirely by women, including his daughters. Later, in 1915, Overton's female staff created a sensation by demonstrating the use of Overton Hygienic beauty products at the Lincoln Jubilee, a national exhibition held in Chicago to celebrate fifty years of African American freedom.

By the middle of the second decade of the twentieth century, Anthony Overton presided over one of the major companies in the growing (and increasingly competitive) African American personal care products industry. In this context, Overton realized that, above and beyond his female-staffed branch office, he needed an advertising venue that allowed his products to truly *stand out* in an increasingly crowded marketplace. Chapter 3 discusses how Overton used the *Half-Century Magazine* to accomplish this aim. Importantly, Overton, in a seeming attempt to deflect charges of shameless self-promotion, shrewdly put forward a female associate as the owner, editor, and public face of this woman-oriented periodical. Moreover, the evidence also suggests that he used anonymous editorials and a pseudonym to convey his beliefs regarding business enterprise and personal conduct to *Half-Century's* readers. In the end, Overton's skillful use of the magazine, which existed from 1916 to 1925, not only helped him to promote products produced by the Overton Hygienic Manufacturing Company but also helped him to promote other components of his growing financial empire.

As Juliet E. K. Walker and John Sibley Butler note, the 1920s represented the high point of a golden age of black business development in the United States.[9] One of the leading figures of this significant decade was Anthony Overton. Perhaps ironically, Overton, who before the 1920s possessed little to no substantive background and experience in the realms of banking and insurance, led two of the most visible African American financial institutions during this period. Besides his ongoing leadership of the Overton Hygienic Manufacturing Company; in 1922 he assumed the presidency of Chicago's Douglass National Bank (the second black-owned bank to receive a national charter). Two years later, Overton organized the Victory Life Insurance Company in Chicago. In 1927, Victory Life accomplished two unprecedented feats. First, it was the only insurance company chartered in Illinois (black or white) granted the right to conduct business in New York State. Second, it also became the first African American insurer granted the right to do business there. After this business coup, Anthony Overton, as Victory Life's president, became viewed by many as America's leading black businessman. This directly contributed to his receipt of the NAACP's 1927 Spingarn Medal and other accolades (including being referred to, in some circles, as the "Merchant Prince of His Race").

To further enhance his growing status as a business magnate during the 1920s, Overton built two major commercial structures in the heart of black Chicago's business district. The Overton building, located at 3619–27 South State Street, housed the Overton Hygienic Manufacturing Company, the Douglass National Bank, and the Victory Life Insurance Company. The *Chicago Bee* Building, located at 3647–55 South State Street, was the headquarters for this Overton-controlled periodical. Chapter 4 elaborates on Anthony Overton's evolution from a moderately successful entrepreneur into a literal tycoon. It also provides a window to observe other aspects of his complex, enigmatic, personality. During the 1920s, Anthony Overton was not only lionized in the African American press as a business genius, but he was also lauded as a humble individual who maintained his "common touch" in the midst of growing fame and fortune. Conversely, the story behind Overton's ascension to the presidency of Douglass National Bank reveals a Machiavellian, if not ruthless, component of his mindset. Moreover, the dark side of Anthony Overton's persona contributed to his commercial and personal decline during the 1930s.

Anthony Overton's success during the 1920s mirrored that of several other entrepreneurs during this decade. However, the Wall Street crash in October 1929 and the subsequent Great Depression put an end to the halcyon days of the Roaring Twenties. One casualty of this economic downturn was Anthony Overton: the 1930s witnessed not only the dissolution of the Douglass National Bank but also his ouster as president of the Victory Life Insurance Company. Chapter 5 explores this aspect of Overton's life and career and some of the business missteps that contributed to his problems.

Anthony Overton's fall from grace during the 1930s appears linked to both external and internal circumstances. When the Douglass National Bank commenced operations in 1922 and Victory Life began two years later, both institutions directed a significant amount of money (in the form of loans and investment capital) toward real estate in the African American community. At the time, this appeared to be a profitable strategy because the 1920s represented a boon period for the real estate market. However, when real estate values plummeted with the onset of the Great Depression, both Douglass National and Victory Life possessed dramatically depreciated assets. In all fairness to Anthony Overton, he was not the only person fooled by the 1920s real estate bubble. However, his long-standing funneling of Victory Life Insurance Company funds into the Douglass National Bank, which Merah S. Stuart refers to as Overton's "perplexing entanglements of the affairs of the two institutions," became increasingly problematic.[10] To make matters worse, Overton's autocratic response to the legitimate concerns of Victory Life shareholders ultimately became a public relations nightmare that led to his ouster as president of the insurer. In addition, despite creative attempts to keep the Douglass National Bank afloat during the early 1930s, this financial institution ultimately became a casualty of the Great Depression. Thus, Overton, the former "Merchant Prince of His Race," became directly associated with business failure.

Although Anthony Overton suffered a significant loss of prestige and wealth during the 1930s, he was not totally devastated by the Great Depression. He maintained control of the Overton Hygienic Manufacturing Company and the *Chicago Bee* newspaper. Yet both ultimately became tenuous financial enterprises. For instance, between 1932 and 1942, Overton Hygienic lost nearly 98 percent of its net worth.[11] Similarly, the *Chicago Bee*, for the last ten years of its existence (1937–47), regularly fell short of meeting its financial obligations to the Associated Negro Press wire service.[12]

Whereas Anthony Overton's post-1930s business portfolio was now much smaller, he remained an important business leader in black Chicago. Moreover, the 1940s witnessed a rehabilitation of Anthony Overton's image. Indeed, by the time of his death in 1946, much of the negativity associated with the early 1930s had dissipated. Nevertheless, while Anthony Overton's reputation had been salvaged, his successors at the helm of Overton Hygienic, son Everett and grandson Anthony Overton III, were unable to re-create the founder's earlier success. Among other things, by the mid-to-late twentieth century, competition within the increasingly profitable African American personal care products industry had become increasingly fierce. In addition, Overton Hygienic's corporate profile diminished further because it did not have the research and development funds to develop Afro hairstyle-related products during the late 1960s and Jheri curl–related products during the late 1970s. Thus, when Anthony Overton's core enterprise closed its doors in 1983, it was barely noticed.[13]

The epilogue examines not only Anthony Overton's final years and the succeeding history of the Overton Hygienic Manufacturing Company but also Overton's ongoing legacy. Ironically, a year after the Overton Hygienic Manufacturing Company ceased operations, a March 7, 1984, proposal submitted to the Commission on Chicago Landmarks (by the Chicago Department of Planning and Development) helped stimulate a renewed interest in the life and career of Anthony Overton. The proposal contends that the neighborhood "centered in the general vicinity of State and 35th Streets on

Chicago's Near South Side" contains some "of the most significant landmarks of African-American urban history in the United States." Two of the buildings spotlighted in this document were the Overton Hygienic Manufacturing Building and the *Chicago Bee* Building.[14] A consortium of Chicagoans subsequently began a successful campaign that resulted in the restoration of the *Chicago Bee* Building and the Overton Hygienic Manufacturing Building, as well as their designations as municipal landmarks.[15]

Besides examining the man and his accomplishments, this biography of Anthony Overton seeks to place his activities in the context of larger societal occurrences. In fact, his life intersected with some of the most important events in American and African American history in the late nineteenth and early twentieth centuries. As a boy, Overton witnessed the nuances of Reconstruction in Monroe, Louisiana. As a teenager, Anthony observed the dynamics of the Exoduster movement (when his family moved to Topeka, Kansas, for their safety). Later, as a young adult, Anthony Overton participated in the 1889 Oklahoma Land Rush. Early in the second decade of the twentieth century, Overton moved to Chicago as one of the forerunners of the Great Migration that would dramatically increase the Windy City's African American population (and would assist Overton and other black entrepreneurs). Finally, Overton personified the boom and bust attributes associated with US business during the 1920s and 1930s.

As one of the twentieth century's most significant black businessmen, Anthony Overton confirmed the ongoing linkage between creativity and perseverance with entrepreneurial success. At his core, Anthony Overton was a master marketer who continually sought new (and creative) ways to present his various products to the buying public. In a related fashion, Overton used the power of persuasion to enhance his professional persona by embellishing his past accomplishments. Yet, notwithstanding his entrepreneurial triumphs, Anthony Overton also experienced numerous trials and tribulations. Even before the trauma he experienced during the 1930s, Overton's early life featured a succession of unfulfilled goals and dreams. Moreover, the same steely determination that ultimately positioned Overton to take advantage of business opportunities in the early twentieth century later helped him to survive after the Great Depression turned his world upside down.

Another important dynamic of Anthony Overton's business success was his relationship with women. As a producer of personal care and beauty products, he was literally a man in a woman's world. Furthermore, in yet another manifestation of Overton's enigmatic persona, this conservative disciple of Booker T. Washington possessed (for the times) a fairly progressive attitude regarding women's "proper" role. Available evidence suggests that his wife, Clara, influenced Overton's thinking in this regard. The daughter of an entrepreneur, Clara Overton appears to have been more than just a dutiful housewife. During Overton Hygienic's formative years, she was an equal partner who supervised the production of the company's product line.

After Clara's death, as previously noted, Overton's daughters and other female personnel provided the company beneficial commercial visibility as product demonstrators. Later in life, after the Great Depression decimated other elements of his business empire, Overton's *Chicago Bee* newspaper had only women on the editorial staff.

Although the significance of Anthony Overton's life and career has been previously acknowledged, this book should further cement his importance as a historical figure. Moreover, by recounting Overton's life story, this biography seeks to more fully illuminate the historic role of business and entrepreneurship in the African American experience. Finally, Anthony Overton's accomplishments may help inspire a new generation of African American entrepreneurs to generate much-needed economic revitalization in black enclaves across the nation.

1. Anthony Overton's Early Life
Myth versus Reality

   Making sense of Anthony Overton's formative years represents a major challenge to anyone seeking to understand this important historical figure. Many depictions of this segment of his life possess glaring inaccuracies and misinformation. In a variety of sources, including encyclopedia entries, magazine articles, book chapters, and obituaries, Overton is incorrectly depicted as a literal young Renaissance man whose activities included owning a successful business as a teenager; earning a law degree; serving as a municipal judge in Topeka, Kansas; starting a general store, sawmill, cotton gin, and bank in the black "land rush" settlement of Wanamaker, Oklahoma; and being elected treasurer of Kingfisher County, Oklahoma. This distorted historiography, some of which Overton was the source of, seemingly sought to create a heroic past that better coincided with Overton's future success. This chapter attempts to separate fact from fiction regarding Anthony Overton Jr.'s path to his later, well-documented, entrepreneurial triumphs. It also discusses how Booker T. Washington's National Negro Business League (and its precedents) encouraged Overton, and other ambitious young black men in the late nineteenth and early twentieth century, to actively seek a place in the nation's growing capitalist economy.

Birthdate at Question

As with nearly all African Americans born as slaves, there are contradictory assertions regarding Anthony Overton's birth. While all accounts cite him as being born in Monroe, Louisiana, his birth date is uncertain. For instance, March 21, 1865, is cited in John N. Ingham and Lynne B. Feldman's 1994 reference book, *African-American Business Leaders*. This date is also used in an extensive obituary that appeared in the July 1947 issue of the *Journal of Negro History*, as well in the 1928–29 edition of *Who's Who in Colored America*. Conversely, the October 1923 issue of the *Sphinx*, the official organ of Alpha Phi Alpha Fraternity Inc., featured a story regarding Overton stating he was born in 1864. Similarly, a 1942 article in the *Chicago Defender* titled "From Slave To Wealth Is Story Of Overton," indicated his birthdate as March 18, 1864. Fortunately, census data provides some clarity, if not total precision, in this regard. In the 1870 federal census, Overton was listed as being six years old, with an estimated birth year of 1864.[1]

Family Lineage

The uncertainty surrounding Anthony Overton's birth is accentuated by a similar uncertainty associated with his parents, Anthony ("Antoine") Overton Sr. and Martha Deberry Overton. In the 1870 federal census, Overton Sr., listed as a mulatto, gave his estimated birth year as 1822 and his birthplace as Louisiana. Ten years later, Overton told census enumerators that his birth date was 1826. Moreover, he cited his father's birthplace as Tennessee and his mother's birthplace as Virginia. From a cursory assessment of Overton's census data, we can reasonably insinuate that his father was white (probably his master) and that he lived in Louisiana during the first decades of his life. However, a local history of Ouachita Parish, Louisiana (where Monroe is located), seemingly disputes this hypothesis. In its discussion of an 1874 court case, where Overton appeared as a witness, the record of his testimony included the following: "Anthony Overton noted that he was 50 years of age, lived in Monroe for 15 to 16 years and kept a family grocery. He had not been a slave of [John Quincy Wesley] Baker's but had been a possession of the McGregor Estate in Tenn. (the McGregors had been related to Baker). He and other slaves had been brought to Ou. Par. [Ouachita Parish] before the war."[2]

If Overton Sr. had, indeed, been born in Louisiana in 1822 or 1826 and returned to the state in 1858 or 1859, this raises several questions. First, where was he during the interim period? Did his Tennessee-born father leave Louisiana and take his slave/son with him? Presuming Antoine Overton's master/father had the surname Overton, when did he apparently sell his slave/son to the McGregor estate?

The background of Martha Deberry Overton, Anthony Overton Jr.'s mother, is also shrouded in mystery. According to the 1880 federal census, Martha Deberry Overton was born in Missouri sometime in 1833. Moreover, she told census enumerators that both of her parents were born in Missouri. Finally,

Oil painting of Anthony Overton Sr. (Courtesy of the Northeast Louisiana Delta African American Museum, Monroe, Louisiana)

since she is listed as a "mulatto," one can surmise that, similar to her husband, her father was white (presumably her master).[3]

Martha Overton's response to the 1880 federal census raises a variety of questions pertaining to her early relationship with Antoine. First and foremost, where did they meet? Did Antoine's early life include a stint in Missouri? Conversely, if they met in Tennessee, how did Martha get there? These questions unfortunately cannot be definitively answered. However, census data, related to their first child, Mack Wilson Overton, does seemingly co-

Martha Deberry Overton. (Courtesy of Sharon F. Patton, digitally restored from original by photographer George Aldridge)

incide with testimony Antoine Overton gave in 1874 regarding when he first arrived in Monroe, Louisiana. In the 1870 federal census, Antoine's oldest son, then twelve years old, is listed as "Wilson Overton." Ten years later, in the 1880 federal census, he is cited as "Mack W. Overton." More important, in both documents, the eldest Overton son is listed as being born in Louisiana sometime in 1858.[4] This appears to corroborate Antoine Overton's 1874 testimony that he arrived in Monroe during that year. Moreover, it appears that Martha accompanied Antoine on this trip as well. Also, according to census data, six years later, in 1864, the couple had their second child, Anthony Jr. Finally, three years later, as was often the case with slave marriages, Antoine and Martha's relationship was legally certified through an April 20, 1867, ceremony in Monroe.[5]

The nebulous backgrounds of Anthony Overton Sr. and Martha Deberry represent a tragic case study of one of slavery's negative effects on generations of transplanted Africans. Because enslaved blacks' vital statistics were generally not recorded, the subsequent construction of African American genealogical connections remains extremely difficult.[6] Fortunately, the contours of Anthony Overton Sr.'s life become much more visible during the Civil War and afterward. This, among other things, reveals how he served as a role model for his namesake's later political and commercial aspirations.

Antoine Overton during the Civil War

Antoine Overton's master during the Civil War was Wesley John Quincy Baker. Born in Rushville, Ohio, on December 5, 1819, Baker moved to Louisiana during the 1840s and established himself both as a lawyer and plantation owner. At the eve of the Civil War, Baker was a trustee for the City of Monroe.[7] Baker's northern background apparently contributed to his subsequent non-alignment with the secessionist movement in Monroe and Ouachita Parish. Consequently, according to a local historian, as a Unionist in an increasingly pro-Confederate area he "had an exciting, dangerous, and sad life during the conflict." Also, perhaps linked with his being a northerner, Baker seemingly did not possess the unmitigated hatred toward blacks often associated with slaveholders in the South. His relationship with one of his slaves, Antoine Overton, provides verification of this assumption. Overton, who later described Baker as his mentor, spoke of conversations they had about blacks gaining their freedom once the war ended. Yet, Baker also warned Overton "not to advertise the freedom issue as the other slaves might think they were free too soon. A situation which would have them shot down by Confederate soldiers in the region."[8]

One example of the special relationship between Wesley John Quincy Baker and Antoine Overton occurred in August 1863, when Federal troops led by General John D. Stephenson were marching toward Monroe and the surrounding area. Outmatched Confederate forces, camped in the yard of Baker's Bon Air plantation, ordered Baker to make his slaves available to them as they prepared to retreat to Texas. At this point, "Overton ordered all Negroes to load into wagons and proceed toward Texas. The slaves went a few miles towards the west, camped out for the night, and secretly slipped back to the plantation and were there when Stephenson's army stopped on their return to Goodrich's Landing on the west bank of the Mississippi River and before their crossing back into Vicksburg."[9] Later, as Union forces solidified their hold of Ouachita Parish, Antoine Overton benefitted from his actions of August 1863. Presumably with assistance from Baker, Overton established a general store in Monroe. Moreover, his activities as an entrepreneur first entered the historical record in October 1865 with an incident involving US Army troops. Frederick W. Williamson and George T. Goodman describe this episode: "An ironic incident is recorded of eight Federal soldiers stationed at the Trenton camp, who crossed the river to rifle the store of a political compatriot, Antoine Overton, a colored man. Antoine prevented their breaking in by giving them the key, whereupon they helped themselves. This gave Antoine time to gather up some of the members of his race who 'pursued the soldiers to the river and shot at them.'"[10] Overton's ability to both act decisively and get others to follow him, which he demonstrated in August 1863 and again in October 1865, reveal his significant leadership qualities. In the period immediately following the Civil War, Antoine Overton further displayed and refined these capabilities in both politics and business.

Antoine Overton and Reconstruction in Louisiana

While we can only presume that Wesley John Quincy Baker helped facilitate Antoine's entry into the realm of business, it is much easier to speculate that Baker helped facilitate Overton's entry into the realm of politics. In August 1865, just a few months after the Civil War ended, Baker chaired a convention in Ouachita Parish with the task of working out a plan to "restore Louisiana to her constitutional relations to the Union." Considering his wartime conversations with Overton, where they discussed the eventuality of African American freedom, Baker's vision of a reconstructed Louisiana no doubt included black participation in the political process. According to one historian, "the reconstruction period in Ouachita Parish is believed to be the bloodiest in the state, if not the bloodiest in the region, as white Democratic forces fought to regain power in their parish against freedmen and Republicans."[11] In this extremely volatile setting, Antoine Overton rose to significant political visibility.

Because blacks had outnumbered whites in Ouachita Parish since the 1840s, it became clear that African Americans would play a major role in the political reorganization of the region.[12] Predictably, to former slaveholders, such a prospect appeared unthinkable. Moreover, because many whites in

Louisiana could not imagine former slaves as their social and political equals, in 1866 the state rejected the proposed Fourteenth Amendment to the US Constitution. Ironically, this recalcitrance had an unintended consequence for former Confederates and their supporters in Louisiana and throughout the South. On March 2, 1867, the US Congress passed the first Reconstruction Act, dividing the eleven ex-Confederate states, excluding Tennessee, into five military districts. Louisiana became part of the Fifth Military District under the supervision of Major General Phil Sheridan.[13]

One of Sheridan's primary duties was to organize a constitutional convention in Louisiana that would, among other things, ratify the Fourteenth Amendment. Significantly, this political exercise had to include the participation of African Americans. During subsequent elections in April 1868, because of the Ouachita Parish's demographics, not only did the 1,235 supporters (34 whites and 1,201 blacks) of a new Louisiana Constitution outnumber the 671 opponents (461 whites and 213 blacks) by a majority of 561, many of the specific political contests generated landslide victories for Republican candidates. One of the more lopsided races in Ouachita Parish was for the position of coroner, with Antoine Overton defeating his Democratic opponent by a count of 1,390 to 3.[14]

Although ex-Confederates were disheartened by political developments after the Reconstruction Act of 1867, ex-slaves such as Antoine Overton were equally encouraged. Moreover, not only did African Americans take full advantage of the opportunity to participate in the body politic, they also took advantage of the opportunity to provide education for their children. For instance, in 1867, Anthony Overton Sr. headed a group of black men who established the first school for African Americans in Monroe and Ouachita Parish.[15]

After the elections of 1868, the Republican Party sought to consolidate its gains in Louisiana and elsewhere. On February 3, 1870, this effort received a major boost with the ratification of the Fifteenth Amendment, giving African American men the vote.

Three months later, in May 1870, Senator Oliver P. Morton from Indiana introduced a bill that sought to strengthen the new legislation by mandating prison time and fines for persons who obstructed officially enfranchised blacks from exercising this constitutional right.[16] Partially due to the newly ratified Fifteenth Amendment, Republicans, once again, scored major victories in the elections of November 1870. In Ouachita Parish, the number of registered black voters had increased by 285 compared to 1868 figures (1,960 vs. 1,675). Conversely, the number of white registered voters had decreased by 86 compared to 1868 (590 vs. 676). One of the important consequences of this election was that the parish coroner, Antoine Overton, received a major political promotion by being elected to the Louisiana State House of Representatives.[17]

In his definitive study of African American state legislators in Louisiana during Reconstruction, Charles Vincent notes that, of the thirty-six black House members who served during the 1871–72 session, twenty-six were new to this position. According to Vincent, the legislative inexperience of most Louisiana African American House members, which mirrored similar data from other southern states during Reconstruction, led to charges (by white critics of black political participation) that these individuals' incompetence "contributed to an end of honest government." Nevertheless, Vincent declares that Louisiana's neophyte black state legislators, among them Antoine Overton, were not preoccupied with crafting vindictive legislation to further punish ex-Confederates. Quite to the contrary, they focused on legislation "designed to finance internal improvements, education . . . and to establish social reforms."[18]

Being elected to and serving in the Louisiana House of Representatives represented a major accomplishment for Anthony Overton Sr. Yet, serving in the state legislature was not financially profitable. At the time, members of the Louisiana House received only $8.00 a day during the legislative session. In the case of Overton, who Vincent describes as owning "a large boarding-house and a 'provisionstore' in Monroe," the inordinate amount of time he spent in New Orleans attending to Louisiana's business, had a negative effect on his own personal business interests.[19] This assertion is verified by Antoine Overton's R. G. Dun & Company's credit reports during this period.

In its first report outlining Overton's financial strength and general credit assessment, Dun's May 1, 1871, edition lists Overton as owning a general store and describes him as "a freeman, was formerly a slave, does a g'd [good] negro trade, makes money, is a member of the State Legis." It goes on to describe his character as fair and notes that Overton had been "in bus (business) 4 yrs." In January 1872, Antoine Overton's Dun entry is promising: "2.5c [$250 capital], making money & has considerable trade with the Negroes, is a member of the State Legis." However, on June 23, 1872, Dun describes Overton as a "Negro member of Legislature, but little capacity in cap. [capital]."[20]

Because Antoine Overton could not simultaneously be an effective legislator and a profitable business owner, he chose not to run for reelection to the Louisiana House in 1872. Subsequent Dun reports demonstrate how this decision dramatically enhanced his financial stature. In January 1873, Dun describes Overton as someone who possessed $1,500 in real estate and $1,500 in capital. Significantly, his available capital had increased 600 percent

Anthony Overton Sr. This may be one of few surviving photographs of Anthony Overton's father. (Courtesy of Robert Branch II)

from the January 1872 listing of $250. In terms of his credit situation, Dun notes that Overton "owes considerable, will pay if he has it." Dun's July 1873 report of Antoine Overton incorrectly lists him as being forty years old. Yet, more importantly, it cites his character, habits, and capital, as "good." It also provides the following estimates: "capl [capital] 2m$ [$2,000] R.E. [real estate] and other ppty [property] 3m$ [$3,000].[21]

In the last available Dun report for Antoine Overton, which appeared in December 1874, his capital and real estate holdings stand at $2,000 and $4,000, respectively. In terms of his credit, he is judged to be "good for advances." The evidence also suggests that, after leaving politics, Antoine Overton introduced his sons Mack and Anthony Jr. to the dynamics of business and entrepreneurship. A 1925 article on the then-evolving business tycoon described Overton Jr. as someone "brought up behind the counter."[22] Moreover, it is reasonable to assume that Antoine also inspired his namesake son's later interest in running for political office.

Antoine Overton and Family Leave Louisiana

By the mid-1870s, Antoine Overton had established a solid economic base in Monroe, Louisiana. This, coupled with his previous political activities, made him a bona fide leader in Ouachita Parish's black community. Yet, in a changing political climate, Overton's visibility soon proved to be a liability. Ultimately, to escape a lynch mob, he fled Louisiana and joined thousands of other Exodusters seeking a new start in Kansas. Curiously, in the 1925 article "Anthony Overton: A Man Who Planned For Success," which appeared in the short-lived African American magazine *Reflexus*, Overton insinuates that his father had not been forced to leave Monroe. Overton Jr. told *Reflexus* that Overton Sr., "a man of importance in the public life of the community as well as a successful merchant" wanted to "give his son every advantage to equip him for his battle with life." Consequently, "at the age of 19, he [Overton Jr.] was sent to Topeka, Kansas to enter the public school."[23]

Notwithstanding Anthony Overton Jr.'s flawed 1925 recollection, the evidence clearly indicates that Anthony Overton Sr. not only left Louisiana in the late 1870s but took some of his cash with him to Topeka. Consequently, the elder Overton rebuilt his life quickly. For instance, the New Advertisements section of the January 30, 1880, edition of Topeka's *Weekly Kansas Herald* features an ad for the Overton House. Readers were informed that this boardinghouse at the corner of Kansas Avenue and First Street was "first class in every respect." Moreover, to enhance his new enterprise's visibility, Antoine Overton, for the next couple months, prominently advertised the Overton House on the front page of this African American newspaper.[24]

Although Antoine Overton subsequently became a prominent entrepreneur in Topeka, he is not discussed in Thomas C. Cox's *Blacks in Topeka, Kansas 1865–1915*. Nevertheless, Overton's extended obituary in the April 5, 1884, issue of the *Topeka Daily Commonwealth* provides important details regarding his abbreviated presence in Kansas. Besides establishing the Overton House, Antoine Overton "acquired considerable property" in the Topeka area. Also, similar to the information contained in his early to mid-1870s R. G. Dun & Company reports, Overton's obituary describes him as "scrupulously particular as to his pledges." Finally, although Antoine Overton had been in Topeka for a relatively brief period, "his friends were numerous in both races."[25]

Activities in Topeka 1880–85

Notwithstanding Anthony Overton Jr.'s flawed memory in 1925 as to how he arrived in Topeka, some later published accounts related to his early activities in the Sunflower State are even more distorted. For instance, James J. Flynn's *Negroes of Achievement in Modern America*—a glaring instance of interjecting hyperbole into history—provides a fantastical account of the future business magnate's first commercial experiences. In all fairness to Flynn, *Negroes of Achievement*, which features an introduction by Roy E. Wilkins, executive secretary of the NAACP, was written not as a scholarly book but primarily for a young adult audience. Yet, because of the relative paucity of works related to Anthony Overton, Flynn's flawed discussion of this African American business leader has served as a reference point for some later studies. For instance, Robert M. Silverman's 2000 book, *Doing Business in Minority Markets: Black and Korean Entrepreneurs in Chicago's Ethnic Beauty Aids Industry*, relies exclusively on Flynn's 1970 book chapter in discussing Overton's early life.[26]

Flynn tells his readers that Overton first exhibited his business acumen in high school while working part-time for an "easy going" storeowner: "Anthony was appalled at his happy-go-lucky-attitude. The first thing young Overton did was to put in a bookkeeping system." Next, he (Overton) "sent out bills to the delinquent customers, much to their annoyance." Later, the teenage Anthony, with the storeowner's permission, "dickered with the wholesalers on the prices of the goods to be bought." Finally, the future tycoon "purchased a scale with some of the money that was saved, and made his boss use it."[27]

According to Flynn, after Overton graduated from high school, he once again demonstrated his entrepreneurial inclinations. After describing Topeka as a growing city that "needed young, energetic, and foresighted businessmen," *Negroes of Achievement* discusses how the young Overton and a business partner started a wholesale fruit business "that proved a most successful venture, again because of Anthony's shrewd and capable handling." As a result, "he [Overton] was not yet twenty years of age, and he was making more annually than most men twice his age.[28]

Given Overton's future entrepreneurial successes, a reasonable person, perhaps, would not immediately dismiss Flynn's narrative as untrue. In fact, Rachel Kranz's 2004 encyclopedic work, *African American Business Leaders and Entrepreneurs* appears to use Flynn as a reference point. The entry on Anthony Overton notes that he "worked at a local grocery store while going to school—and his talent for business was such that the store showed a profit for the first time in its existence." Moreover, after graduating from high school, Overton "went into the fruit business, where once again his flair for business led him to success. For example, he often went to growers directly so he could get the best of their crop."[29]

Anthony Overton, himself, further complicated the literature related to his first years in Topeka in a December 26, 1942, *Chicago Defender* article. Apparently not remembering what he told *Reflexus* magazine seventeen years earlier, Overton declared that his father, had indeed, left Louisiana "when the Ku Klux Klan started riding—murdering and terrorizing Negroes who had become prominent political figures." Moreover, after the family arrived in Topeka, Antoine Overton never "got on his feet." Consequently, the *Defender* reports that, at the age of nineteen, "Anthony quit school and went to work. He got a job as a pullman porter and saved his money."[30]

At the same time Flynn and Kranz situated Overton as the owner of a thriving wholesale fruit business, as well as when Overton Jr. claims he started working as a Pullman porter, the younger Overton was, in fact, a student at Topeka's Washburn College, which matriculated both white and African American students.[31] Washburn, an institution linked with the Congregational Church, began at Lincoln College in early 1865 but was renamed Lincoln Monumental College that same year, and then renamed Washburn in 1868. Ichabod Washburn of Worcester, Massachusetts, was the institution's chief donor during its formative years.[32]

Anthony Overton Jr. entered Washburn during the 1882–83 academic year as a student in its English and Business Curriculum Program. The college catalog describes this course of study as one "intended to meet the wants of many who have neither the time nor the means for pursuing more extended course of study. As will be seen, it gives a good basis for practical business education. Special lessons in penmanship free." The courses associated with Washburn's English and Business Curriculum Program included English Grammar, Arithmetic, General Reading (History of England, History of France, History of Greece, History of Rome), Bookkeeping, Law of Contracts, Algebra, Geometry, and Parliamentary Rules.[33] Because relevant records from Washburn's Registrar's Office are not extant, it is not possible to determine how the young Overton performed in his classes during the 1882–83 and 1883–84 academic years.[34] We do definitively know that he left Washburn after two years and later enrolled in the University of Kansas's embryonic law school.

The first building constructed on the campus of Washburn College, ca. early 1880s. Anthony Overton took classes here 1882–83 and 1883–84. (Courtesy of University Archives, Mabee Library, Washburn University)

The University of Kansas Law School

While available evidence does place Anthony Overton Jr. as a law student at the University of Kansas during the mid-to-late 1880s, his experiences in Lawrence and immediately afterward remain relatively unclear. Moreover, the flawed historiography related to this segment of Overton's life contributes to this lack of clarity. Ingham and Feldman's *African-American Business Leaders* provides one of the best depictions of the life of Anthony Overton. To their credit, Ingham and Feldman, in their listing of the sources consulted to compile the Overton entry, identify James J. Flynn's work as a "lengthy although somewhat flawed biography of Overton." Yet, Ingham's and Feldman's summary of Overton's early life, too, feature several incorrect assertions. For instance, they state that Overton received a bachelor of law degree from the University of Kansas in 1888, which he never did. Moreover, "he was admitted to the Kansas state bar upon graduation and began practicing law in Topeka. Shortly thereafter he served for one year as a judge of the municipal court in Shawnee County."[35] Ingham and Feldman apparently copied these assertions, almost verbatim, from an Overton obituary published in the July 1947 issue of the *Journal of Negro History*, as well as an Overton entry in the 1965 edition of *The National Cyclopedia of American Biography*. Moreover, to demonstrate the credence given to Ingham and Feldman's assessment of Overton's early life, an entry on Overton that appears in the 1999 *Encyclopedia of African American Business History* reiterates the narrative (related to Overton's alleged law-related activities) presented in *African-American Business Leaders: A Biographical Dictionary*.[36]

Finally, the evidence indicates that a primary source of misinformation about this aspect of Anthony Overton's life was Overton himself. A December 26, 1942, *Chicago Defender* article depicting Overton's rise "from slave to wealth" includes the following declarations (based on an interview with Overton). First, "he [Overton] desired to enter some business but he wanted to be prepared before doing so." Consequently, "he applied to admission at the University of Kansas where he asked to specialize in business law. The school officials insisted, however, that he take a complete law course and when he graduated in 1888 he was admitted to the bar." Finally, the *Defender* told its readers that Overton's "first job was not in business, but as a judge. His brother, who was six years older than he, had entered politics and was a power in Topeka as a Negro leader. He saw that his younger brother was placed on the Republican ticket and elected a judge of the Municipal Court of the city."[37]

Significantly, after Antoine Overton's death in April 1884, his widow and sons left Topeka to settle on land that the deceased entrepreneur had purchased in Soldier Township, outside of the city. Consequently, the 1885 Kansas State Census lists the Overton family (including an adopted sister, Mary Upshaw) as deriving their income from farming. Again to separate fact from fiction, this census data disputes Anthony Overton's later assertion that he became a municipal judge in Topeka through the intercession of his power-broker elder brother, Mack Wilson.[38]

Circumstantial evidence suggests that, shortly after the 1885 Kansas State Census placing the Overton family in Soldier Township outside of Topeka, the ambitious Anthony Overton Jr. left farm life behind to begin law studies. As with incorrect assertions about Overton as a teenage business prodigy, the young Overton's subsequent experiences with law school and the legal profession were far less successful than the literature suggests. Nevertheless, Overton, while in Lawrence, met his future wife and business partner, Clara Gregg.

Notwithstanding Topeka's later significance as a destination for African American migrants to Kansas, Lawrence was the state's first important refuge for blacks. For instance, in 1860, there were no African Americans residing

Mack Wilson Overton, ca.1886. Like his younger brother and father, Mack (who continued to live in Topeka, Kansas) was a prominent entrepreneur. In 1938 the city honored him for being Topeka's oldest active grocer by renaming Center Street from Chandler to Edison as Overton Street. (Courtesy of the Everett and Ida Overton Collection)

in Topeka. Yet, in 1861, Lawrence's *Kansas State Journal* reported that "our colored population is now not far from one hundred."[39]

Moreover, by the end of the Civil War, the number of African Americans living in Lawrence and Douglas County had swelled to over two thousand. One reason for this dramatic growth was the "large presence of black soldiers stationed in Lawrence at the end of the Civil War, some of whom remained to raise families and participate in public life." Another reason for this significant demographic development involved former slaves from neighboring Missouri who, even before the war ended, escaped and resettled in Lawrence and other Kansas towns.[40]

One escaped slave from Missouri was Alexander Gregg. Born in Kentucky in 1824, Gregg was the offspring of his slave mother and slave master father. In 1851 he was taken to Missouri where, among other things, he learned the craft of shoemaking. During the Civil War, he escaped with his second wife and six children to Lawrence, where he established himself as a leader in the embryonic black community there.[41] The industrious Gregg purchased property at 903 Tennessee Street that he converted into a cobbler's shop and living quarters. The profits he generated from his custom-made boot and shoe repair business "went into city lots on the east and west side [of Lawrence], and his children's education."[42] Besides establishing an economic presence in Lawrence, Alexander Gregg also established a political presence; he was a prominent black Republican whose interests included supporting the prohibition of alcoholic beverages in the state. For example, in 1881, he helped organize Lawrence's annual Emancipation Day celebration, which featured a speech by Kansas governor John P. St. John (who had been elected in 1878 on a Prohibitionist platform).[43]

Lawrence was not only the home of such African American migrants as Alexander Gregg but, from 1866, was also the home of the University of Kansas. Open to students of all races from its founding, in 1870 the school reportedly enrolled its first black student, Selina Wilson.[44] Wilson and other African American pioneers at the University of Kansas had a mixed experience on campus. On one hand, "they participated in varsity athletics, joined clubs, and attended concerts and athletic events." Yet, at the same time, "in the classroom they sat in the back of the room. They could not live in campus housing. Housing had to be sought off-campus in the homes of African Americans willing to rent rooms."[45] When Anthony Overton arrived in Lawrence to study law, he also undoubtedly had to find an off-campus location to reside. Lawrence city directories reveal that Overton found such quarters at the home of Alexander Gregg at 903 Tennessee Street.[46] Moreover, the evidence indicates that the young Overton also found a romantic interest at Alexander Gregg's residence, one of his daughters, Clara.

While Overton spent some of his time in Lawrence building a relationship with the woman who would later become his wife, he spent most of his time working toward a law degree from the University of Kansas. Although extant institutional records associated with Overton's matriculation at KU do not include documentation of his admission or graduation, the school's 1886–87

Anthony Overton Jr., ca. 1886. (Courtesy of the Everett and Ida Overton Collection)

Register of Student Withdrawal lists Overton. Moreover, the University of Kansas's Registrar's Office records for 1887–88 indicate that he had reenrolled in the law school.[47] Determining Overton's association with the University of Kansas becomes all the murkier because of a December 1927 University of Kansas Alumni Association publication listing him as an 1891 graduate.[48] This is highly unlikely because, in 1891, as discussed below, Overton was in the recently opened Oklahoma Territory seeking to make the black settlement of Wanamaker a successful venture.

Clara Gregg, ca.1885–86. (Courtesy of the Everett and Ida Overton Collection)

Despite considerable nebulosity regarding Overton's activities at the University of Kansas, substantive information about its law school during his enrollment does exist. Furthermore, while Overton apparently did not earn a law degree from this institution, according to the requirements of the day he possessed the qualifications to do so. In the late nineteenth century, it was relatively easy to become a lawyer in the state of Kansas. As a history of the Kansas Bar Association notes, "for a good many years, the Association had cocked a critical eye at the casual requirements for practicing law in

James W. Green established the University of Kansas Law School in 1878. He coordinated its activities during the time of Anthony Overton's aborted matriculation in the mid-1880s. (Courtesy of Kenneth Spencer Research Library, University of Kansas Libraries)

Kansas. From the beginning of statehood, it was required only that an applicant be of good moral character and well qualified in the knowledge of law. Examinations were conducted by the several district judges and were often indifferent, at best, whether administered by the judge himself or by a common committee selected from the local bar."[49]

The law school at the University of Kansas began rather inauspiciously in October 1878. According to a report issued by its sole faculty member, James Woods Green, it started "without a library, without any pecuniary support and without previous advertising or notice." The history of the Kansas Bar Association reveals that the embryonic University of Kansas law school had admission requirements that "were virtually nonexistent . . . Applicants without a high school diploma could be admitted by passing a simple examination in English and American and English history; high school and college graduates were admitted without examination." Also, students were charged a "matriculation fee" of $25 that "provided the sole faculty compensation."[50]

His previous studies at Washburn College meant that Anthony Overton Jr. was fully qualified to study law and be a lawyer in late nineteenth-century Kansas. It remains unclear as to why he never actually received a law degree. Yet, it is equally clear that Overton, later in life, embellished this aspect of his personal history. Also, in a bizarre twist, some later commentators asserted that Overton received a law degree from Washburn College and not the University of Kansas. The spring 1997 issue of the online journal *Issues and Views* carries an article asserting that Anthony received his law degree from Topeka's Washburn College in 1888. Even more interesting, an article in the November 21, 2004, *Topeka Capital-Journal* also states that Overton received a bachelor of law degree from Washburn in 1888. In the end, these assertions are no more credible than those regarding Overton and the University of Kansas law program—particularly since the Washburn College School of Law did not open until September 1903.[51]

Part of the self-created mythology surrounding the young Anthony Overton is that, after graduating from the University of Kansas (or Washburn College) law school, he became a member of the Kansas Bar Association, an assertion that is not borne out by the Kansas Bar Association directories for 1883–1901.[52] Also, since Anthony Overton graduated from neither the University of Kansas nor Washburn College schools of law, and he was not a member of the Kansas Bar Association, it appears impossible for him to have been elected as a municipal judge in Topeka. Research confirms this assumption. Overton is not listed in the Topeka city directory (under the category of "Attorneys") from 1888 to 1897, nor is he listed as a candidate for judge during 1889 and 1890 local elections.[53]

The 1889 Oklahoma Land Rush

While Anthony Overton's activities related to law during the late 1880s remains uncertain, he did take an important, and documented, step in his personal life during this period. On June 14, 1888, he and Clara M. Gregg were married in Lawrence.[54] Given that his anticipated career in the legal profession had seemingly stalled, this appeared to be less than an opportune time to commit to marriage. Yet, the ambitious and mobile Anthony Overton Jr. seemingly had a plan to secure the economic future of his new family. By the late 1880s, a group of African Americans based in Topeka became convinced that establishing settlements in the soon-to-be-opened Indian lands in Oklahoma would be blacks' best strategy to enhance both personal and group power and autonomy. This sentiment became actualized in a group called the Oklahoma Immigration Association (OIA).[55]

The apparent instigator of this movement was Topeka newspaper editor W. L. Eagleson. Shortly after the Oklahoma Land Rush commenced on April 22, 1889, Eagleson's *American Citizen*, which had agents in various southern cities, informed its readers that "there never was a more favorable time than now for you to secure good homes in land where you will be free and your rights respected. Oklahoma is now open for settlement. Come in and help make it one of the best states in the union." Southern blacks were also informed that "five hundred of the best colored citizens of Topeka have gone there within the last month. They send back word for others to come on, there is room for many more."[56]

Although the records of the OIA appear not to have survived, other evidence indicates that Anthony Overton was part of the initial contingent of Kansas blacks who resettled in Oklahoma. The 1890 Territorial Census situates Overton, his wife, Clara, and their ten-month-old son, Everett, in Kingfisher County.[57] Moreover, circumstantial evidence suggests that Overton, as the perceived leader of this contingent of settlers, convinced them to name their new home Wanamaker. In addition to his father, the Philadelphia merchant John Wanamaker was an important business role model for the young Overton. Regarded as a consequential figure in the evolution of US department stores, Wanamaker is also regarded as a pioneer in the evolution of US advertising. Known for his extensive and clever use of newspaper marketing, Wanamaker presided over the largest retail operation in the United States by the 1880s. In addition, besides also being known for his philanthropy, Wanamaker, who came from an abolitionist family, was also perceived to be an advocate for African American rights.[58]

While economic considerations no doubt motivated Anthony Overton and other blacks to move to Oklahoma, an important political dynamic animated this significant demographic development. Eagleson's OIA believed that Oklahoma could subsequently be a black-controlled state. In a bid to bring this about, the OIA started a petition drive requesting that President Benjamin Harrison appoint Edward Preston McCabe, arguably the most distinguished black Kansan during this period, as territorial governor.[59] Born in Troy, New York, in 1850, McCabe possessed a nonconventional background for a late nineteenth-century African American. Before moving to Nicodemus, Kansas, in 1878 to establish a law and real estate office, McCabe had reportedly worked as a clerk on Wall Street, a clerk for Chicago hotel magnate Potter Palmer, and had served as a clerk in the US Treasury Department's Cook County (Illinois) office. After arriving in Nicodemus, McCabe quickly established himself as a political leader. In 1880, he represented Kansas as a delegate-at-large to the Republican Party's national convention in Chicago. Two years later, in 1882, McCabe made history as the first African American elected to statewide office in Kansas; he was reelected to the post of state auditor in 1884.[60]

For his part, McCabe, then living in Washington, DC, reacted enthusiastically to efforts to have him named the territorial governor of Oklahoma. However, while McCabe, Eagleson, and other African Americans were encouraged by this possibility, white settlers were far less so. In fact, as Jimmie Franklin writes, one white settler in Oklahoma "conjectured that if President Harrison named a black to the executive post, he would not 'give five cents for his life.'"[61] In the end, McCabe was not named territorial governor of Oklahoma, nor was he named secretary of the territory (another position his supporters sought for him). As an alternative, after moving to the Oklahoma Territory settlement of Guthrie in 1890, McCabe was appointed the first treasurer of Logan County. He would go on to play a major role in the establishment of Langston, one of the most successful all-black towns in Oklahoma.[62]

While Edward McCabe sought to establish his stake in the newly opened Oklahoma Territory, Anthony Overton Jr. sought to do likewise. Available evidence suggests that, notwithstanding the very positive assessment of this process promoted by Eagleson's *American Citizen* and the OIA, the experiences of Oklahoma's first black settlers were fraught with hardship. Although Anthony Overton and other early black Oklahoma migrants successfully staked out claims in Kingfisher County, the physical environment of the area that became Wanamaker was far from hospitable. As one study has noted, rather than rely on farming, migrants' best hope for survival laid in "selling wild game, fence posts, and firewood."[63]

Significantly, most of the early settlers in Kingfisher County, black and white, started their new lives in marginal housing. A mid-twentieth-century commemoration of the area's initial settlement asserted that "many families had as their only shelter the spaces under their wagons. Other more fortunate families had large covered wagons, small tents, or even small shacks for shelter." To make matters worse, settlers' substandard housing provided little protection from "the fierce plains storms" that caused many pioneers to spend "sleepless nights watching the clouds." Because of the harsh conditions faced by early black settlers to Kingfisher County, Oklahoma, some immediately returned to Kansas.[64] Anthony Overton Jr. was not among them. Determined to make his mark in the world, he persevered in the midst of a difficult situation. Unfortunately, Overton's experiences in Oklahoma remain, for the most part, a mystery. Moreover, available documentary evidence reveals that most of the previous depictions of Overton's life in Oklahoma are flawed. Perhaps the major contributing factor to this historiographical uncertainty is the fact that the first Kingfisher County courthouse burned down in 1900. Thus, relevant tax records that could provide a concrete glimpse of Overton's activities in Oklahoma are gone forever.[65]

Because of a paucity of substantive information regarding Anthony Overton's experiences in Oklahoma, interested scholars have had to rely on other, dubious, assessments of this phase of his life. A 1925 article titled "Anthony Overton: A Man Who Planned for Success" epitomizes this genre. According to this account, because the opening of Indian territory "offered unlimited opportunities at the time to enterprising young businessmen with a little capital and a large capacity for hard work," the ambitious, recently married Overton moved to Oklahoma. Moreover, the article reiterates that Overton, the apparent leader of the contingent that established Wanamaker, named the town after "the world famous merchant prince of Philadelphia, John Wanamaker, who was one of Overton's 'little tin gods.'"[66]

After settling in Wanamaker, Overton, similar to his father's example, "established a mercantile store." Moreover, the aggressive young man "was later appointed United States postmaster for the district by President Harrison." The article continues that, within a short period of time "as the community around Wanamaker began to grow and the lumber and cotton industries flourished, he [Overton] added to his interests a sawmill and a cotton gin." Consequently, "Overton was by far the leading citizen of the town, socially, economically, and politically. It was he who applied for a charter for the town, it was he who got out the vote for the Republican Party in the district, and in 1892 it was he who organized the first Bank of Wanamaker."[67]

While this account of Overton's activities in Oklahoma no doubt enthralled readers in 1925, the evidence indicates that it was patently false. Jimmie Lewis Franklin's 1982 book *Journey toward Hope: A History of Blacks in Oklahoma* remains the still-definitive work on the subject. If Anthony Overton *had* established a grocery store, sawmill, cotton gin, and bank during the early days of black settlement in Oklahoma, this significant accomplishment would surely be mentioned in *Journey toward Hope*. Consequently, Anthony Overton's *complete absence* in this important work is revelatory.

Another source, the Oklahoma Historic Preservation Survey, originating from the History Department at Oklahoma State University, all but dispels the assertion that Wanamaker was a thriving community. In fact, it refers to Wanamaker as a "bubble town," one of several Oklahoma land rush communities that "just 'bubbled up' after the run and then collapsed almost as quickly." Moreover, it states that, because of the harsh conditions, many of the inhabitants of Wanamaker ended up abandoning the all-black enclave and moved to the nearby (predominantly white) town of Kingfisher. Finally, Wanamaker's total absence from *Journey toward Hope* and Arthur L. Tolson's 1966 doctoral dissertation examining the early African American experience in Oklahoma further confirms Wanamaker's very short and relatively insignificant lifespan. Interestingly enough, there is one aspect of "Anthony Overton: A Man Who Planned for Success" that is partially correct: instead of Anthony Overton, it appears that his wife, Clara, was Wanamaker's first postmaster.[68]

Besides the dramatically overblown 1925 assessment of Overton's business activities in Oklahoma, partially incorrect information persists regarding his political activities there. For instance, Ingham and Feldman's *African-American Business Leaders* states that "in 1892 Overton was elected treasurer of Kingfisher County [Oklahoma]."[69] In fact, Overton *unsuccessfully* ran for this position. Nevertheless, his defeat indicates that, while Overton may not have been the business titan described in "Anthony Overton: A Man Who Planned for Success," he had established himself as a person of substance in early Oklahoma.

From a political standpoint, Kingfisher County was a staunchly Republican area in 1892. Because of Overton's own qualifications, as well as the fact that his father had been a GOP elected official, it appears reasonable to assume that local Republicans placed him on their slate of candidates to ensure that Kingfisher County blacks would support the Republican ticket. In fact, the October 13, 1892, issue of the *Kingfisher Free Press*, a Republican-leaning publication notes that "the republicans of Kingfisher county are as happy as clams; they have a good ticket of honest, able, upright men; there is not a single fly on the ticket and we have yet to hear of a single republican who will not go straight to the polls on the 8 of November and Vote the republican ticket."[70]

Although the *Kingfisher Free Press* conveys a sense of Republican unity going into the November elections, a major racial rift had recently developed in the area. In late September 1892, members of the board of directors of the public school in North Kingfisher voted to deny its black students future access to the school. As an alternative, these young people were to be sent to a blacks-only school being built in the area. For their part, black adults in

Kingfisher responded by hiring a lawyer to fight this blatant discrimination in court and urged black parents not to send their children to the separate school. Because most of the North Kingfisher School board of directors were white Republicans, their actions had political implications. As the September 29, 1892, issue of the *Kingfisher Free Press* reported in this regard, some local African American leaders declared that "this trouble will result in the defeat of the Republican party of the county."[71]

Ironically, when the votes were counted after the November 8, 1892, election, Anthony Overton was the *only* Republican candidate *not* elected to office in Kingfisher County. He lost by 123 votes to the People's Party candidate.[72] This election defeat must have been especially crushing for Overton. In fact, a survey of his young adult life indicates it was just the latest instance of apparent personal failure. Within the matter of a few years, he had failed to earn a law degree, failed to start a successful business, and failed to be elected to political office.

Founding the Overton Hygienic Manufacturing Company

After his election defeat, Overton's immediate next move remains a question. For instance, Ingham and Feldman assert that Overton subsequently moved to Oklahoma City, where he started a general store, though this cannot be verified because no Oklahoma City directories are known to survive from 1890 to 1898. Also, the nebulosity surrounding the details of Overton's immediate activities after 1892 is intensified by yet another dubious assertion regarding his early personal history. Instead of subsequently leaving the future Sooner state because of his failure to establish a suitable stake there, the 1925 "Anthony Overton: A Man Who Planned for Success" declares that an encounter with the infamous Dalton Gang prompted Overton to return to Kansas. According to this account, derived from an interview with Anthony Overton, one of the consequences of the settlement of Oklahoma territory was "the vast expanse of grazing land for cattle was slowly but surely diminishing." As a result, a growing number of cowboys "found themselves out of employment." Moreover, these individuals, "reckless and daring by nature from hardships and Indian fighting, banded together and proceeded to live by preying upon the settlers whom they regarded as the cause of their misfortune."[73]

As Overton continued, because "it was certain that so prosperous and thriving a town as Wanamaker would not be overlooked by the outlaws," the infamous Dalton Gang paid a late night visit to his store in late 1892. During this encounter, Overton lost one hundred dollars in cash and was unhurt.

Nevertheless, "fearing for the safety of his family and his interests, he decided to return to Kansas. He sold out his sawmill, his cotton gin, and store and in 1893 he returned with his family to Kansas City, Kansas." Significantly, Overton's fantastical explanation for leaving Oklahoma extends beyond the boundaries of the 1925 article about him. In fact, a July 12, 1946, obituary of the recently deceased business magnate in the black-owned *Kansas City Call* states that Overton and his family left Oklahoma after "they were victims of a daring robbery staged by the infamous Dalton brothers."[74]

Three facts complicate the linkage between Anthony Overton and the Dalton Gang. First, around the time that Overton claimed the Daltons robbed his store (late 1892), they were all but destroyed during a famous October 5, 1892, gun battle in Coffeyville, Kansas. Second, the Dalton Gang, before its end, focused on such dramatic crimes as train and bank robberies. Third, no documented information suggests that Overton then possessed the wealth that would have made him a desirable target for the Daltons.[75]

To again separate fact from fiction and speculation, the 1895 Kansas City, Kansas, city directory does list Anthony Overton—not as a businessman, but as a "porter" residing at 838 State Street. Yet, within two years, the 1897 Kansas City, Missouri, city directory listed him as a "grocer" residing at 1517 East Seventeenth Street. As Charles E. Coulter writes, "no physical feature separates much of Kansas City, Missouri, from Kansas City Kansas, or the rest of the Kansas suburbs." Moreover, "in the African American community, the boundary between the two Kansas Cities consistently appeared permeable."[76]

The 1900 Federal Census may provide a clue as to Overton's enhanced motivation for success during the mid-1890s. Census data reveal that Anthony and Clara had three more children during this decade: Mabel (b. 1892), Eva (b. 1894), and Frances (b. 1895).[77] Because Anthony Overton, after moving to Kansas City, had four children to provide for, it is plausible to assume that this additional responsibility inspired him to push forward even harder.

Most of Overton historiography asserts that he expanded his grocery business by establishing the Overton Hygienic Manufacturing Company in 1898. The 1900 edition of the *Kansas State Gazetteer and Business Directory* verifies these claims. This document listed Overton as a "mnfrs agent" (manufacturer's agent) for "extracts" doing business at 405 West Sixth Street in Kansas City, Missouri.[78] Among other things, this coincides with declarations that the Overton Hygienic Manufacturing Company's first products were baking powder and flavoring extracts.[79]

Although Anthony Overton Jr. got off to a relatively late start as a serious businessman, his uncanny ability to determine and influence consumer wants and desires became apparent shortly after he established the Overton

Clara Gregg Overton and children, ca. mid-1890s. Left to right: Mabel, Frances (on lap), Everett; Eva in front. (Courtesy of the Everett and Ida Overton Collection)

Hygienic Manufacturing Company. In the beginning, Overton's primary product was baking powder. However, he quickly realized there was a potentially bigger market for face powder that complimented and enhanced the complexions of African American women. Thus, around 1900, he launched his pioneering High-Brown Face Powder. Moreover, within a few years, Overton expanded the High-Brown product line to include a variety of beauty preparations aimed at black female consumers.[80]

The National Negro Business League

In 1901, Overton's rising commercial visibility contributed to his inclusion as a speaker at the second annual meeting of the National Negro Business League (NNBL) in Chicago. The NNBL, established in 1900 by Booker T. Washington, represented the culmination of a movement that began in the years immediately following the end of Reconstruction. After the South's "redemption" by ex-Confederates and their sympathizers, the political power conveyed to African American men through the Fifteenth Amendment quickly became illusionary, rather than factual. Consequently, years before Booker T. Washington became a national celebrity, the recently freed African American population, especially its men, began to view business development as the primary means to exhibit agency and self-determination.

Two 1879 conferences epitomized this phenomenon. During the spring of that year, blacks from across the country traveled to Kansas City, Missouri, to participate in the Colored Laborers' and Business Men's Industrial Convention. Among other things, this meeting's reported resolutions state that African Americans should "engage in individual enterprises of a mercantile nature." Also, blacks should "open a store, office, or place of business on their own account" because, if successful, it would "create a confidence and establish a precedent that shall induce others to join labor and capital in larger and better enterprises or business operations." Later that year, the National Conference of Colored Men convened in Nashville, Tennessee. The proceedings of this meeting clearly indicate that the end of Reconstruction—and the federal government's apparent lack of interest in forcefully protecting the rights of the ex-slave population—did not go unnoticed by blacks. Delegates articulated the belief that "blacks were to a great extent the architects of their own fortunes and should rely mainly upon their own exertions for success." Moreover, "black youths were challenged to observe strict morality and temperate habits, acquire land, engage in agriculture [and] advance to mercantile positions."[81]

Most historians consider the "Negro in Business" conference, convened by W. E. B. Du Bois at Atlanta University May 30–31, 1899, to be a direct precursor to the National Negro Business League established the following year. Although Du Bois's and Booker T. Washington's public disagreement over civil rights and black political activity is well documented, at the turn of the twentieth century both men agreed on the importance of black business development.[82] In his prepared remarks at the meeting, Du Bois proposed "the organization in every town and hamlet where colored people dwell, of National Business Men's Leagues, and the gradual federation from these of state and national organizations."[83] Moreover, this historic gathering produced the first comprehensive assessment of the state of black business in the United States including an attempt to enumerate the number of businesses owned by African American men.[84]

Besides Du Bois's admirable quest to present qualitative and quantitative data related to the status of black business in America, his 1899 "Negro in Business" conference featured an illuminating presentation by Professor John Hope of Atlanta Baptist College (later renamed Morehouse College) titled "The Meaning of Business." Hope, who later became the first black president of Atlanta Baptist College/Morehouse College, provided a variety of rationales as to why it was important for blacks to establish commercial enterprises in the United States. In discussing what African Americans' ultimate contributions to civilization would include, Hope declared that there were "emotional, spiritual elements that presage gifts from the Negro more ennobling and enduring than factories, rail-roads, and banks." Nevertheless, "without these factories, railroads and banks, He [the Negro] cannot accomplish his highest aim." Moreover, Hope told the audience that "we are living among the so-called Anglo-Saxons and dealing with them. They are a conquering people who turn their conquests into their pockets. The vanquished may not always recognize this as true, but the fact remains." As Hope continued, "business seems to be not simply the raw material of the Anglo-Saxon civilization, but almost the civilization itself." Because of this reality, Hope concluded, "living among such a people is it not obvious that we cannot escape its most powerful motive and survive? To the finite vision, to say the least, the policy of avoiding entrance in the world's *business* would be suicidal to the Negro."[85]

Although Hope urged African Americans to engage in commercial activities, like their "Anglo-Saxon" fellow countrymen, he did not call for prospective black entrepreneurs to emulate the actions of the era's so-called robber barons whose commercial success came at the expense of others. Quite to the contrary, Hope urged blacks to use business enterprise as a means to uplift the entire black community. Specifically, he declared that "more money diffused among the masses through Negro capital" would assist a variety of individuals and groups (not just the entrepreneurial class). Furthermore, Hope declared that African American men should be at the forefront of this movement, stating "I know of no men who as a class go so far for the good of others as do Negro men for the good of the race."[86]

Later in 1899, after Du Bois's successful Atlanta University conference; the National Afro-American Council (NAAC), a pioneering civil rights organization that began in 1890, appointed Du Bois at its annual meeting to "the post of director of a 'Negro business bureau' with responsibility for organizing local business leagues as suggested by him in the Atlanta meeting."[87] For his part, Booker T. Washington, who did not attend the 1899 meeting of the NAAC, sought to establish a business-related organization that he could control. What became the National Negro Business League differed from the National Afro-American Council's business agenda in that it reversed "the order of Du Bois' organizational priorities, Washington stressed the importance of a 'national organization' out of which 'will grow local business leagues that will tend to improve the Negro as a business factor.'" Also, Washington, cognizant that his proposed NNBL could be construed as an attempt to undermine the NAAC, declared that he wanted to create something that "is expected to do a distinct work that no other organization now in existence can do so well."[88]

The first annual meeting of the NNBL took place in Boston August 23–24, 1900. Attracting a hundred delegates from across the United States, the convention's proceedings were tightly controlled by Washington. As one observer remarked about this convention's sessions, they featured "no point-of-order squabbles, no parliamentary wrangles, no disgruntled individuals to air grievances . . . no whining or lugubrious complaints." Instead, all of the speakers were "brim full of business." An important order of business at the first annual meeting of the NNBL was the election of officers. Predictably, Booker T. Washington was elected president of the fledgling organization. In addition, persons elected to the organization's executive committee were individuals linked to Washington in one way or another. According to John Burrows, this was significant because the NNBL's executive committee "was given the authority to set the time for future conventions and review all proposed resolutions before their presentation in the open sessions."[89]

The proceedings of the 1901 NNBL annual meeting in Chicago were similar to those of the previous year's inaugural conclave. A published report of this gathering proudly mentions that, unlike some African American meetings that placed a premium on oratory skills, this convention featured speakers who "were plain, practical, serious, and sincere." Moreover, the preface to the published official proceedings of the 1901 meeting notes that "there were no complaints, no indignations, no lamentations, and no resolutions denouncing anybody or anything." Indeed, the mood of the meeting indicated that "the old sentiment of political servitude and dependence upon politics and politicians for relief from all our ills was fast giving way to the newer sentiment of self-help and self-reliance." Therefore, the persons who attended this meeting talked about "schools, homes, factories, stores, banks, corporations, insurance, improved agriculture, merchandising and business ethics, with as much animation and hopefulness as the colored men of twenty-five years ago 'in Convention assembled' talked of candidates, resolutions, and offices."[90]

Although Booker T. Washington was, arguably, the most well-known black person in the nation at the beginning of the twentieth century, most of the attendees at the second annual NNBL meeting, such as Anthony Overton Jr., were not then notable individuals. As the published report of this convention declares, "there were no Honorables, no Colonels, and no Ex-anybodys. With two or three exceptions, the delegates were but little known outside of their respective communities." Nevertheless, they were individuals who were "creating a source of new strength for further [racial] advancement." Considering his previous struggles, Anthony Overton, no doubt, relished the opportunity to be among persons regarded as "the architects of our future, giving their thought and talents towards the problems that are near, real, and possible of solution."[91]

Overton's August 23, 1901, presentation titled "The Negro as a Manufacturer and Jobber," exemplifies the "plain, practical, serious, and sincere" nature of the papers delivered at this conference. He discussed such subjects as how to extend credit to customers, the intersection between personal morality and business practices, and how to effectively advertise.[92] Two other more nuanced topics that Overton spoke about were racial prejudice in the commercial world and how the growing proliferation of business conglomerates ("trusts") affected black entrepreneurs.

In keeping with the overall upbeat tone of NNBL conventions, Overton declared that "while there is no denying the fact that the negro is subject to some disadvantages on account of race prejudice . . . I am pleased to state however, from personal experience as a salesman, I can attribute the failure to make a sale to very few instances to this cause alone." He went on to discuss how successful commercial transactions with "a noble hearted Anglo-Saxon brother" made up "for the sales I might occasionally lose from unwarranted prejudice." In terms of business conglomerates, Overton asserted "I will state very candidly the trusts have been a benefit to the negro." He went on to declare that "these soulless corporations to their credit have uniform prices and terms, and a negro manufacturer with good commercial rating can now buy raw material as low as his white competitor."[93]

As a result of his well-received remarks at the second NNBL convention in Chicago, Anthony Overton became a protégé and friend of Booker T. Washington. In fact, subsequent correspondence between Washington and Overton provides additional insights as to how the Wizard of Tuskegee conducted his affairs during this period. In a March 1904 letter to Overton marked "Personal and Confidential," Washington asked Overton's help regarding Dr.

William D. Crum's stalled confirmation in the US Senate to become collector of the Port of Charleston (South Carolina). Although President Theodore Roosevelt stated his intent to name Crum, an African American, to the post in 1902, white opposition had kept Crum's appointment from being quickly confirmed in the Senate. In the interim, Crum served in this capacity through a series of presidential recess appointments.[94]

Washington urged Overton in the letter "to arrange to have a number of strong colored men in your state send at once a large number of telegrams and letters to your Senators urging them to have the Crum case called up and favorably acted upon at once. If you can get Negro organizations to do the same it will help much." Washington, who preferred to keep his advocacy for such causes underground, further instructed Overton to "please do not let this letter pass out of your hands." Moreover, Washington concluded by declaring "I shall depend upon you to see that my name does not appear in any manner in connection with the telegrams and letters." In his reply, Overton, "with pleasure," agreed to assist Washington with the Crum matter. Moreover, he assured Washington that "you can fully depend upon my handling your communication with the due caution as you have suggested."[95]

Historians have long commented on Booker T. Washington's complex personality. For instance, as his biographer Louis R. Harlan notes, "perhaps psychoanalysis or role psychology would help us solve Booker T. Washington's behavioral riddle, if we could only put him on the couch." Harlan suggests that "if we could remove [Washington's] layers of secrecy as one peels an onion, perhaps at the center of Washington's being would be revealed a person with a single-minded concern with power, a minotaur, a fox, or Brer Rabbit, some frightened little man like the Wizard of Oz, or in the case of the onion, nothing—a personality that had vanished into the roles it played."[96] Informed conjecture suggests that his mentor's preoccupation with secrecy may have had an effect on Anthony Overton's subsequent business affairs. As discussed in chapter 3, when Overton established the *Half-Century Magazine* in 1916 he employed a clandestine strategy that included putting forward a female associate as the owner, editor, and public face of this woman-oriented periodical; and using anonymous editorials and a pseudonym to convey his beliefs regarding business enterprise and personal conduct to *Half-Century*'s readers.

Business Disaster and Recovery

Besides establishing a personal relationship with Booker T. Washington, Anthony Overton, after the 1901 NNBL annual meeting, undoubtedly felt more energized and confident as he proceeded to grow his company. Unfortunately, in the context of these aspirations, severe flooding submerged Kansas City, Missouri, in 1903 ultimately destroying Overton Hygienic and a host of other commercial enterprises in the area. Overton's March 1904 letter to Booker T. Washington provides an intimate glimpse as to how he responded to this business reversal. Although Overton laments that the previous year's flood had destroyed his manufacturing facilities, he optimistically claims that "adversities sometimes tend to make a man of one . . . unless some new ones develops, within another six months, from a business standpoint we will be doing a larger and better business than before." Overton's confidence appears linked to an offer from a supplier to loan him the money necessary to rebuild his enterprise.[97] Curiously, in this same letter Overton also tells Washington that his manufacturing facility in Topeka had also been destroyed in the June 1903 flood. Yet, Topeka city directories have no listing for Anthony Overton or the Hygienic Manufacturing Company during the period in question.[98]

Indeed, Overton's reference to a Topeka factory appears to have been another instance of personal hyperbole. Nevertheless, although company records from this period are not extant, his business recovery is documented in Kansas City, Kansas, annual city directories. The 1907 directory there lists the Hygienic Manufacturing Company at 2033 North Third Street, and Overton and his family lived next door at 2031 North Third Street. Moreover, the 1910 edition provides a detailed inside glimpse of the company's operations. This publication lists Overton as the manager of the Hygienic Manufacturing Company; his wife Clara is identified as the company "forelady" (suggesting she directly supervised the workers who produced the products); his daughters Eva and Mabel are cited as Overton Hygienic's stenographer and bookkeeper, respectively, and his son Everett is listed as a salesman for the firm.[99] The business model of using family members as the core employees of an enterprise had been employed by his father (as well as many other entrepreneurs). In fact, as succeeding chapters discuss, Overton later expanded this template to include his sons-in-law.

Another aspect of the reborn Overton Hygienic Manufacturing Company that would manifest itself in a variety of ways in succeeding years was Anthony Overton's employment of innovative marketing campaigns. An early manifestation of Overton's creativity in this regard was his underwriting of the 1911 *National Negro Almanac and Yearbook*. Besides spotlighting such information as the black population of major cities and the location of the nation's black banks, this work also features a plethora of advertisements for Overton Hygienic Manufacturing Company products. For instance, an ad describing High-Brown De Luxe Face Powder informs readers that it "is the first and only face powder that was ever made especially for the complexion of colored ladies." Moreover, African American female consumers were told that "the use of face powders made by white concerns for the white woman, make you look as if you had fallen into a flour barrel."[100]

Another Move

Notwithstanding the *National Negro Almanac and Yearbook*, other records insinuate that both the initial and reborn Overton Hygienic Manufacturing Company had a negligible commercial presence in either the Kansas City of Missouri or of Kansas.[101] For example, Anthony Overton is not mentioned in Charles E. Coulter's 2006 *"Take Up the Black Man's Burden": Kansas City's African American Communities, 1865–1939*.[102] Also, a contemporary economic overview of both Kansas Cities notes that "half of the Negro property in Greater Kansas City is owned by fifty persons. One fourth of this half is owned by ten persons, which shows that like the white man, the wealth of the Negroes is in the hands of a few persons."[103] Since Anthony Overton was not a member of Kansas City's black economic elite, his local prospects appeared limited. Consequently, in 1911, he, like thousands of African Americans before and after him, migrated to Chicago seeking a better life and more opportunity. Among other things, the ambitious Overton believed that Chicago, with its network of railroads that facilitated the distribution of products, would be an economic boon to his young business. Also, unlike previous moves that resulted in failure or lower than expected rewards, Overton's move to Chicago would result in entrepreneurial success beyond his wildest dreams.

2. A Star Is Born

Initial Years in Chicago

Anthony Overton's decision to relocate his family and business to Chicago in 1911 proved to be one of the wisest moves of his life. Within a relatively short period of time, the once frustrated entrepreneur established an important business niche in one of the nation's leading cities. The thirteenth annual convention of the NNBL, held in Chicago on August 21–23, 1912, contributed mightily to Overton's enhanced status. His presentation at this meeting provided Anthony Overton an opportunity to shine in his new hometown and helped open up other opportunities in the Windy City. For instance, in 1913, Overton assumed the presidency of the Chicago Negro Business League. Yet, Anthony Overton's first years in Chicago were not without challenges. Within a year after his arrival, Clara Overton's sudden death forced Overton to reorient both his personal and business affairs. In the period following his wife's death, Overton began to more fully incorporate his daughters into company operations. In 1915, Overton opened a new company branch office staffed by all females (including his three daughters). Later that year, Overton Hygienic's female personnel were a hit at the Lincoln Jubilee convened in Chicago. In the end, Anthony Overton's increased use of attractive young women, as the public face of his enterprise, helped him increase his prominence in a female-oriented industry. This marketing strategy appeared crucial because both of his primary competitors, Annie Turnbo-Malone and the woman who built an empire as Madam C. J. Walker, possessed more extensive business infrastructures. By 1916, Overton Hygienic held its first convention which allowed Anthony Overton to both savor his current good fortune and to begin visualizing even greater business success in the future.

Black Chicago in 1900

Given his background and interests, Anthony Overton moved to Chicago at an especially opportune time. During the late nineteenth century, Chicago's black leaders focused their attention on desegregating all areas of civic life and concurrently deemphasized the importance of race-based institutions. For instance, as Allan H. Spear asserted, "a proposal to establish a Negro YMCA in 1889 met with loud cries of protest and after a spirited indignation meeting the idea was shelved." However, after 1900, in the wake of growing white hostility, black Chicago leaders increasingly adopted "a northern variation of the philosophy of racial solidarity and self-help that had emerged in the post-Reconstruction South and had found its greatest vogue in the teachings of Booker T. Washington."[1] Moreover, from a business standpoint, as Chicago's African American population steadily increased, it became conceivable to believe that black Chicago could sustain a separate economic infrastructure.

The Thirteenth Annual Convention of the NNBL

The Thirteenth Annual Convention of the National Negro Business League, convened in Chicago from August 21 to August 23, 1912, helped solidify the ascendancy of local black leaders who espoused the Washingtonian philosophy of racial solidarity and self-help. It also provided Anthony Overton, a long-time associate of Booker T. Washington, an opportunity to increase his visibility in his new hometown. Before Overton's appearance at the 1912 NNBL meeting in Chicago, his initial experiences in the Windy City have scant documentary evidence. A display advertisement in the March 16, 1912, issue of the *Chicago Defender* indicates that the company's first headquarters was at 5752–54 South State Street. Also, after Clara Overton's sudden death in July 1912, the *Defender*'s July 27 listing of recent deaths reported that the Overtons' first Chicago home was at 5830 South Wabash Avenue.[2]

The recorded proceedings of the thirteenth annual NNBL meeting proudly declared how much African American business development had progressed since the organization had convened its second annual convention in Chicago in 1901. For instance, a summary report candidly admitted "that first convention held in Chicago seemed to many of us more of an experiment than an expression of things possible." Moreover, "at the time we could not talk much about banks, insurance companies, big land holders, factories, and town builders."[3]

Despite the organization's relatively humble beginnings, the 1912 Chicago meeting of the NNBL acknowledged "an increase of banks, an increase of corporations, an increase of farm lands and crops, [and a] remarkable increase of men and women who are branching out in new lines of business." In addition, by 1912 the NNBL had spawned a growing number of affiliated organizations including "the National Negro Bankers Association, the National Funeral Directors' Association, the National Negro Bar Association, and the National Negro Press Association."[4]

Just as the NNBL (and African American business enterprise) had evolved during its embryonic years, its 1912 convention indicated that Chicago had similarly evolved as a locale favorable to African American business development. In his welcoming remarks made on behalf of "the Local Negro Business League of Chicago," Attorney S. Laing Williams, a longtime supporter of Booker T. Washington, told the audience "the city of Chicago is fast becoming a great Negro center; thousands of members of our race have come and settled here from practically every State in the Union; perhaps there are not more than two or three cities in the entire country having a larger percentage of our people in the make-up of their population than the city of Chicago." He further told the assemblage of business proponents "we feel that your coming will be the means of infusing new life, encouragement, and inspiration into the hearts of all our people" and that "your sessions will demonstrate to this city and the public in general the remarkable progress we have made along business lines, thereby justifying faith in the race and furnishing an incentive for enlarged opportunities and greater economic development."[5]

Dr. George C. Hall, a prominent black Chicago physician and president of the local NNBL branch, followed up S. Laing Williams's remarks with a rousing speech where, among other things, he declared "the world has heard of how the Indians have been helped by our Government, but instead of being helped from the *outside*, we are here to-day to welcome a group of men and women . . . who have arisen from obscurity to a measure of success in the business world largely as a result of helping themselves." Hall then introduced Booker T. Washington, who officially gaveled the thirteenth annual meeting to order.[6]

One of the most well-received addresses at this convention was Overton's Thursday, August 22, 1912, presentation, "The Largest Negro Manufacturing Enterprise in the United States—'The Overton-Hygienic Mfg. Co., Chicago, Ill.'" Interspersing humorous anecdotes with concrete information about his business growth, Overton presented himself as one of the most experienced entrepreneurs at the meeting. John H. Burrows, in his critical study of the NNBL, cited the tendency of the organization's convention speakers, for the purpose of inspiring their audiences, to exaggerate their business success. Considering that Anthony Overton did, at various times, provide other hyperbolic observations about his past, Burrows's observations appear especially relevant in this instance. Nevertheless, because Overton Hygienic records from this period were destroyed, commentators have referenced Overton's own comments at the NNBL's 1912 convention to assess his early entrepreneurial career.[7]

Overton told the 1912 attendees that he began Overton Hygienic with $1,960 in capital, while providing no information as to how he raised that significant sum of money. With Hygienic Pet Baking Powder the first, other products were "added from time to time as experience, capital and other conditions would warrant." He further asserted that "at present, we manufacture fifty-two different articles." To his listeners he described Overton Hygienic's early marketing plan, in which salaried salesmen sold the "products at wholesale only to merchants, large schools, and public institutions." Moreover, the embryonic Overton Hygienic Manufacturing Company utilized "agents on commission, selling our products from house to house."[8]

The official proceedings note that Overton received applause when he proudly declared "having abiding faith in our own people, we have conducted our business strictly as a Negro enterprise, and have none but Negroes employed in any capacity." Early on, it had been suggested to him that he needed to employ white salesmen because whites and even some blacks would not buy a black-owned company's products. To illustrate the correctness of his decision to ignore such advice, Overton shared his experiences with a white storeowner in Lawrence, Kansas. After looking at various product samples, the prospective buyer reportedly asked, "Are these articles made by colored people?" Overton, wary about the motivation for this question, replied, "yes, does it make a difference?" To Overton's pleasant surprise, the white merchant replied: "it does; there are so few of your people that really try to do anything worthwhile that, in appreciation for your effort, I am going to give you an order and will take special interest in pushing your goods."[9]

By utilizing a variety of marketing and sales strategies, Overton sought to reach the embryonic black female consumer market. As he told the NNBL in 1912, "when we added our line of toilet articles, we placed colored girls' pictures on our Talcum Powder, Hair Pomades, and other toilet articles, and later we originated and made a face powder, especially for our own colored women." In speaking about Overton Hygienic's pioneering High-Brown Face Powder, which was sold in "the most handsome and expensive face-powder-box that has ever been made," Overton generated laughter and applause with his declaration that "on top of the said box . . . is printed the explanation that the said space is reserved for the picture of the most beautiful colored woman in the United States, which we propose to put on the box later as soon as we find her."[10]

Besides demonstrating his sense of humor and chronicling the early history of the Overton Hygienic Manufacturing Company, Overton discussed some of the possibilities and challenges facing entrepreneurially-minded blacks. On a positive note, he asserted that "there are openings for our people to engage in many mercantile and manufacturing lines, some of which are: department stores, the manufacture of shoes, clothing, soaps, candles, etc." Yet he also lamented "that it is becoming more and more difficult to do so, for the reason that each year more experience and capital are required."[11]

To buttress his assertions, Overton provided a personal business testimony related to his first product, baking powder. In 1898, when he started Overton Hygienic, he told the audience that he could buy the materials to produce baking powder only one barrel at a time. However, "that was before the era of the trusts. After the formation of the trusts, they required us to buy at least ten barrels of each material or else purchase the same from other firms that did." Moreover, "two or three years later, they raised the requirement to car-load lots. This year, the requirements have again been raised . . . we are required to contract for five car loads of each ingredient during the year, although we are permitted to take the same in single car-lots as we desire."[12]

Notwithstanding these increasing business requirements, which Overton told the audience his company could meet, he reiterated the positive comments he made about trusts in his presentation at the 1901 NNBL meeting, "The Negro as a Manufacturer and Jobber." Specifically, Overton asserted that "as Negroes we find the trust a benefit to us, for the reason that previous to the forming of these large combines, our white competitors could often buy various raw materials at a price lower than we could, for previous to the combinations the several raw material houses in competition with each other would give their sales representatives the right to cut prices on their products in special cases." Moreover, these "deductions would always be given to the house that could buy the largest quantities, or whose buyer would entertain the said representative with a box party at the grand opera, an after-theater supper, or by other social courtesies." Finally, because black companies could not offer "such social favors," they "would not likely get the benefit of the lower prices." According to Overton, the formation of trusts eliminated an unequal price structure for raw materials. As he told his NNBL audience, "the trusts have only one price, based upon the market quotations for certain designated quantities, and whether you are black or white, rich or poor (provided you are not too poor to buy and pay for the quantities ordered), the price is the same to all."[13]

During the question-and-answer period after Overton's presentation, George Knox, the publisher of the *Indianapolis Freeman* and a longtime

NNBL supporter, declared, "I arise to ask this convention for a few minutes of its time to hear a remarkable woman . . . She is the woman who gave $1,000 to the Young Men's Christian Association of Indianapolis,—Madam Walker, the lady I refer to, is the manufacturer of hair goods and preparations."[14] As A'Lelia Bundles has written, Booker T. Washington, who presided over this part of the meeting, dismissed Knox's request on the pretext that it was now time to discuss "the question of [NNBL] life membership." Both Knox and Walker perceived this to be a snub because Washington possessed the power to alter the convention program as he saw fit. Washington's actions in this regard appeared linked to his long-standing antipathy toward black female beauty products, which he believed fostered an imitation of white beauty standards. Moreover, his refusal to acknowledge Walker's presence, even after she publicly confronted him the following day, suggests that Washington's apparent sexism prevented him from celebrating the activities of a successful African American female entrepreneur.[15]

Anthony Overton's favorable placement in the 1912 National Negro Business League's convention schedule reinforces the theory that Washington's sexism, rather than a dislike for black female beauty products, motivated his dismissal of Walker at the 1912 NNBL convention. Davarian Baldwin has assessed this phenomenon by insinuating that "an alliance was made between Overton and Washington's NNBL because of the shared desire for black male enterprise to fashion black female conduct and beauty." Yet, Baldwin does not supply a substantive source that verifies this claim. The citation associated with the presumed alliance between Washington and Overton only discusses Overton's later commercial building projects.[16] Finally, beyond hypotheses related to conspiracy and Booker T. Washington's attitudes toward women, the evidence suggests the dichotomy between how Washington regarded Anthony Overton and Madam C. J. Walker could be linked to one simple fact: whereas Booker T. Washington knew and trusted Anthony Overton, he did not, at the time, have a similar relationship with Walker.

Personal Tragedy, Professional Advancement

Notwithstanding the interesting dynamics of its immediate aftermath, Anthony Overton's August 1912 presentation at the annual NNBL convention represented a personal and professional triumph that dramatically enhanced his stature in the Windy City. Yet, this growing positive visibility contained a bittersweet component. During the previous month, Overton's wife Clara suddenly passed away. Clara Overton's obituary, which appeared in the July 20, 1912, issue of the *Chicago Defender*, provides additional important insights

Anthony Overton, ca. 1913. (Courtesy of Sharon F. Patton)

about this period. For instance, it notes that, besides business considerations, the family moved to Chicago so "their children may get better educational advantages." The article states that the Overtons had "two girls at Chicago University, one girl attending high school, and a son in his last year at Lane [Tech], a great friend of [Fritz] Pollard."[17]

Clara Overton's obituary suggests that she had been more than just a dutiful, supportive spouse. Specifically, it describes the "wife of the high brown powder manufacturer" as "the prime mover of the business and did lots to give it the reputtion [*sic*] it has."[18] Among other things, Clara Overton supervised the production of Overton Hygienic products and presumably played a major role in helping the young company successfully relocate its operations to a new city.[19] The positive local response to his appearance at the 1912 annual NNBL meeting may well have provided her grieving husband with additional duties and recognition that helped take his mind off of the loss of his wife and business partner.

In 1913, Overton assumed the presidency of the Chicago Negro Business League, which extended his influence beyond the Overton Hygienic Manufacturing Company. The evidence also suggests that Overton, to buttress his growing visibility as a black Chicago community leader, began to consciously embellish his past activities and accomplishments. Clara Overton, the only person who knew otherwise, was now deceased. This seemingly facilitated Overton's reinvention of his pre-Chicago career.

Christopher R. Reed, in his 2014 study of African American migration to Chicago between 1900 and 1919, asserts that many of the period's local black elite considered advanced formal education as a prerequisite for assuming community leadership. Given this mindset, some of Chicago's African American upper class, among them physician Charles E. Bentley and attorney Ferdinand L. Barnett, looked down even on Booker T. Washington. As Reed declared, such individuals "despaired of Washington's lack of formal educational training and equated it with an inability to provide leadership for their racial group." Considering this reality, Overton seemingly felt compelled to reshape himself into a Renaissance man whose background included serving as a municipal judge in Topeka, Kansas.[20] In retrospect, Overton's embellishment of his past life seems sadly misguided. His overcoming of early trials and tribulations, through perseverance and determination, appear far more complimentary to his legacy than the Renaissance man myth he created.

Although Anthony Overton overstated his credentials to enhance his persona as a business and community leader, his early accomplishments in Chicago indicate that he engaged in more than mere puffery. For instance, under his leadership, the Chicago Negro Business League became affiliated with the Chicago Chamber of Commerce. This prompted the *Chicago Defender* to declare in March 1914 that "the Chicago league is now one of the strongest branches of the nation's Negro Business League." As president of the Chicago Negro Business League, Anthony Overton also became a sought-after speaker in the city. One of his favorite venues was Olivet Baptist Church, at Twenty-Seventh and South Dearborn Street. On May 18, 1913, Olivet's Standard Literary Society convened their first Sunday afternoon mass meeting, which sought to attract "every person interested in the welfare of the Negro in Chicago, with special reference to his business activity and employment." Besides Anthony Overton, speakers included the real estate magnate and banker Jesse Binga and the noted activist Ida B. Wells-Barnett. Also, Olivet's Standard Literary Society encouraged other black Chicago clubs and organizations to host their own mass meetings "for the purpose of creating sentiment and interest along these specific lines [business activity and employment]." Within a couple of years, Anthony Overton regularly received top billing for his presentations at Olivet Baptist Church's Sunday afternoon mass meetings and similar venues. A June 1915 *Chicago Defender* article acknowledged Overton's oratorical talents: "President of Local League Rivals Booker T. Washington in His Plea for Race Unity."[21]

A New Business Plan = Greater Business Success

Anthony Overton's enhanced visibility as president of the Chicago Negro Business League helped create additional visibility for his Overton Hygienic Manufacturing Company. Also, during this period, Overton began to more fully incorporate his children into company operations. This process evolved to the point that, by 1915, Overton's daughters were actively engaged in the public marketing of Overton Hygienic products. Moreover, the success of Overton's March 6, 1915, opening of a new company branch office at 3519 South State Street (featuring his daughters and other female employees) and his extremely popular exhibit at the Lincoln Jubilee later that year (that also spotlighted his female sales force) provide important clues as to how he, as a male entrepreneur, heightened his prominence in a female-oriented industry. Specifically, Overton decided to put forward his daughters and other attractive young female employees as the public face of his enterprise.

Between the time of their mother's death and their increased participation in the family business, Eva, Mabel, and Frances Overton became ever more active members of black Chicago's young elite. For instance, all three young women participated in a September 11, 1913, suffragettes' convention held at Grace Presbyterian Church at 3409 South Dearborn Street. The following year, Eva and Frances participated in a *Chicago Defender*–sponsored contest, "Who Is the Most Popular Girl in Chicago?" Finally, Eva achieved additional distinction by being a charter member of Alpha Kappa Alpha Sorority Inc.'s first undergraduate chapter established in the Midwest. Alpha Kappa Alpha, the first African American Greek-letter sorority, chartered its Beta chapter in Chicago on October 13, 1913.[22]

Before the spring of 1915, Overton Hygienic conducted its business at 5200–02 South Wabash Avenue. After Clara's death, Overton moved the entire family business as well as the family residence to this multiuse facility. The opening of the 3519 South State Street branch office, among other things, reflected a larger industry trend. As Kathy Peiss has written, during the early twentieth century beauty product manufacturers increased their employment of product demonstrators to increase sales. For instance, "as Helena Rubenstein and Elizabeth Arden expanded from salon services to product sales, they converted the demonstrator into a sales representative who toured exclusive shops and department stores throughout the country, demonstrating cosmetics, training saleswomen, and generating publicity."[23] Yet, notwithstanding the activities of beauty industry giants, Anthony Overton, because of racism, would have found it impossible to place Overton Hygienic product demonstrators in mainstream department and drugstores. Thus, he shrewdly developed his own facility for this purpose.

Evidence indicates that favorable press coverage of Overton Hygienic's expansion assisted Overton's quest for greater commercial visibility. For instance, a March 1915 *Chicago Defender* article about the new South State Street facility declares that "Mr. Overton manufactures all of his goods and are copyrighted, so many others having tried to imitate." Moreover, *Defender* readers were told that "no woman of today who looks sweet and charming is without 'High Brown' powder or perfumes made by this house." Within a month, the new branch office had, indeed, generated increased interest in Overton's various personal care products, as in another *Chicago Defender* article: "thousands of people have become acquainted with the powders and perfumes manufactured by Mr. Overton only and they claim his goods to be the very best on the market." Moreover, readers were urged to visit Overton's State Street facility to see "the pretty girls who will be in charge."[24]

Overton's use of physically attractive female employees at his State Street branch office to generate increased excitement about his products set the stage for another major entrepreneurial triumph. Later that year he used the same strategy to become a sensation at the Lincoln Jubilee, a national celebration, held in Chicago, to celebrate fifty years of African American freedom. The Lincoln Jubilee, which convened at the Chicago Coliseum between August 22 and September 16, attracted delegates from throughout the country. Financed by contributions from Illinois and nineteen other states, this event celebrated African American progress in such areas as education, religion, agriculture, business, and the arts. In its front-page coverage of this event, the *Chicago Broad Ax* quoted the opening-day keynote speaker, Dr. J. W. E. Bowen of Atlanta's Gammon Theological Seminary: "the Negro should not be judged by the American people on the progress they have made in fifty years; give them a hundred, a hundred fifty, yes, two hundred years if you please."[25]

Predictably, the *Chicago Defender*, the city's leading African American newspaper, extensively covered this historic gathering. In an August 1915 article, readers were informed that "the biggest and most attractive exhibit is from a Chicago concern. It is the Overton Hygienic Company."[26]

Although Overton, himself, was at this exhibit, his seven female assistants, including his three daughters, were spotlighted. In fact, as the journalist who wrote the story noted, "it was a pleasure for the Defender reporter to pass by and have a girl who uses the 'High Brown Powder' beckon him over and fill the lapel of his coat with a perfume that was as sweet as magnolia." The *Defender* continued its coverage of the twenty-six-day Lincoln Jubilee and the public's response to the Overton Hygienic Company's exhibit, noting that "Overton's Still Drawing." Readers were informed that "a Defender reporter could hardly make his way to the exhibit, the crowd was so thick."[27]

A later summary report of the Lincoln Jubilee puts Overton Hygienic's visibility in clearer perspective. Besides Anthony Overton's company, the numerous other exhibits included such diverse phenomena as the all-black town of Mound Bayou, Mississippi; the prominent black inventor Elijah Mc-Coy; John Brown's daughter (who showed a lock of her father's hair); and a box reportedly used to transport fugitive slaves on the Underground Railroad. Moreover, this publication declared that "the demonstrations mentioned however, do not by any means complete the splendid list of exhibits which literally crowded all the available space in the Coliseum."[28]

Primary Competitors

In retrospect, Anthony Overton's decision to put forward female employees as the public face of the Overton Hygienic Manufacturing Company represented a pragmatic response to his gender-based disadvantage in the evolving African American personal care products industry. For instance, Annie Turnbo-Malone later reminisced about how she initially generated consumer interest in her products: "I went around in the buggy and made speeches, demonstrated the shampoo on myself, and talked about cleanliness and hygiene, until they realized I was right." Similarly, Sarah Breedlove, one of Malone's early students who would later gain fame under the business name (also her married name) of Madam C. J. Walker, utilized a personal testimonial in her advertising—the classic "before" and "after" images—to assist her marketing campaigns.[29] Consequently, as a man who did not use his feminine beauty products, Overton had to rely on female surrogates to extol the benefits of his High-Brown Face Powder and other toiletries.

Although Walker has been regarded as the pioneering figure in the embryonic black-owned personal care products industry, that distinction rightfully belongs to her teacher (and later bitter competitor) Annie Turnbo-Malone. The evidence clearly indicates that Turnbo-Malone created personal care products for other blacks long before Walker did. Moreover, Malone created a distribution and marketing system for these products that were later employed by Walker, Overton, and other competitors.

Annie Turnbo was born on August 9, 1869, on a small farm near Metropolis, Illinois. When both parents, Robert and Isabella Cook-Turnbo, died before she reached school age, Annie's nine older brothers and sisters took care of her. After graduating from elementary school in Metropolis, she went to live with a married sister in Peoria, Illinois, to attend high school. Although ill health kept her from graduating, Annie's favorite class during her abbreviated high school career was chemistry. Significantly, her growing interest in chemistry melded with her long-standing interest in hair care. Apparently, as a little girl, "her sisters and their friends humored her by allowing her to plait their hair—a play game which was to develop into a dignified and profitable profession."[30]

In 1900, Annie moved with another older sister to Lovejoy, Illinois. Here, she rented office space for five dollars a month and began conducting experiments to develop a product to help black women better manage their hair. These efforts culminated in the creation of her Wonderful Hair Grower. Within a short period of time, this product, which she marketed from door to door, became a local sensation. As one biographical sketch of Annie Turnbo-Malone has described this period of her life, "women liked Annie's hair formula. It was different from the goose fat, soap and other oils they had been using to manage their hair. It did not damage their scalps like stronger products on the market did."[31]

Significantly, the positive response of black female consumers in Lovejoy to Turnbo's Wonderful Hair Grower soon generated interest in the product in nearby St. Louis, Missouri. In an astute business decision, Turnbo, moved to St. Louis in 1902 to take advantage of its larger African American consumer market. Moreover, the 1904 World's Fair, scheduled to be held in St. Louis, provided Turnbo with the potential to market her Wonderful Hair Grower and other products to black female visitors to the city.[32]

As she had with her initial marketing campaign in Lovejoy, Annie Turnbo relied on "diligent house-to-house canvassing to advertise her preparations, enlisting customers by prevailing upon women and girls to permit her to treat their hair and scalps." Moreover, to maximize her potential profit, Malone hired and trained assistants to duplicate her efforts. Because blacks in St.

Louis and elsewhere were denied access to traditional distribution systems, this process of door-to-door sales, coupled with free demonstrations, would become the industry's marketing template.[33]

During the 1904 World's Fair in St. Louis, Turnbo, indeed, was able to reach a broader market through a retail outlet she established. The success of this endeavor prompted Turnbo-Malone to expand the marketing of her products even further. Later in 1904, "she launched her first extensive advertising program which consisted of a tour through the South demonstrating her preparations and methods, and she had advertisements of her preparations printed in Negro newspapers." While in the South, just as she had done in St. Louis, Turnbo hired and trained women to serve as local sales agents. These individuals, in turn, recruited others. Consequently, by 1910, Turnbo had a national distribution network in place.[34]

One of Annie Turnbo's earliest sales agents was Sarah Breedlove, a southern migrant working as a washerwoman in early twentieth-century St. Louis, who had begun to experience serious hair loss. It remains unclear as to how Breedlove and Malone actually met. A'Lelia Bundles, Walker's biographer and her great-great-granddaughter, has offered the several informed speculations. First, "after hearing of her [Malone's] reputation for hair restoration, Sarah may have sought her out." Also, Bundles suggests that they could have met through Sarah's widowed sister-in-law, Hettie Martin Breedlove, whose family, similar to Turnbo's, was also from tiny Metropolis, Illinois. Finally, Bundles surmises that "their meeting could have been the result of a fortuitous knock on Sarah's door" during one of Turnbo's house-to-house canvassing campaigns.[35]

Besides the nebulosity concerning how Turnbo and Breedlove actually met, there is intense controversy regarding how Turnbo's *agent* Sarah Breedlove evolved into the *independent* Madam C. J. Walker. According to Bundles, when Breedlove left St. Louis to resettle in Denver on July 19, 1905, her bag was filled with Turnbo's Wonderful Hair Grower. However, shortly after arriving in Denver, the ambitious Breedlove decided to cut ties with Turnbo and establish her own product line. According to Breedlove, her quest for independence was motivated by a dream where "a big black man appeared before me and told me what to mix for my hair. Some of the remedy was from Africa, but I sent for it, mixed it, put it on my scalp and in a few weeks my hair was coming in faster than it had ever fallen out."[36]

Also, according to Bundles's self-admitted speculation, the inspiration for the subsequent appearance of Madam C. J. Walker's eponymous products could have been Edmund L. Scholtz, a white Denver druggist, rather than a "big black man" seen in a dream. Specifically, Scholtz was a boarder in a

Denver rooming house where Breedlove worked as a cook. During the course of a conversation, Scholtz allegedly told Breedlove that he would analyze Turnbo-Malone's Wonderful Hair Grower and tell her how she could modify it to create a new product.[37]

Perhaps ironically, Breedlove, while making plans to develop her own product line, continued to market Turnbo's products in Colorado. In fact, she used Turnbo's grassroots marketing strategy in this regard: "I made house-to-house canvasses among people of my race, and after awhile I got going pretty well." By the summer of 1906, Sarah, now married to Charles J. Walker, emerged with a new public persona, Madam C. J. Walker, and a new product line bearing her assumed name. Moreover, she demonstrated what else she had gleaned from her association with Turnbo. Walker and her new husband announced a September tour "to place their goods on the market through the southern and eastern states."[38]

Turnbo, who regarded Sarah Breedlove's transformation into Madam C. J. Walker as a "fraudulent imitation," moved quickly to protect her financial interests. In 1906, Turnbo adopted and copyrighted the trade name Poro, apparently derived from a West African word associated with mutual aid societies.[39]

While Walker borrowed liberally from Turnbo's business plan (if not product base), the former Sarah Breedlove supplied her own personal drive and determination to turn her company and herself into an economic juggernaut. At the time of Walker's death in 1919, her business and personal assets were valued at $600,000, equivalent to approximately $6 million today. Also, to her distinct credit, Walker not only sought to enrich herself but also sought to empower other black women and to assist less fortunate African Americans (especially children). Her Madam Walker's Hair Culturists' Union, comprised of company agents, not only provided thousands of African American women an alternative to working in domestic service occupations but also sought to "encourage them to harness their prosperity for improving their communities." One of her more noteworthy personal philanthropic contributions was a 1910 contribution of $1,000 to help build an African American YMCA in Indianapolis, where she was then living. At the time, her yearly income was approximately $10,000, which made her gift "a near tithe of her annual earnings."[40]

At the same time Walker was building her financial empire, Annie Turnbo continued to expand hers. In 1910, she moved to larger commercial space in St. Louis. In 1914, Annie, who since childhood had been plagued with bouts of illness, had to turn over company operations to trusted associates. During her recuperation, she became reacquainted with Aaron Eugene Malone, a former schoolmate she had not seen for several years. They subsequently married and the two, with Annie now Turnbo-Malone, planned what subsequently became known as Poro College. Originally opened in 1918 and later expanded, this facility at the "Poro Corner" in St. Louis (Pendleton and St. Ferdinand Avenues) became the showplace of St. Louis's African American community. Besides facilities directly associated with the production of the Poro product line and the training of company agents, the Poro College building complex also included an auditorium, dining facilities, a theater, a gymnasium, a chapel, and a roof garden. At a time when St. Louis blacks were denied access to other entertainment and hospitality venues, the Poro College complex represented a literal godsend.[41]

Like Madam C. J. Walker, Annie Turnbo-Malone was a philanthropist with a special interest in uplifting African American children. For instance, "at one time it is believed that she was supporting two full-time students at every black land-grant college in the United States." Closer to home, her donations helped to build the St. Louis Colored YWCA and the St. Louis Colored Orphans' Home. In fact, it has been asserted that the construction of the Poro College building complex took place at the corner of Pendleton and St. Ferdinand Avenues "because of its proximity to a number of public schools. She [Turnbo-Malone] felt that in this location the Institution would serve as an inspiration to the thousands of children who pass daily to and from neighborhood schools."[42]

Another similarity between the business careers of Turnbo-Malone and Walker was that both regarded their agents as the cornerstone of their respective companies. Just as Walker's agents felt a special sense of kinship through the Madam Walker's Hair Culturists' Union, Turnbo-Malone's agents felt a special kinship working under the Poro banner. As one scholar has written, "to become a PORO agent-operator, one had to attend a series of trainings and commit to the PORO mission. In a sense, a person was initiated into PORO."[43]

In the end, both Annie Turnbo-Malone and Madam C. J. Walker established impressive commercial infrastructures that operated as near vertical monopolies. Conversely, irrespective of the issue of gender, Anthony Overton's personal care products business infrastructure, early on, was far less extensive than Turnbo-Malone's and Walker's. As discussed in chapter 4, Overton later established a beauty college whose graduates would exclusively use Overton Hygienic products. But in the meantime, he sought to lessen the distance between his chief competitors and himself through creative marketing strategies.

Overton Hygienic's 1916 Convention

Perhaps ironically, despite his increasing use of attractive female surrogates, the cornerstone of Overton Hygienic's marketing operations were the all-male traveling sales corps who operated across the country. As Overton mentioned during his 1912 NNBL presentation, the company employed these individuals to sell products wholesale to merchants, large schools, and public institutions. Also, available evidence suggests that they were an elite group within the company's hierarchy. At a June 1916 company convention in Chicago, Overton told the salesmen present that, as the company's administrative infrastructure expanded, they would be called on to assume such future positions as sales manager, advertising manager, purchasing agent, and factory superintendent.[44] Overton Hygienic salesmen who attended this convention included Warren Roane, who covered the U.S. Northeast; William Gales, whose territory included Oklahoma, Texas, Arkansas, and Louisiana; Bruce K. Tucker, whose territory included Mississippi, Tennessee, and western Alabama; William S. Bester, whose territory included the District of Columbia and Maryland; C. E. Howard, whose territory included eastern Alabama, Georgia, Florida, and South Carolina; and A. E. Jordan, who covered Illinois, Ohio, Indiana, and Kentucky for the company.[45]

At Overton Hygienic's June 1916 convention, Overton not only discussed possible future roles for company salesmen but shared his related, grandiose vision of the company's future. He boldly declared that he envisioned seeing his firm grow to become not just "the largest Negro enterprise in the United States" but indeed "the largest business concern, white or colored, on the western Continent. Not even second to the Standard Oil Company or the Steel trust." Clearly, Overton's declaration, on its surface, appeared extremely hyperbolic, if not delusional. Yet, considering his previous trials and tribulations, it must have been truly exhilarating for him to preside over his company's first convention. Moreover, as Overton continued his presentation, he revealed the source of his optimism: "[while] we labor under some disadvantages, we also have something in our favor that could be used to materially assist in our up-building." He further explained: "each year our people are growing more loyal to their support of race efforts, and as it seems we rightfully are the pioneers in the manufacturing efforts, we rightfully should receive their first consideration."[46]

Within five years of moving to Chicago, Anthony Overton made great strides toward erasing the pain and frustration associated with his earlier life endeavors. As his personal and entrepreneurial triumph at the 1915 Lincoln Jubilee suggested, he was becoming a businessman who possessed positive

Anthony Overton surrounded by company salesmen at the 1916 Overton Hygienic convention in Chicago. (Courtesy of the Everett and Ida Overton Collection)

name recognition across the country. Seeking to fully capitalize on his growing success, the ambitious Overton established the *Half-Century Magazine* during the summer of 1916. This magazine not only helped him to increase his market share in the increasingly competitive African American personal care products industry but also facilitated his transformation from a moderately successful entrepreneur into a tycoon.

3. The *Half-Century Magazine*
1916–1925

One of the consequences of the Overton Hygienic Manufacturing Company's growth, after the enterprise moved to Chicago, was that Anthony Overton diversified his business interests. In 1916, he established the *Half-Century Magazine*, shrewdly putting forward a female employee as the owner, editor, and public face of this woman-oriented periodical. Because of the increasing number of various purveyors of African American personal care products in the marketplace, Overton wanted a venue—which the magazine became—in which his various marketing messages could feature prominently. Moreover, not publicly identifying himself as the owner of the *Half-Century* allowed him to deflect charges of shameless self-promotion. In addition, Overton's use of anonymous editorials and a pseudonym to convey his beliefs regarding business enterprise, racial identity, and personal conduct, represented another manifestation of his clandestine strategy regarding *Half-Century*. Still, above and beyond Overton's skullduggery, the magazine created a commercial environment where black female readers were not exposed to racially insulting personal care products ads that made outrageous claims. This advertising policy (which featured Overton Hygienic products), along with *Half-Century's* sponsorship of a contest extolling the beauty of African American women, enhanced Overton Hygienic's position in the marketplace. Finally, as Anthony Overton's business interests expanded to include a national bank and a legal reserve insurance company, the magazine promoted these enterprises as well. Similarly, as Anthony Overton's family expanded to include sons-in-law Julian Lewis and Richard Hill, the *Half-Century Magazine* employed them both as columnists, which enhanced both their careers and the quality of the periodical.

Contested Terrain

Circumstantial evidence suggests that Anthony Overton developed the *Half-Century Magazine* as a means to capitalize on the positive attention his company received at the 1915 Lincoln Jubilee. Among other things, the magazine's use of the words *half century* in its title is a subliminal link to the Lincoln Jubilee, which sought to celebrate a *half century* of African American freedom. Despite an apparent connection between Overton Hygienic's success at the 1915 Lincoln Jubilee and the founding of the *Half-Century Magazine* in 1916, the magazine's initial "Statement of Ownership" cites Katherine E. Williams at its owner. Nevertheless, an in-depth examination of this periodical provides compelling evidence that Overton had a major influence on its operations and hints that he used Williams as a front for this female-oriented publication.

In her 2004 *Ladies' Pages: African American Women's Magazines and the Culture That Made Them*, Noliwe Rooks, based on the magazine's "Statement of Ownership," situates Williams as the *Half-Century Magazine*'s "owner and editor in chief." Yet, Rooks provides no sense of how the twenty-one-year-old Williams generated the capital to start this enterprise.[1] Williams's youth is further illustrated by the fact that, a mere two years earlier, she, along with two of Overton's daughters (Eva and Frances), was a contestant in the *Chicago Defender*'s "Who Is the Most Popular Girl in Chicago?" promotion.[2]

What we do know is that, in less than a year, the offices of the *Half-Century Magazine* moved from 3708 South Wabash Avenue to Overton-owned commercial space at 5202 South Wabash Avenue. Furthermore, the magazine's November 1918 "Statement of Ownership" lists the then-married Katherine Williams-Irvin as a tenant living in an Overton-owned apartment at 5200 South Wabash Avenue. But the proverbial "smoking gun" in terms of establishing who actually owned the magazine appears in a July 1946 edition of the *Chicago Bee* newspaper: a photo caption describing a January 1946 Overton reunion lists Katherine Williams-Irvin as "a former Overton Hygienic employee."[3]

Marketing Overton Hygienic Manufacturing Company Products

Perhaps, the most compelling evidence associated with determining Anthony Overton's role with the *Half-Century Magazine* involves both the quantity and placement of his advertisements in this periodical. In fact, in a marketplace becoming increasingly crowded with a myriad of African American personal care products, Overton established the magazine as a venue where his various marketing messages faced little, if any, competition.

The inaugural August 1916 issue features not only a predominance of ads marketing various Overton Hygienic products but also their most advantageous placement for maximum commercial effect. For instance, two large display ads for Overton Hygienic's Rozol Complexion Clarifier and High-Brown Hair Grower appear on a recto page directly across from a "Beauty Hints" section article. For good measure, the article conclusion shares space with display ads for Overton Hygienic's Perfumes and Toilet Waters, Peroxide Vanishing Cream, and High-Brown Soap.[4]

A special offer was announced in the September 1916 issue to further stimulate black female readership of both the *Half-Century Magazine* and Overton Hygienic ads: "to ascertain how many people read the 'Ads' in this magazine . . . we are going to print a coupon in the Sept., Oct., Nov., and Dec. issues. To each person who will send us three consecutive monthly coupons filled out and signed on or before Dec. 20th, 1916, we will send FREE, a 2cent box of *High-Brown Face Powder* or a 25 cent box of *Ro-zol Face Bleach*."[5]

Besides using clever ad placement strategies and contests to effectively promote his personal care products, Overton also employed advantageous ad placements to increase sales of Hygienic Pet Baking Powder. For example, the May 1918 edition of the *Half-Century Magazine* carries an article titled "Maytime in the Kitchen." Informed that the increasing availability of strawberries could result in "a splendid pie," female readers are asked "who wouldn't smile at the sight of a strawberry short cake for supper?" Significantly, directly across from the preparation instructions for these and other items was a large display ad for Hygienic Pet Baking Powder that assures readers this is an ideal product "For Cakes, Pastries, Biscuits, and ALL Particular Baking."[6]

Another instance of Anthony Overton's business acumen with the magazine was its "Satisfaction or Money Back" advertising policy. Readers were told that "the publishers of THE HALF-CENTURY MAGAZINE guarantee the reliability of every advertisement in this magazine." Consumers were assured that, if any product marketed in the magazine proved unsatisfactory within thirty days of purchase, their money would "be refunded by either the manufacturer or by us."[7] Considering that Overton Hygienic Manufacturing Company products were prominently marketed in the *Half-Century Magazine*, these items, in the minds of readers, were directly associated with the periodical's money-back guarantee. Consequently, this reinforced, in the minds of consumers, the quality of Overton's products.

Race Pride and Promoting African American Beauty

Besides its "Satisfaction or Money Back" policy, another aspect of the *Half-Century Magazine* that endeared it to its readers was the publication's advertising policy. The March 1917 issue of *Half-Century* states the magazine's advertising policy: "The Following Classes of 'Ads' Will Not Be Accepted by THE HALF-CENTURY MAGAZINE: Clairvoyants, Fortune-Tellers, Saloons, Intoxicating Liquors, Get-Rich-Quick Oil Wells or Mining Stocks, Buffet Flats, or Pictures Ridiculing Colored People."[8] This is significant since, eager for the revenue many African American publications in the early twentieth century accepted any and all advertisements, regardless of how offensive and demeaning they may have been.[9]

In the context of personal care products, Overton created a commercial environment that protected black female readers from derogatory ads making outrageous claims. Moreover, the *Half-Century Magazine* periodically attacked black periodicals that published racially insulting personal care products advertisements. For instance, the April 1919 issue features an editorial titled "That Bleaching Proposition." The essay begins by sadly asserting that "concerns advertising face bleaches have stepped beyond the bounds of decency in advertising." It describes an ad from another periodical: "Miss _____ with a very black face, very coarse hair, and very distinct Negro features scowls at us in one picture, while in the next picture sunshine lights up her face, a new head of hair has been grown, her coarse features made fine and a white skin produced." The editor goes on to scold any consumer not "possess[ing] horse sense enough to refuse to buy any paper that accepts such trashy and ridiculing advertisements."[10]

Two months later, a *Half-Century* editorial titled "Take Out the Kinks" continued in this regard. It lamented the following advertising text that appeared in a popular African American newspaper: "Race men and women may easily have straight, soft, long hair by simply applying _____ Hair Dressing and in a short time all your kinky, snarly, ugly, curly hair, becomes soft, silky smooth, straight, long." The *Half-Century* editor went on to chastise the unnamed culprit—"Shame on the Colored editor who will print such degrading trash!"[11] Finally, the provocatively titled "Betrayers of the Race" editorial in the February 1920 *Half-Century* takes up nearly a full page on the same subject: "[some black editors] will help a white man swindle the race solely because they are receiving good pay for printing their ads."[12]

Overton's *Half-Century*, besides merely criticizing the shortcomings of *some contemporary African American newspapers*, sought to proactively promote the notion of African American feminine beauty. For instance, the June 1919 issue features a page of African American female photos titled "Types of Racial Beauty" with the accompanying caption: "our race has produced more varieties of beauty than any other race on earth."[13] These images, which feature both lighter- and darker-complexioned black women, suggest that *Half-Century* sought to provide a counter narrative to the widely held belief that women of European descent represented the pinnacle of female attractiveness. In 1921, the magazine stepped up its interest in promoting the beauty of African American women by urging readers to send in photos responding to the question "Who Is the Prettiest Colored Girl in the United States?" The seven judges who evaluated the submitted pictures included Mrs. Robert Abbott, Ida B. Wells-Barnett, and Anthony Overton. As Susannah Walker writes about this phenomenon, "the [*Half-Century*] 1921 contest was explicitly framed as a way to 'prove' that African American women were beautiful."[14]

In retrospect, the *Half-Century Magazine*'s advertising policy, its public denigration of black publications that featured racially demeaning and offensive personal care advertisements, along with its attempt to consciously acknowledge and celebrate the beauty of African American women, were ways it sought to distinguish itself in the marketplace. In fact, *Half-Century* may have pioneered what is currently called a niche market magazine. Specifically, Overton sought to attract African Americans interested in seeing positive portrayals of black life. Moreover, this business plan not only expanded the readership of the *Half-Century* but expanded the sales of the Overton Hygienic Manufacturing Company products marketed extensively in the periodical.

The Bottom Line

In 1920, *Half-Century* reported its monthly circulation to readers: "our magazine goes into 41,000 homes of Colored people in every walk of life, and approximately 6,000 of the intelligent white people who favor fair play for the black man."[15] While historic black periodicals tended to inflate their circulation rates, the records of Dun & Bradstreet, the preeminent business financial reporting agency, reveals a clear linkage between the *Half-Century Magazine* and Overton Hygienic Manufacturing Company product sales.

Before the appearance of *Half-Century*, Dun & Bradstreet reports that Overton Hygienic was a moderately successful enterprise. In 1912, the company's first appearance in the *Dun & Bradstreet Reference Book*, Overton Hygienic received a financial strength rating of E ($20,000-$35,000 in company assets) and a credit rating of 2½ (good). Three years later, in 1915, Overton

This drugstore in Hot Springs, Arkansas, prominently features Overton Hygienic products. Besides being spotlighted in Chicago, Anthony Overton used the widely circulated *Half-Century Magazine* to create product recognition and consumer support across the country. (Courtesy of the Everett and Ida Overton Collection)

Hygienic received a financial strength rating of D+ ($50,000-$75,000 in assets) and a credit rating of 2 (good).[16]

After the 1916 inauguration of the *Half-Century Magazine*, subsequent *Dun & Bradstreet Reference Book* editions reveal Overton Hygienic's steady ascent as a commercial enterprise. In 1917, Dun & Bradstreet gave Overton Hygienic a financial strength rating of C+ ($125,000-$200,000 in assets) and a credit rating of 1 (high—the top rating). Three years later, in 1920, Overton Hygienic received a financial strength rating of B ($200,000-$300,000 in assets) and a credit rating of 1 (high). In 1922, the *Dun & Bradstreet Reference Book* gave the Overton Hygienic Manufacturing Company a financial strength rating of B+ ($300,000-$500,000 in assets) and a credit rating of 1 (high).[17]

Although I was unable to locate copies of the *Dun & Bradstreet Reference Book* (retitled the *R. G. Dun & Company Reference Book*) for the mid-to-late

1920s, the September 1928 issue of the National Urban League's *Opportunity* magazine provides a secondhand account of Overton Hygienic's Dun ratings during this period. In a summary of Overton's burgeoning financial empire, including the Douglass National Bank, the Victory Life Insurance Company, and the *Chicago Bee* newspaper, *Opportunity* cites Dun as providing Overton Hygienic with a $1,000,000 financial and credit rating.[18] This assertion is seemingly confirmed by the 1930 edition of the *R. G. Dun & Company Reference Book*. Even in the midst of a deepening economic depression, R. G. Dun gave Overton Hygienic a financial strength rating of A ($500,000-$750,000 in assets) and a credit rating of A1 (high).[19]

Overton's Corporate Expansion

Although Overton extensively used his *Half-Century Magazine* to market Hygienic Manufacturing Company products, as his financial empire expanded, his later entrepreneurial involvements likewise received high-profile coverage and advantageous placement in this periodical. For instance, beginning with the July–August 1922 issue, and continuing until the magazine's (final) January–February 1925 issue, the inside cover of the periodical features a prominent full-page advertisement of the Overton-led Douglass National Bank.[20] Moreover, the July–August 1922 issue features a full-page article on the newly formed Douglass Bank and offers a favorable assessment of its president: "The same wisdom and commercial ability that popularized and made profitable the sale of High Brown Toilet Preparations and the same sound judgment and integrity that placed the Overton Hygienic Company in the first rank among commercial institutions, regardless of color, is guiding the Douglass National Bank to its rightful place among the foremost banking institutions of the world."[21] Overton's involvement with the Douglass National Bank is examined in depth in Chapter 4.

Besides the Douglass National Bank, Overton's quest to construct a new commercial headquarters on South State Street received considerable coverage and support in *Half-Century*. By the early 1920s, the Overton Hygienic Manufacturing Company, through Anthony Overton's creative use of the magazine, was a rapidly growing African American enterprise. It was also becoming increasingly clear that the company had outgrown its manufacturing facilities at 5200–5202 South Wabash. Thus, Overton, to satisfy his growing customer base, expanded the company's productive capacity by building a new manufacturing facility. To facilitate this process, which included selling bonds to the public, he once again relied on the *Half-Century Magazine*. From its April 1922 issue to its March–April 1924 issue, *Half-Century* sought financial support from readers to build a new headquarters for Overton Hygienic and Overton's other business interests (including the Douglass National Bank) at 3619–27 South State Street.[22]

Overton possessed the funds to build three stories of what would be called a "Monument to Negro Thrift and Industry"—a multiuse six-story building projected to be "the finest building ever erected and owned by Colored People." To generate funds to build the remaining three floors, the newly created Overton Building Corporation initiated a $200,000 bond campaign (in denominations of $100 and $500) promising investors a 7 percent return on their money. Moreover, prospective financial backers were told that "it is our firm belief that those who have a genuine interest in race development will prove it by buying some of these bonds."[23]

When Anthony Overton's Victory Life Insurance Company began operations on March 3, 1924, this enterprise, too, received favorable coverage in his *Half-Century Magazine*.[24] An article in the January–February 1925 issue reports on the first annual meeting of the insurer's stockholders. Readers are informed that "the annual reports of the various officers indicate that the company ends its first year, though licensed less than ten months, in a particularly strong position." The same issue features a full-page advertisement for Victory Life with the headline "The evidence of a Dependable Life Insurance Company Is the Prompt Payment of Its Death Claims." The ad tells about Mr. Leon W. Thomas, "who took out a $4,000 policy in the Victory Life Insurance Co. July 16, 1924 and paid one quarterly premium of $22.08." Unfortunately, Thomas was injured in an automobile accident on August 11, 1924, and died on September 2, 1924. When his widow notified Victory Life of his death on September 4, 1924, "the claim was paid in full on the same day." To fully impress on readers the significance of this transaction, the advertisement includes, in bold, "**$4,000 for $22.08.**"[25] Chapter 4 examines in-depth the establishment and early history of the Victory Life Insurance Company.

Overton's Writing Career

Although the *Half-Century Magazine* was essentially a vehicle to promote Anthony Overton's various commercial projects, the magazine also provided him the opportunity to pursue a writing career under a pseudonym. Predictably, the works apparently attributable to Overton reinforced *Half-Century*'s promotion of personal responsibility, racial pride, and black economic development.

What is likely Overton's first literary contribution to the magazine is an unsigned October 1916 editorial, "Have You a Bank Account"? After noting that "one of the criticisms of the race is the practice that most of us have of spending all our earnings, instead of exercising the saving habit," the author quotes Benjamin Franklin: "if you know how to spend less than you get, you have the philosopher's stone." Furthermore, this editorial's following discussion of John Wanamaker, as a case study of the power of saving, provides strong circumstantial evidence that Anthony Overton was its author: "young John Wanamaker, by hard work and severe economy, saved $100 while he was employed in a clothing store where he had worked for years for $1.50 a week. By a wise real estate investment his $100 became $2,000 and with this sum he started in the clothing business for himself."[26]

Just as Anthony Overton often provided hyperbolic recollections about his own past, John Wanamaker's rise to prominence did not coincide with Overton's October 1916 glowing analysis. As a biographer of Wanamaker notes, Wanamaker entered the retail industry through money saved from working as the secretary of the Philadelphia YMCA as well as his partnership with "Nathan Brown, the son of a wealthy grocer."[27] These apparent facts, clearly, are not as "interesting" as Overton's depiction of John Wanamaker's evolution as an entrepreneur. Yet, in all fairness to Anthony Overton, rather than his Wanamaker reference being the result of conscious falsification, it appears more likely that he simply reiterated to *Half-Century* readers an embellished version of Wanamaker's youth that he (Overton) had discovered.

Above and beyond the John Wanamaker reference, "Have You a Bank Account?" provides a window to view other nuances of Anthony Overton's mindset. To Overton, developing the habit of saving demonstrated a "desire to lift one's head out of the crowd, a desire to stand for something in the world, to be independent, self-reliant, one's own man. In other words, the habit of thrift means character; it means stability; it means self-control. It is a proof that a man is not a hopeless victim of his appetites, his weaknesses."[28] This conservatism, reflective of a worldview promoted by Overton's recently deceased friend Booker T. Washington, formed the cornerstone of his other literary contributions to the *Half-Century Magazine*.

Beginning in its June 1917 issue, one of the magazine's periodic contributors was the financial writer "McAdoo Baker." Considering the content of his articles, as well as the fact that Baker's background and credentials were never revealed in *Half-Century*, it is plausible that Overton used this pseudonym to further instill in readers the importance of supporting race-based commercial enterprises. Baker's first appearance in the *Half-Century Magazine* was as the author of a June 1917 column, "Business and Finance." This article begins by asserting "possibly the most urgent need of the race is co-operation." Reminiscent of Booker T. Washington, Baker continues: "if members of the race owned and controlled several large manufacturing and mercantile enterprises to the extent that we would become a factor in the financial and commercial world, much of the prejudice that we are now undergoing would be done away with." Finally, because the "building up of such enterprises can be accomplished only by co-operation," Baker exhorts blacks to start "pooling our resources, our ability, our experience and our dollars."[29]

Besides offering a strategy for African American economic success, Baker also used this column to announce the opening of *Half-Century*'s "Investors' Guide Department," which would "investigate, upon request of our subscribers, the standing of any enterprise, new or old, Colored or white, which is offering to sell stocks or bonds to our people." Also appearing for the first time, and conveniently placed alongside Baker's column, is the *Half-Century* "Investors' Guide" column, which offers assessments of four potential investments and answers a reader's question about purchasing life insurance. Also on the same page is a display ad for "The U.S. Securities Corporation," which offered readers a convenient way to buy and sell stocks and bonds. Considering their office was located in Overton-controlled commercial space at 5200 South Wabash Avenue, this appears to be another instance of his strategic use of commercially advantageous ad placements to generate additional income.[30]

The September and October 1917 issues of the *Half-Century* include a two-part Baker column titled "Making a Business Man of the Negro." This piece provides practical (and still relevant) observations about going into business. Among other things, Baker asserts that "a new man in any field, in order to deserve public consideration, must be a BENEFACTOR in some way to his community." To generate this mindset, Baker notes that a prospective entrepreneur, especially if they are a merchant or grocer, "must not overlook the fact that the public was buying and consuming groceries before he ever thought of opening up in business." Consequently, someone seeking to carve out a new niche among consumers "must . . . in some way render some additional conveniences or accommodations."[31]

While Baker had previously declared the importance of African American economic cooperation, in the September 1917 section of "Making a Business Man of the Negro" he provides an important clarification. He reasonably contends that until new black entrepreneurs establish themselves as community benefactors, they cannot demand "the patronage of every Colored resident of the neighborhood." Moreover, the wise prospective black business person would work on earning this support, whereas the unwise prospective black business person "goes out of his way to back-bite those that fail to patronize him, thereby making enemies not only of persons so maligned, but also of these persons' friends."[32]

The March and April 1918 issues of the magazine feature another extended Baker article, "How a Colored Merchant Can Secure Credit." Once again, Baker provides practical advice that remains relevant a century later. Moreover, this particular work, as does the October 1916 unsigned "Have You a Bank Account?" editorial, explicitly links economic and moral conduct.

After providing a general discussion of the importance of a business securing "a substantial Credit Rating," Baker's narrative takes an almost evangelical turn: "The Good Book tells us that the three essentials of a good Christian are faith, hope and charity and the greatest of these is charity; likewise the requirements of a good credit [rating] are ability, experience and integrity, and the greatest of these is *integrity*." According to Baker, "integrity means that you will abstain from intoxicating liquors; that you will not gamble or take part in unbecoming conduct. Business statistics show that a large percentage of failures can be attributed to such short-comings." He elaborates further: "when intoxicated, men have been known to sign checks or notes without a valued consideration causing a failure of the firms with which they were connected." Moreover, "men have been known to lose at the gambling table, not only their own, but the money and property of others." Finally, after Baker enumerates the moral prerequisites for securing a good commercial credit rating, he provides specific instructions to black merchants on how to register their businesses with the Dun and Bradstreet Mercantile Agencies, as well as explains how Dun and Bradstreet monitored commercial credit in the United States.[33]

The April 1918 issue of the *Half-Century Magazine* features the second part of Baker's article "How a Colored Merchant Can Secure Credit" article. In this installment, which features examples of Dun and Bradstreet credit reports, "McAdoo Baker" all but reveals his true identity. Baker begins by declaring that "the following are examples of good, medium, and bad reports as made on some of our Colored Merchants. On inquiry, copies of these reports were sent to one of their [Dun and Bradstreet] subscribers, which happens in this case to be a Colored Manufacturing concern in Chicago." It seems clear that the "Colored Manufacturing concern in Chicago" Baker refers to was the Overton Hygienic Manufacturing Company. Moreover, Baker later explicitly cites the Overton Hygienic Manufacturing Company in a hypothetical example of how companies determine the creditworthiness of potential clients. Finally, after presenting more details (and tips) about how black merchants could maximize their Dun and Bradstreet ratings, Baker returns to his earlier evangelical tone: "a good credit rating is compared with a good Christian, for it is a fact that a person that can successfully pass the scrutiny of an up-to-date Credit Man, should have no trouble in passing St. Peter at the Pearly Gates."[34]

Baker's next article, titled "Banks," appears in the January 1919 issue of the *Half-Century Magazine*. This essay not only educates readers on how banks operate but also stresses the need for "a bank in Chicago under Colored ownership and management."[35]

Considering Overton's later involvement with the Douglass National Bank (see chapter 4), this article provides insights into his thinking about this aspect of African American economic development. To Baker, it makes absolutely no sense for blacks in Chicago to have millions of dollars in the city's white-owned banks when "very rarely can a loan be secured from any of the [white] banks of our city, by any of our people." In addition, Baker decries white banks' concurrent acceptance of black deposits and their refusal "to give any of our people employment." Baker also asserts that, even worse, "these same Negro funds are *loaned to white* business institutions, that likewise would not give employment to one of our race in any capacity. The Negro's money is used to close the door of opportunity in his own face" (original emphasis).[36]

Echoing his first *Half-Century* article, where he discusses the importance of racial economic cooperation, Baker concludes his article on banks by asserting that black Chicagoans needed a financial institution where they could "gather into large workable funds, the deposits of our people so that the same can likewise be loaned in turn to our people at a *reasonable* rate on their real estate by mortgage securities or to our business people to encourage their race business development" (original emphasis).[37]

The next article attributed to Baker, "The Evolution of a Negro Merchant," appears in the June 1920 issue of the magazine. For the most part, it is a reworked, nearly verbatim, version of his earlier two-part (September and October 1917) "Making a Business Man of the Negro" article. In both the 1917 and 1920 versions, Baker offers the following encouragement to prospective black merchants: "every captain of industry—Morgan, Carnegie, Rockefeller, Schwab—was once a private in the ranks. . . . The man at the top got there because he made the right start, because every step he took was forward, because his purpose was big."[38]

Besides his interest in assisting black business development, Baker also expresses an interest in providing financial advice to individual African American families. For instance, his January 1922 *Half-Century* article, "Is Your Family Amply Protected?," encourages readers to have a will drawn up: "A rich man can afford to die without a will; there will be enough left of his estate after the lawyers and courts get through to provide for his family. But a poor man—one whose estate is less than ten thousand dollars—cannot afford to take such chances." For readers unable to afford a lawyer (to draw up their will), Baker provides a template for a do-it-yourself last will and testament.[39]

Besides Overton's apparent employment of the McAdoo Baker pseudonym to express certain of his beliefs in the *Half-Century Magazine*, circumstantial evidence suggests that he also used the magazine to promote his anonymously published book, *How a Negro Should Conduct a Business*, through another apparent front enterprise, Progressive Book Publishers. This business had multiple advertisements in the inaugural August 1916 issue of the *Half-Century Magazine*. Located at 3519 South State Street—the same address as Overton Hygienic's branch office—the company's first ad in *Half-Century* informs readers that books written by African American authors were their specialty.[40]

The listed owner of Progressive Book Publishers was Beulah Haynes. Yet, a closer examination of Haynes's background suggests that she, like Katherine Williams, probably served as the front for another enterprise controlled by Anthony Overton. For instance, a March 1915 *Chicago Defender* article about the opening of Overton's new branch office at 3519 South State Street cites the names of Overton Hygienic female employees who staffed this location, including Overton's three daughters (Mabel, Eva, and Frances), and Beulah Haynes.[41]

Given the documents available now, it cannot be definitively determined whether Overton was an "angel investor" who loaned Haynes the money to start Progressive Book Publishers or whether Haynes served as the figurehead owner of yet another Overton-controlled enterprise. However, the August 1916 issue of the *Half-Century Magazine* featured a half-page ad from Progressive Book Publishers for a book, by an *anonymous* author, titled *How a Negro Should Conduct a Business*. Moreover, this book's table of contents not only suggests that it was another of Anthony Overton's unattributed publications, but that some sections of *How a Negro Should Conduct a Business* were later published in *Half-Century* as written by "McAdoo Baker." For example, chapter 5 of *How a Negro Should Conduct a Business* is titled "What Is Necessary to Secure Patronage of Our Own People?" In his September 1917 "Making a Business Man of the Negro" article, McAdoo Baker declares that black businesspeople had to become community "benefactors" (through better prices and/or better customer service) to secure the patronage of fellow blacks.[42] Because no known copies survive of *How a Negro Should Conduct a Business*, it is not possible to prove or disprove the link. The ongoing connection between Anthony Overton and Progressive Book Publishers can be substantiated, however. By the early 1920s, Progressive Book Publishers, as had the *Half-Century Magazine*, had moved its operations to the very busy commercial space owned by Overton on South Wabash Avenue.[43] Moreover, by 1928, Progressive Book Publishers, now known as Progressive Book Company, produced a widely marketed pamphlet, *Songs and Spirituals of Negro Composition; Also Patriotic Songs, Songs of Colleges and College Fraternities and Sororities*. Nearly half of this booklet (27 of its 65 pages) carries a promotional advertisement for one or another Overton business or product.[44]

The Libranian Movement

As a conservative and as a secretive disciple of Booker T. Washington, Anthony Overton primarily used the *Half-Century Magazine* to simultaneously promote African American economic development in general and his own enterprises in particular. However, he also, for a short time, used the periodical to enter into the realm of (still) contentious discourse related to how persons of African descent in the United States should refer to themselves. While Overton's motivation for doing this remains unknown, *Half-Century* contributed to this discussion by urging African Americans to stop referring to themselves as "Negro" or "Colored" and assume the label of "Libranians."

In a front-page editorial, "By What Name Shall the Race Be Known?," the November 1919 issue of *Half-Century* examines the issue of "synonymous terms applied to our people." After raising objections with the existing terms Negro, African, Afro-American, and Colored, the magazine declares that a more proper identifying term would be Libranian. It offers a historical and geographical rationale for this assertion: "The first of our race in the United States were brought from that section of the west coast of Africa, just beyond the gold coast, that lies about four hundred miles east of the country known as Liberia. At that time the country was unnamed; then why not give to that section of the country from which our ancestors came, the name of Librania and designate the descendants of those who came from that section of country as Libranians."[45] According to the periodical, both Liberia and Librania were derived "from the Latin word 'Liber,' meaning free." This grammatical linkage, moreover, should serve as "a constant reminder to us and to the Liberians that we are by blood closely related." Yet, at the same time, "the difference in ending serves to distinguish our race in America, the Libranians, from the citizens of Liberia, who are known as Liberians." "By What Name Shall the Race Be Known?" concludes by declaring that "we recommend that our churches, schools, and the press adopt this name for the good of the people of Libranian lineage in America and place a complete boycott on all other terms."[46]

"Are We Ashamed of Our Lineage?," the front-page editorial in the January 1920 issue, provides additional rationale for *Half-Century's* campaign involving the term Libranian. It points out that such identifiers as "Negro" and "white" do not capture the complexity of ethnic differences within racial groups. Moreover, persons of African descent in America have a unique experience worthy of special designation. In fact, notwithstanding the accomplishments of blacks in the ancient world, the magazine declares, "no group of people have crowded so much in half a century as the descendants of that little band of blacks who were brought to America three hundred years ago. Let us not be ashamed of the struggles of our ancestors, but rather proud enough of their progress to call ourselves by a name that explains our lineage—Libranians."[47]

For the next couple of years—from its November 1919 issue to its November 1921 issue—the *Half-Century Magazine* actively used its "General Race News" section to promote the use of the term Libranians. Readers were told that, "as explained in the November, 1919 issue of THE HALF-CENTURY, we are using the term LIBRANIAN to apply to members of the race who were born in America. We do this because so many object to the term NEGRO."[48] Significantly, *Half-Century's* "General Race News" section disappeared from the publication between January 1922 and May–June 1923. When it reappeared, there was no mention of Libranians. Instead blacks were primarily referred to as "colored."[49]

We can reasonably assume that Overton, who later in 1922 began using the *Half-Century Magazine* to sell bonds to help build a new commercial headquarters, did not want the fairly controversial Libranian campaign to impede his bond-selling campaign. Another, more documentable, instance of Anthony Overton's essentially pragmatic mindset was his use of sons-in-law Julian H. Lewis and Richard Hill Jr. to enhance this publication.

A Family Affair

Julian Lewis, who received a doctorate in pathology and physiology from the University of Chicago in 1915 and a medical degree from the Rush Medical School in 1917, already had an impressive professional track record before his association with the *Half-Century Magazine*.[50] A June 1915 article in the *Chicago Defender* about black participants in University of Chicago graduation ceremonies notes that Lewis "is a research student and his work has attracted national attention, having been appointed by the faculty of the University to make such studies." Six months later, the *Defender* proudly proclaims that "the name of Julian Lewis now appears on the official list of the faculty as an associate instructor in Pathology. This makes the second man of the race to be on the faculty of our big universities." The evidence suggests that, besides pursuing medical research at the University of Chicago, Lewis also began his pursuit of Eva Overton. Described in the June 1915 *Defender* article about University of Chicago black graduates as "one of the younger set's prettiest and most cultured girls," she and Lewis were married three years later.[51]

In the June 1919 issue of the *Half-Century Magazine*, Dr. Julian H. Lewis appears in the "In the Limelight" section. Here readers are informed of his impressive educational and professional background, though his 1918 marriage to Eva Overton is omitted from this biographical sketch. The following *Half-Century* issue announces that Dr. Lewis will write periodic columns on African American health issues and will answer readers' health-related questions. One of his more interesting columns, titled "The Health of the Negro," appears in the September 1919 issue. Dr. Lewis used this space to refute claims that blacks suffered more diseases than whites because of blacks' inherent "degeneracy" and immorality.[52]

In the context of interesting timing, the July 1919 issue of the *Half-Century Magazine* not only announces Dr. Julian Lewis's forthcoming columns but also features another Anthony Overton son-in-law, Richard Hill Jr., in its "In the Limelight Section." This biographical sketch, similar to the previous month's article on Lewis, makes no mention of Hill's marriage to Overton's youngest daughter, Frances. Yet, it provides readers with background information about another dynamic young professional who, like Lewis, would subsequently have his own column in *Half-Century*.

Born in Nashville in 1887, Richard Hill Jr. received his elementary and secondary education in that city's public schools and later entered Fisk University, also in Nashville. After graduating in 1908, he enrolled in the University of Michigan Law School. In 1910, his oratorical skills landed him on the school's Jeffersonian Cup Debating team. The following year, he secured his law degree and subsequently moved to Chicago.[53] In Chicago, Hill established himself as one of the city's most successful civil lawyers, having an almost exclusively white client base. An African American business and professional directory of the era notes that on October 11, 1916, he married Frances M. Overton. After Hill's introduction to *Half-Century* readers in the July 1919 issue, the magazine's August issue features the introduction of a new section, the "Half-Century Law Department," coordinated by Hill: "for the benefit of our many readers, Atty. Richard Hill will answer legal questions of general interest through this column."[54]

Anthony Overton's utilization of his sons-in-law Julian Lewis and Richard Hill Jr. to enrich the content of the *Half-Century Magazine* was yet another shrewd business decision. Moreover, as is discussed in chapters 4 and 5, Lewis's and Hill's connection with their father-in-law's business activities extended far beyond submitting periodic columns to *Half-Century*. Both men would play important roles in the administration of the Douglass National Bank and the Victory Life Insurance Company.

Historical Context

Although the *Half-Century Magazine* helped Overton to effectively promote a variety of business projects, he phased it out after the January–February 1925 issue and replaced it with the *Chicago Bee* newspaper. This ensured that his plethora of marketing messages would reach consumers once a week instead of monthly or bimonthly. Moreover, the subsequent success of Overton's newest publishing venture led to the 1929 construction of the *Chicago Bee* Building at 3647–55 South State Street (one block south from his primary commercial headquarters at 3519–27 South State).[55]

The *Half-Century Magazine*, which existed from 1916 to 1925, is a fascinating historical artifact that has been examined from a variety of perspectives. Noliwe Rooks's *Ladies' Pages* examines this periodical in the context of the broader history of African American women's magazines. Another important work, Albert Lee Kreiling's dissertation on race journalism in Chicago from 1878 to 1929, includes content analysis of the various short stories that appeared in *Half-Century* and the revelation that editor Katherine Williams-Irvin, as had Anthony Overton, used a pseudonym ("Bettie Mason") to contribute various works of fiction to the periodical.[56]

In the end, just as sophisticated observers of television contend that its entertainment programming is essentially bulk filler between its marketing messages, a similar dynamic was true for the *Half-Century Magazine*. Notwithstanding Anthony Overton's personal literary contributions through the pseudonym "McAdoo Baker," he, from the beginning, viewed *Half-Century* primarily as a vehicle to enhance his entrepreneurial presence and status through frequent and strategically placed advertising. Moreover, this business strategy proved to be extremely successful. In 1916, when the magazine began publication, Anthony Overton was a moderately successful businessperson. By 1925, when *Half-Century* transitioned into the *Chicago Bee* newspaper, he had become a literal tycoon. The next chapter examines how the once struggling and frustrated entrepreneur presided over a financial empire that the *Half-Century Magazine* had helped create.

4. Business Titan

The Douglass National Bank and the Victory Life Insurance Company

In late 1921, Anthony Overton received a significant opportunity to further diversify his financial interests by participating in the opening of the Douglass National Bank. This Chicago-based institution was the second black-owned bank to receive a national charter. Three years later, Overton started the Victory Life Insurance Company in Chicago. In 1927, Victory Life accomplished an unprecedented feat: it was the only black-owned insurance company granted the right to conduct business in the state of New York. Following this business coup, Overton, in some circles, became regarded as "the merchant prince of his race." To further enhance his growing status as a business magnate during the 1920s, Overton built two major commercial structures in the heart of black Chicago's business district. The Overton Building, at 3619–27 South State Street, housed the Overton Hygienic Manufacturing Company, the Douglass National Bank, and the Victory Life Insurance Company. At 3647–55 South State Street, the *Chicago Bee* Building served as the headquarters for the successor to the *Half-Century Magazine*.

Overton and the Douglass National Bank

Contradictions in the record characterize Overton's involvement with the Douglass National Bank, reminiscent of some aspects of his pre-Chicago career. On the one hand, a variety of sources explicitly identify him as the organizer and founder of the Douglass National Bank.[1] A March 1929 *Opportunity: A Journal of Negro Life* article notes: "at first he [Overton] had his Hygienic plant, turning out cosmetics and hair preparations. Then, because he saw the great need for a banking institution which would take care of certain developments, he founded his National Bank." Similarly, an extended obituary of Overton, published in 1947 in the *Journal of Negro History*, asserts that "as a manufacturer he was eminently successful, and he became ambitious to invade other fields. Negroes had never before conducted a national bank, and he decided that he would make the step beyond the small private banking firms which Negroes as a rule operated." Decades later, John N. Ingham and Lynne B. Feldman's 1994 *African-American Business Leaders: A Biographical Dictionary* and Juliet E. K. Walker's 1999 *Encyclopedia of African American Business History* likewise situate Overton as the organizer of the Douglass National Bank.[2]

Notwithstanding long-held beliefs regarding Overton and the founding of the Douglass National Bank, Madrue Chavers-Wright provides indisputable evidence corroborated by contemporary newspapers that her father, Pearl William (P. W.) Chavers, actually organized this historic institution. Moreover, in her biography of her father, *The Guarantee*, Chavers-Wright insinuates that Overton was part of a conspiracy that ultimately resulted in Chavers being administratively removed from the institution he organized.[3]

According to Chavers-Wright, the road toward the establishment of the Douglass National Bank began in early 1920, when black Chicago depositors of the financially troubled R. W. Woodford Bank approached Chavers for assistance. Chavers, who moved to Chicago from Columbus, Ohio, in 1917, owned a female garment manufacturing factory at 534 East Forty-Third Street and had quickly gained a local reputation as someone committed to racial uplift.[4]

During the spring of 1920, Chavers, after attending several meetings of worried Woodford Bank depositors, agreed to become the trustee of the ailing institution. Later, with advice and encouragement from Jesse Binga, a local black banker, and from J. Gray Lucas, the attorney representing the interests of Woodford Bank depositors, Chavers worked out a deal with the Woodford Bank's court-appointed receiver whereby its assets would be transferred to a new institution, the Merchants and People's Bank. Moreover, to maintain a positive sense of continuity, the proposed Merchants and People's Bank would be housed at 3201 South State Street (the site of the old R. W. Woodford Bank).[5]

In 1921, when a new Illinois law went into effect prohibiting individual ownership of banks, Chavers dramatically enhanced his visibility in the realm of banking. Unlike Binga, who secured a state charter for his previously privately owned Binga Bank, Chavers announced his intent to seek a federal charter for the Merchants and People's Bank. This, in fact, was the first time that a black-controlled institution sought to become a national bank.[6]

In her biography, Chavers-Wright states that her father, beginning in November 1921, began drafting speeches that included his suggestion that the national bank be named after the venerable Frederick Douglass.[7] However, contemporary newspaper reports indicate that the evolution from the Merchants and People's Bank to the Douglass National Bank took place earlier that year. A short, front-page article titled "The 1st National Bank among Colored People in the United States Opens in Chicago" appears in an April issue of the *Chicago Broad Ax*. Although the bank was not yet open for business, the article notes that the "Douglass National Bank" received its federal charter on April 27, 1921, and identifies P. W. Chavers as its president.[8] This indicates that Chavers, well before November 1921, had decided to name his proposed national bank after Frederick Douglass.

Two weeks later, the *Broad Ax* lists the officers of this fledgling financial institution. Besides Chavers, Major Robert R. Jackson, alderman of Chicago's Third Ward, is cited as the vice president of Douglass National Bank. Its board of directors included chairman O. F. Smith, president of Citizens' Trust Bank (the only non–African American in the group); Rev. John W. Robinson, pastor of St. Mark's Methodist Episcopal Church; and physician Dr. Edward S. Miller. Significantly, Anthony Overton was *not* among the original officers of this bank.[9]

P. W. Chavers, by early 1921, had secured a federal charter for the Douglass National Bank. Nevertheless, he soon faced the even more daunting task of raising the $200,000 necessary for the bank to commence operations. Moreover, as Christopher Reed cogently observes, while Chavers received the bank charter, the US Office of the Comptroller of the Currency began raising "legitimate questions about the capabilities of the board of directors Chavers had assembled. These were basically inexperienced men in the world of banking who desired to operate an institution authorized under federal auspices."[10]

To address the issue of raising the necessary capitalization for the Douglass National Bank, Chavers undertook a grassroots stock-selling campaign. Chavers's plan to fund this institution, based on stock sales to numerous smaller investors, reflected what Madrue Chavers-Wright has called her father's desire to create "a People's National Bank!" To attract potential stockholders, the embryonic Douglass National Bank staffed informational booths at community events. For example, as noted in a June issue of the *Broad Ax*, the Douglass National Bank's exhibit attracted the largest crowds at a festival held at the Eighth Regiment Armory. The visually striking display featured a poster outlining the history of African Americans surrounded by three portraits. According to the *Broad Ax*, "on the left of the sign appears a picture of the Sainted Frederick Douglass, 'typifying physical freedom,' in the center Booker T. Washington representing 'industrial freedom' and on the right a portrait of P. W. Chavers, president of the bank showing 'economic freedom,' the three great steps in the upward development of the race."[11]

In the short term, Chavers's attempts to generate grassroots interest in the Douglass National Bank appeared to be working. As the *Broad Ax* reported, at the bank's well-attended July 26, 1921, stockholders' meeting, Chavers, to stimulate even more stock sales, offered prizes to those that recruited additional investors. Also, while the Douglass National Bank would be housed in Chicago's South Side black enclave, Chavers did not ignore African Americans who resided in the city's West Side black community. That September, the *Broad Ax* reported that a recent bank-sponsored meeting held at the Friendship Baptist Church at Lake and Ada Streets attracted a large crowd that "listened to several well delivered addresses on the most vital subject: 'the economic development of our group.'"[12]

By December 1921, according to the *Broad Ax,* interest in the Douglass National Bank had reached a fever pitch. A December 3 article informs readers that the bank's officers had just returned from a recent stock-selling campaign in Indianapolis, where "the population turned out 'en masse' to welcome the bank representatives and indicated their interest by subscribing and paying for a large number of shares." Moreover, the *Broad Ax* notes that "similar meetings have been held in St. Louis and Detroit and Mr. Chavers and the board are much elated with the evident awakening of the race to its industrial and commercial needs and predict that within a short time we will obtain REAL freedom: that of economic emancipation." The article concludes this upbeat assessment of the Douglass National Bank's progress: "all necessary equipment, such as pass books, check books, etc., have been ordered and will be installed as soon as the contractor completes the renovation of the building [at 3201 South State Street] and makes it ready for the formal opening early in January, 1922."[13]

By late 1921, national media had joined local African American newspapers in following the Douglass National Bank story. On December 7, the *New York Times* wrote about the soon-to-be-opened institution. Citing a December 6, 1921, announcement by president Chavers, Douglass National Bank's grand opening, scheduled for January 2, 1922, would include "a parade of more than 5,000 negro school children, members of churches and business organizations." Moreover, "store fronts and electric lamp posts along South State Street will be decorated with flags and bunting."[14]

The fall of 1921 witnessed efforts not only by P. W. Chavers and his board of directors to raise the necessary capital to actually open the Douglass National

Bank, but also by Anthony Overton to increase his growing market share in the African American personal care products industry. As discussed in chapter 2, Overton's primary competitors, Annie Turnbo-Malone and Madam C. J. Walker, generated revenue not only from selling beauty preparations but also from training beauticians who subsequently used their product lines. Consequently, Overton used the November 1921 issue of the *Half-Century Magazine* to promote a new venture, the Overton High-Brown Beauty College. To distinguish his training program from that of Turnbo-Malone's and Walker's, an ad in *Half-Century* informed prospective students that "in addition to beauty culture, our curriculum includes a course in business." Moreover, "graduates get the advantage of our twenty-three years in the commercial world."[15]

Shortly after Anthony Overton introduced his Overton High-Brown Beauty College, a meeting with one of the Douglass National Bank's board members, Rev. John W. Robinson, prompted Overton to redirect his entrepreneurial focus. Notwithstanding positive newspaper articles to the contrary, Chavers's grassroots capitalization process had proceeded only slowly, so that by December 1921, the bank was still short of the money needed to open its doors. Moreover, Chavers's announcement in December 1921 of a grand opening parade on January 2, 1922, placed further pressure on the situation. Thus, to help avert both public embarrassment and financial disaster, Robinson asked Anthony Overton to consider joining the Douglass National Bank's board of directors and becoming the institution's chief investor. Overton subsequently accepted the invitation due to his long-standing interest in banking. As discussed in chapter 3, he wrote a 1919 article on the importance of banking for the *Half-Century* under the pseudonym McAdoo Baker.[16]

Part of Robinson's motivation for seeking Anthony Overton's involvement with the Douglass National Bank was because he had been informed that "Washington officials wanted someone who was either Caucasian or an African American of Anthony Overton's financial stature to head the bank." Perhaps predictably, Chavers dismissed this information when Robinson shared it with him. After his enormous investment of time and energy, Chavers apparently could not accept the fact that the bank would not open with him as president. In February 1922, Chavers, sensing the threat that Overton's potential presence on the bank board posed to his leadership, requested an extension from the deputy in the Office of the Comptroller of the Currency. Among other things, he hoped that he could still generate the grassroots-based funding necessary to open the Douglass National Bank and regain the confidence of Robinson and other nervous board members. Unfortunately, for Chavers, this strategy failed, and in April he reluctantly agreed to accept Overton as a bank board member.[17]

In a last-ditch effort to salvage his weakening stature within the embryonic Douglass National Bank, Chavers, in June, circumvented Chicago obstacles and used his Ohio political contacts to secure the sought-after finalized federal bank charter. In fact, with the assistance of fellow Ohioan, President Warren G. Harding, Chavers, during a trip to Washington, DC, indeed secured a finalized federal charter for the Douglass National Bank on June 27, 1922. On the surface, it appeared that the trip to Washington resulted in a major personal victory for P. W. Chavers. Against all odds, including the opposition of some Douglass National Bank board members, he had persevered and won. Yet, on his return to Chicago, Chavers's exhilaration and sense of vindication soon turned to shock and dismay. According to Chavers-Wright, the Douglass National Bank opened its doors for business on June 29, 1922. Moreover, she asserts that on July 10, at the bank's initial board meeting, the first order of business was a motion for Chavers to resign from the presidency and for him to accept an uncompensated position as vice president. While Chavers was in Washington, the board had apparently elected Overton as the bank's new president. In recounting this episode, in a chapter titled "The Coup," Chavers-Wright contends that the Douglass board of directors, who wanted to be rid of Chavers, offered him an insulting proposal "that they knew he would be too embarrassed to accept." Their strategy worked, and Chavers stormed out of the meeting.[18]

While there is no doubt that the Douglass National Bank board of directors sought to remove P. W. Chavers as its president, the evidence suggests that Chavers was not as totally unaware of their intentions as *The Guarantee* implies. The Saturday, July 8, 1922, edition of the *Chicago Defender* carried an article titled "National Bank to Open on South Side: Pioneer Institution to Have Formal Opening July 12, Overton Is Head." In addition to explicitly citing Anthony Overton as the bank's president, the article lists P. W. Chavers only as a member of the board of directors.[19] Considering the hoopla surrounding the opening of the Douglass National Bank and considering the *Chicago Defender*'s stature as the top black newspaper in the city, the chance is remote that P. W. Chavers was *not* aware of this article before he attended the Monday, July 10, 1922, board meeting.

In her book, Chavers-Wright focuses on the actions of the Douglass National Bank's board of directors as it relates to her father's ouster from the leadership of the bank. While the board's summary dismissal of her father was, indeed, stunning, the evidence suggests that the board may have been emboldened by the US government's tacit approval of this action. In recounting her father's reaction to the July 10, 1922, Douglass National Bank board of directors meeting, Wright-Chavers asserts that the other board members' attitude toward P. W. Chavers was "that he had acted for the bank in securing the charter like an ordinary political emissary."[20] Considering long-standing government concerns about the original constitution of the bank's board of directors, it is not implausible to contend that, at the very time Chavers was in Washington securing the charter, the Douglass National Bank board of directors was informing the Office of the Comptroller of the Currency that Overton would assume the leadership of this historic African American financial institution. Moreover, the government's response to a subsequent lawsuit filed by Chavers against the Douglass National Bank implies that it approved of the simultaneous ascent of Anthony Overton and descent of P. W. Chavers within the Douglass National Bank's administrative hierarchy.

On November 22, 1922, Chavers filed a suit in federal court against the Douglass National Bank, claiming that "the bank is insolvent, that its charter was fraudulently obtained, and a move is on to unfairly and illegally dispose of its assets." Specifically, Chavers's lawsuit contended that "the officers of the bank are planning to float a bond issue totaling some $175,000, practically all of the bank's capital, for the construction of a building at 36th Place and State Street for the Overton Building Company whose head is Anthony Overton. Mr. Overton is also president of the Douglass bank." For his part, Overton told the *Chicago Defender* that he had been asked to take charge of the Douglass National Bank after "Chavers had struggled for a year." Moreover, he characterized "the charge that the bank is insolvent [as] absurd. The National bank department would not permit us to run a day if we were insolvent." Finally, Overton, responded to Chavers's charge that the bank charter had been secured through fraudulent means by reminding the former president that he had singularly undertaken that task.[21]

Chavers received a crushing defeat a month after filing his lawsuit, when the case was thrown out of court. As the *Chicago Defender* reported just before Christmas that the Douglass National Bank had been thoroughly examined by the comptroller of the currency and it was found "to be solvent and in splendid condition." Moreover, to P. W. Chavers's embarrassment, the *Defender* notes that "Comptroller Crissinger complimented Anthony Overton, president of the bank, and the officers upon the wonderful showing the institution had made during the first six months of business."[22]

Even before the administratively reconfigured Douglass National Bank received legal vindication in late 1922, Overton used the *Half-Century Magazine* to extol his rise to the institution's presidency. The July–August 1922 issue features a full-page article announcing the opening of the Douglass National Bank and praising the business acumen of its president: "The same wisdom and commercial ability that popularized and made profitable the sale of

Anthony Overton Jr., ca. 1920s. (Courtesy of the Everett and Ida
Overton Collection)

High Brown Toilet Preparations and the same sound judgment and integrity
that placed the Overton Hygienic Company in the first rank of commercial
institutions, regardless of color, is guiding the Douglass National Bank to its
rightful place among the foremost banking institutions of the world." The
"Have You Seen Them?" editorial in the very next issue of the *Half-Century*
declares that "there are some new bank notes in circulation that should attract and hold the attention of the entire race." With undisguised pride, the
Half-Century continues: "these bright, new, crispy bank-notes are being issued by the United States government through the Douglass National Bank

of Chicago in denominations of $5.00 and more. These bills are worthless unless they bear the signature of Anthony Overton, the president of the bank. The Douglass National Bank is the first Colored Organization ever granted the privilege of putting money into circulation."[23]

The following issue provides even more encouraging news about the newly opened Douglass National Bank. An editorial titled "A Monument to Racial Industry" announces that ground had been broken for a new commercial structure that would house several African American enterprises including the Douglass National Bank and the Overton Hygienic Manufacturing Company. Moreover, to help minimize negative publicity associated with P. W. Chavers's pending lawsuit against the Douglass National Bank, *Half-Century* presents this construction project as a racial victory. In addition to contending that the new Overton Building, when completed, "will be the finest structure of its kind owned by Negroes," the magazine claims that "it is impossible to place a monetary value on this very interesting building project—for its value to the race is immeasurable."[24]

Ironically, although P. W. Chavers had been removed from the Douglass National Bank's administrative team after the July 10, 1922, board of directors meeting, his name still appears (as a vice president) in full-page bank advertisements in the July–August and September–October issues of the *Half-Century*. However, his name disappeared from the ad in the November–December issue, which, not coincidentally, came out at the time he filed his lawsuit against the institution.[25] In the final analysis, by the end of 1922, the Douglass National Bank had become an integral part of Anthony Overton's growing financial empire and an embittered P. W. Chavers had to reorganize his commercial and personal life.[26]

Douglass National Bank versus Binga State Bank

Besides seeking to silence the recalcitrant P. W. Chavers, the fledgling Douglass National Bank had to contend with a formidable local black competitor for bank deposits, the Binga State Bank. This financial institution, presided over by Jesse Binga, commenced operations on January 3, 1921. Moreover, unlike Anthony Overton, who had only recently entered into banking, Binga had organized a Chicago private bank in 1908 (which evolved into a state-regulated financial institution).[27] Although Overton and Binga headed rival black banks, according to Dempsey J. Travis, the two men had earlier discussed starting a bank together. In fact, "the Binga State Bank permit was issued in 1920 over the signatures of Jesse Binga and Anthony Overton."

Yet, because the two men subsequently "had a disagreement over a business transaction," when the Binga State Bank opened in 1921, Overton had already severed his ties with this enterprise.[28]

Although unaffiliated, the two banks were often linked together as praiseworthy demonstrations of African American performance in the realm of finance. For instance, in his classic 1936 work *The Negro as Capitalist*, Abram Harris notes that "in 1929 these two banks [the Douglass National Bank and the Binga State Bank] possessed 36 percent of the combined resources of all Negro banks in the United States. A similar relationship existed in other years."[29] It appears that the entrepreneurial competition between Overton and Binga contributed to this noteworthy distinction.

Table 4-1 reports the total deposits in the Douglass National Bank and the Binga State Bank from 1921 to 1929. The figures reveal that, although the Binga State Bank had eighteen months' head start on the Douglass National Bank, by the end of the decade Overton's bank held a slight edge in deposits over Binga's financial institution. One of the primary ways that Overton and Binga competed for depositors was through impressive banking facilities. When the flamboyant Jesse Binga opened the Binga State Bank on January 3, 1921, he set the proverbial bar high in this regard. The *Chicago Broad Ax* recounted this event in a front-page story with the extended title "The Opening of Binga State Bank: Monday, January Third, 1921, Was a History-Making Event among Colored People Residing in Chicago." According to the *Broad Ax*, the new Binga State Bank at State Street and Thirty-Sixth Place "was beautifully decorated with many rare and beautiful flowers, ferns and potted plants in honor of the history making occasion." The article reports that, on the bank's opening day, "thousands of men and women were . . . depositing all kinds of money right and left, some of them for the first time in their lives opened savings accounts."[30]

The enthusiastic public response to the opening of the Binga State Bank may have been another contributing factor to Anthony Overton's acceptance of Robinson's invitation to become involved with the fledgling Douglass National Bank later that year. Although Overton had already distinguished himself as an entrepreneur by 1921, the banking world potentially held more personal and business prestige. As discussed in chapter 3, the *Half-Century Magazine* began, with its April 1922 issue, to market bonds to help Overton construct a large new commercial complex on South State Street. It may be more than coincidental that this campaign started at the same time Overton officially joined the Douglass National Bank board of directors. Overton was likely already positioning himself to acquire additional space to someday house the Douglass National Bank. This assumption is given credence by

Table 4-1: Comparative Total Deposits in the Binga State Bank and the Douglass National Bank, 1921–29

	Binga State Bank	Douglass National Bank
1921	$300,082.95	N.A.
1922	572,450.23	$56,030.32
1923	953,370.11	412,654.59
1924	1,181,704.15	927,025.26
1925	1,333,320.59	1,076,314.36
1926	1,414,959.07	1,391,734.93
1927	1,380,850.44	1,399,628.24
1928	1,474,680.96	1,403,402.03
1929	1,465,266.62	1,507,336.70

Source: Abram Harris, *The Negro as Capitalist: A Study of Banking and Business among American Negroes* (Chicago: Urban Research Press, 1992 originally published in 1936), 174, 185.

an announcement in the November–December 1922 *Half-Century* issue that the future Overton Hygienic Manufacturing Building would also house the bank that Overton had assumed the presidency of a few months earlier.[31]

When the Douglass National Bank reopened at its new address in the Overton Building on Saturday, September 22, 1923, it generated excitement similar to that created by the opening of the Binga State Bank two years earlier. According to the *Chicago Defender*, "more than 3,000 persons witnessed the formal opening and receipts show that the deposits for the day exceeded $100,000." To impress on visitors the stability of this relocated financial institution, tours were provided to show its "mammoth burglar proof time safe" built "at the cost of $10,000." The *Defender* further elaborates that "the most interesting feature of this safe is the drill proof door which has a net weight of seven tons and is operated by four time clocks."[32]

Besides favorable local coverage of Anthony Overton's burgeoning financial empire, Alpha Phi Alpha Fraternity, the first African American Greek-lettered intercollegiate fraternity, also looked with pride on its fraternity brother's entrepreneurial accomplishments. The October 1923 issue of the *Sphinx*, the organization's magazine, features a story on Overton and cited other fraternity members associated with Overton's various enterprises. After stating that Overton's Douglass National Bank was "the only bank operated by Negroes with the authority to issue bank notes," the *Sphinx* further declares that "he [Overton] is recognized as a peer among the Captains of Industry as shown from the fact that The Overton-Hygienic Manufacturing Company has the highest credit rating of any Negro mercantile institution in the United States." Besides Ted Roane and Arthur Jewell Wilson, who served as the eastern sales representative and auditor of Overton Hygienic, respectively, the *Sphinx* cites two other fraternity brothers who worked with Overton Hygienic: "Brother Richard Hill, Jr. is its attorney . . . Brother Julian Lewis is corporation physician and adviser in the laboratories for dermatological research."[33]

As discussed in chapter 3, Anthony Overton utilized the skills of his physician and attorney sons-in-law in a variety of ways. Although the *Sphinx* does not mention it, another role that Hill and Lewis played in their father-in-law's business conglomerate was serving on the Douglass National Bank's board of directors. In fact, as is discussed in chapter 5, Hill assumed the presidency of the institution during its final troubled days.[34]

For his part, Jesse Binga, also a member of Alpha Phi Alpha, was not to be outdone by the favorable publicity generated by Overton's relocated Douglass National Bank. Consequently, Binga made plans to relocate the Binga State Bank, which reopened on October 20, 1924, at 3442 South State Street. Christopher Reed describes this new facility: "architecturally the structure was imposing, featuring white bricks and two massive Ionic pillars over its one-and-one-half stories." Moreover, "its interior featured 'lofty reaches of marble and bronze, and . . . massive steel vaults and . . . mellow walnut paneling and . . . subdued hangings.'" Finally, "as a special touch to match its physical elegance, a somewhat formally attired Binga personally greeted customers each morning with the assurance that he was in charge and the institution reflected his confidence and strength in them as residents of a Black Metropolis."[35]

The Associated Business Clubs

Notwithstanding the obvious competition between Anthony Overton and Jesse Binga, the two men worked together on certain occasions. In fact, Overton and Binga, along with *Defender* editor Robert Abbott, headed a local initiative called the Associated Business Clubs (ABC), which sought to better coordinate the activities of black Chicago entrepreneurs. As Juliet E. K. Walker and John Sibley Butler observe in their respective studies of African American business history, the 1920s represented the high point of what could rightfully be called a golden age of black business activity. Motivated by a spirit of economic cooperation and coupled with the reality of US apartheid, African American entrepreneurs in a variety of industries were able to establish an impressive number of commercial enterprises.[36] The establishment of Chicago's ABC in January 1924 epitomized the spirit of African American economic cooperation during this period. Considered the acknowledged leaders of this group, Anthony Overton, Jesse Binga, and Robert Abbott directly competed with one another in the marketplace.

Besides the simultaneous quest of Overton and Binga to secure more depositors for their banks, Overton's *Half-Century Magazine* was a competitor of Robert Abbott's *Chicago Defender*. Nevertheless, to the distinct credit of all three men, they sometimes (as characterized by the ABC) moved beyond self-aggrandizement and used their power and influence to assist the development of Bronzeville's broader economic community.

The Chicago ABC deployed a variety of strategies to enhance black Chicago's business infrastructure. First, it established seminars on effective business management techniques to assist smaller African American enterprises in their quest to attract and keep customers. It also established clusters where entrepreneurs in a similar industry could work collectively to maximize profits for all. In addition, at the suggestion of Binga, the ABC started a coupon program whereby consumers could get discounts by purchasing items at ABC-affiliated businesses. Finally, in 1925, when the ABC reached the threshold of a thousand participating members—and had become a de facto black chamber of commerce—the organization purchased a meeting place at 3632 South Michigan Avenue, which further increased its visibility and credibility. Among other things, after 1925, ABC members officially pledged to deliver "high standards and good service" to customers.[37]

The evidence indicates that Overton, Binga, and Abbott were more than detached titular leaders of the ABC. They freely gave of their time to assist less successful ABC members. For instance, in November 1923, Overton delivered a presentation at an ABC luncheon "Merchandising" seminar that included the following observations and advice: "The average Colored business man does not realize that 95 per cent of all business is done on credit. If you so conduct your establishment and live up to your obligations with such integrity that you are properly accredited in Dun's or Bradstreet's, the good book or bible of commercial life, and then properly apply the principles of merchandising, you are bound to succeed."[38]

Another manifestation of the spirit of economic cooperation that permeated 1920s black Chicago was the relationship between the upstart ABC and the long-standing Chicago branch of the NNBL. Frank Gillespie, the president and founder of Chicago's Liberty Life Insurance Company, assumed the presidency of the Chicago Negro Business League in 1923. On hearing about the establishment of the ABC, he declared that "for the 35 years I have been living in Chicago I have been waiting to see the 'big Negro' join hands and start a co-operative movement like this. With such an example as the Abbott-Binga-Overton combination functioning in unison before them, the smaller business men will take heart and back them up. It means a new day for better, bigger, Negro business." For its part, the ABC used its growing influence to work with the Chicago Negro Business League to insure that the Twenty-Fifth Anniversary NNBL Convention, held in Chicago in August 1924, was an unqualified success.[39]

Although Overton and Binga, through the ABC, promoted economic cooperation, when all was said and done they harbored no ideas of merging their financial institutions for the sake of racial unity. Moreover, from the standpoint of African American consumers in 1920s black Chicago, the competition between the two men for bank deposits was not necessarily a negative phenomenon. Part of their quest to outdo each other in the realm of banking was to provide superior customer service to black Chicagoans. Yet, notwithstanding Overton and Binga's pleas for racial cooperation and their provision of first-class banking facilities to Bronzeville residents, the vast majority of black Chicagoans during the 1920s chose to put their money in white banks. Ironically, these institutions, for the most part, did not hire African Americans.[40] Later in the decade, when Anthony Overton became a national advocate for African American economic development, he decried blacks' tendency not to act in their own economic self-interest.

Entering the Insurance Industry

If Anthony Overton's decision to become involved with the Douglass National Bank helped raise his entrepreneurial profile, his subsequent establishment of the Victory Life Insurance Company catapulted him to greater public recognition. Significantly, when Overton began formulating the idea of starting an insurance company, he sought to enter an industry filled with formidable African American competitors. Nevertheless, Overton's decision to start Victory Life reflected the enormous self-confidence he had developed by the mid-1920s. The frustrations from his past had seemingly dissipated, and Anthony Overton audaciously believed that, even without a background in the industry, he could create a viable insurance company.

African American insurance companies, as with other black institutions during the early twentieth century, were by-products of US apartheid. While historians have tended to focus on the social and educational dynamics of Jim Crow racial segregation, overt racial discrimination also existed in the US commercial sphere. In fact, the evolution of the nation's insurance industry is a classic example of how the reality of "separate and unequal" operated in the realm of business. As early as 1875, large white insurance companies insured African Americans. Moreover, during their initial contact with blacks, companies such as the Prudential Insurance Company of Newark and Metropolitan Life of New York offered blacks and whites identical coverage at identical cost. Nevertheless, over the next couple of decades, overt racism surfaced in the mainstream insurance industry. Consequently, at the dawn of the twentieth century, some companies, such as Prudential, refused to insure blacks altogether. Others, such as Metropolitan Life, continued to insure blacks but charged them higher premiums than their white counterparts.[41] This new reality, among other things, directly contributed to the establishment of African American–owned insurance companies.

The North Carolina Mutual Life Insurance Company, established in Durham in 1898, has the distinction of being the first legal reserve insurance company organized by African Americans. Yet, even before the appearance of North Carolina Mutual, African American fraternal organizations, starting in the late eighteenth century, provided insurance coverage to their members and families.[42] One late nineteenth-century fraternal organization that stands out in this regard was William Washington Browne's Grand United Order of the True Reformers organized in Richmond, Virginia, in 1881. At its peak, the True Reformers, in addition to providing insurance benefits for its members, operated a bank, published a weekly newspaper, owned a cooperative department store and farm, and offered undertaking services. Moreover, there appears to be a direct linkage between the True Reformers and North Carolina Mutual. Durham's John Merrick, the principal founder of North Carolina Mutual, initially learned about the dynamics of insurance as a member-agent of William Washington Browne's True Reformers.[43]

Although Merrick, unlike Overton, had some exposure to the insurance business before starting North Carolina Mutual, he primarily earned his living as a barber. Moreover, the six other founders of what would become the largest African American insurance company were also otherwise employed: Dr. Aaron M. Moore as a physician, William G. Pearson as a teacher, Edward A. Johnson as dean of the Law School at Shaw University, James E. Shepard as a preacher-politician-pharmacist, Pinkney W. Dawkins as a teacher, and Dock Watson as a tinsmith.[44]

Of this group, Merrick clearly possessed the most background in business enterprise. Moreover, as Walter B. Weare asserts, "At the peak of his barbering career, Merrick owned six barbershops—three for whites three for blacks. Managing this small empire was no simple task, and his success indicates that he had learned well the principles of business. As head barber at his Main Street shop, where he attended only to special white customers, Merrick spent a good part of his life in the company of the South's leading capitalists. Only a deaf man could have escaped the profound influence of this indirect tutelage."[45]

One of Merrick's clients at his Main Street barber shop was Washington Duke, founder of the American Tobacco Company. Some have, in fact, asserted that Duke actually gave Merrick the idea to start a black insurance company. According to one white Durham resident who condescendingly re-created this scenario, Duke told Merrick that he should "organize an insurance company and make every dinged nigger in the United States pay you twenty-five dollars a year." A similar, more sanitized, depiction of the motivation for North Carolina Mutual's founding contends that "lower-class blacks, so the story goes, often interrupted Merrick and his patrons to 'pass the hat' for a Negro funeral. One day, 'Mr. Duke watched the proceeding with quiet interest and after the beggar had left . . . he suggested to Mr. Merrick that the colored people should organize an insurance company.'"[46]

While the details of the founding of North Carolina Mutual remain hazy, it is nonetheless clear that African American self-determination and agency helped the company grow as a commercial enterprise. After a difficult first couple of years—which prompted five of the seven founders to abandon the embryonic North Carolina Mutual—John Merrick and Dr. Aaron Moore made a fateful decision that would positively impact the fledgling enterprise. On July 1, 1900, they reorganized the company's administrative structure by naming Charles Clinton Spaulding, who previously served as a part-time insurance agent, to the position of general manager. Walter Weare describes the impact of this decision: "Charles Clinton Spaulding is often remembered as a one-man staff who 'came to work early in the morning, rolled up his sleeves and did janitor's work. Then . . . rolled down his sleeves and worked as an agent. And a little later in the day he put on his coat and was general manager.' Thus, in a success story of epic proportions, he appeared as the savior of a flagging enterprise and transformed it into the unparalleled pride of black capitalism." Before his promotion, Spaulding had attracted Merrick's and Moore's attention by being the young North Carolina Mutual's most productive agent. "He [Spaulding] was bold, almost rash, and could hawk insurance without the slightest diffidence on street corners, in Jim Crow cars, or wherever he found a listener." After his promotion, Spaulding's skill set and enthusiasm helped North Carolina Mutual simultaneously increase its agent corps and market (by moving into other states). Merrick and Moore, the two other members of the North Carolina Mutual triumvirate, used their personal financial resources to help keep the fledgling insurer solvent.[47]

Another strategy that the North Carolina Mutual triumvirate employed to grow its corporate structure was to take over distressed smaller black insurers. This maneuver had a twofold purpose. First, it increased the number of policyholders, which prompted the company to declare on its letterhead in 1907 (after the number of policyholders exceeded 100,000) that it was the "Greatest Negro Insurance Company in the South." Second, North Carolina

Mutual took over smaller distressed black insurers because "unless these companies were heavily encumbered with debts, the Mutual knew that it was better to buy them out than to watch them fail and further erode public confidence in black business."[48] Consequently, by the 1920s, the North Carolina Mutual Life Insurance Company, given a variety of factors, had evolved from a tenuous enterprise into a black business powerhouse (see appendix A for more details).

Another of Anthony Overton's competitors in the 1920s black insurance industry was the Atlanta Life Insurance Company. Like North Carolina Mutual's John Merrick, Alonzo B. Herndon, the founder of Atlanta Life, was a black barber. And, like Merrick, Herndon owned multiple barbershops in Atlanta. His largest shop, located at 66 Peachtree Street, was considered one of the finest in the country. Extending an entire block in length, it "boasted twenty-five chairs and eighteen baths with tubs and showers, had the finest furniture, fixtures, and equipment available, and was set off by handsome sixteen-foot front doors of solid mahogany and beveled plate glass which Herndon had copied from a pair he had seen on the Avenue de l'Opera in Paris." Also, like Merrick's Main Street barbershop in Durham, Herndon's Peachtree establishment "served an all-white clientele made up of some of the state's leading judges, lawyers, politicians, ministers, and businessmen. As proprietor, Herndon saw personally to the tonsorial services provided to some of the most important figures in the state, earning their acquaintance and goodwill."[49]

Despite the striking similarities between the founders of North Carolina Mutual and Atlanta Life, there were also important differences. First, Herndon, unlike Merrick, had no previous exposure to the insurance business before he established Atlanta Life in 1905. Yet, as a community-minded entrepreneur, Herndon responded affirmatively to a request to buy the Atlanta Benevolent Protective Association, a small black insurer that faced closure because it couldn't meet a new state requirement directing insurance companies to deposit $5,000 with the Georgia insurance commission. After completing his purchase of the Atlanta Benevolent Protection Association, Herndon secured a state charter for the renamed Atlanta Mutual Insurance Association and deposited the requested $5,000. This scenario illustrates another apparent difference between Merrick's and Herndon's entries into the realm of insurance. While, as Walter Weare writes, some believe that Duke encouraged Merrick to establish North Carolina Mutual, it does not appear that any of Herndon's wealthy white clients gave him similar advice. In fact, as Alexa B. Henderson writes, "Alonzo Herndon joined the long line of economic and religious leaders whose efforts helped advance the ideals of self-help and race independence. . . . Herndon belonged to a group of black capitalists whose activities transformed mutual aid societies, church and secret societies, and other benevolent endeavors into more efficient secular operations."[50]

While Herndon, like Merrick, possessed the financial wherewithal to establish an insurance company, a major challenge both men faced was finding skilled personnel to grow their enterprises. As discussed earlier, Merrick's discovery of Charles Clinton Spaulding helped facilitate North Carolina Mutual's survival and growth. Herndon, after purchasing the renamed Atlanta Mutual Insurance Association, filled his new board of directors with individuals who possessed expertise in the realm of insurance. For instance, one board member, Wade Aaron Aderhold, "had worked for the Union Mutual Relief Association, the first chartered insurance association by blacks in Georgia." Moreover, "Aderhold was a self-taught insurance wizard, and much of the business done by Union Mutual was credited to his knowledge of insurance and organizational skills." Besides his board service, Aderhold worked as the company's first vice president and treasurer.[51]

Along with utilizing the talent of persons such as Wade Aderhold, Herndon and his board, as with North Carolina Mutual's triumvirate, enhanced Atlanta Mutual's corporate stature by purchasing smaller black insurers. As Alexa Henderson, the company's historian asserts, "Herndon and the other officers began with the idea that one strong, reliable firm with ample assets would be more profitable and beneficial to the community than a dozen or more smaller, less efficient organizations. . . . By taking over these weaker competitors, the directors of Atlanta Mutual hoped to strengthen the enterprise and, at the same time, build confidence in insurance firms operated by African Americans by saving the business of the less stable groups."[52]

In 1916, Herndon undertook another corporate maneuver to strengthen the company's financial foundation. During its first decade of operation, Atlanta Mutual's income came from assessments paid by policyholders. This, at times, became problematic for the company because some policyholders allowed their policies to lapse, making it sometimes difficult for Atlanta Mutual to pay its obligations. To address this situation, Herndon and his board decided to reorganize Atlanta Mutual as a stock corporation. "In contrast to the frailties of a mutual assessment organization, a stock corporation offered greater potential for security and advancement. It was controlled by stockholders, and resources could be obtained through the sale of stock." On August 19, 1912, the newly approved Georgia Insurance Act allowed companies such as Atlanta Mutual to reorganize as a stock company for an additional $25,000 deposit. On September 27, 1916, Herndon, with $25,000 generated from stock sale proceeds, took advantage of this opportunity and received a new corporate charter. Moreover, six years later, Herndon took advantage of Atlanta Mutual's status as a stock company by raising the additional $75,000 deposit necessary to reorganize Atlanta Mutual into Atlanta Life, a legal reserve company authorized to issue all classes of life insurance.[53]

Notwithstanding Herndon's and his board's shrewd business maneuvers, agents represented the cornerstone of Atlanta Life (and all insurance companies). To strengthen this aspect of corporate operations, "in 1922 Atlanta Life became the first black company to meet the pressing need to train agents by creating an educational department and 'furnishing its workers with a complete course of study in Life Insurance Salesmanship.'" Not coincidentally, after establishing its agent education program, Atlanta Life began to expand its operations beyond the state of Georgia.[54] Thus, by the mid-1920s, Atlanta Life, like North Carolina Mutual, represented a powerful, growing, presence in the African American insurance industry (see appendix B for more details).

It is not coincidental that the embryonic black insurance industry had decidedly southern roots. During the first years of the twentieth century, the vast majority of African Americans still lived in the South. Yet, during World War I, a significant number of southern blacks participated in a phenomenon referred to as the Great Migration. Between 1915 and 1918, southern black migrants swelled into northern cities to take advantage of war-related job opportunities. Chicago was an especially attractive destination; its black population grew from 44,103 in 1910 to 109,458 in just a decade.[55] Moreover, the dramatic growth of Chicago's black community convinced Frank Gillespie, a local African American with a significant background in insurance, of the feasibility of establishing an insurance company to cater to this growing consumer market.

Gillespie, a native of Arkansas, possessed a diverse occupational background before securing a salesman position with the Royal Life Insurance Company of Chicago in 1916. He quickly rose to the position of agency superintendent, making him the first African American to hold a management position with a white-owned northern insurer. Despite this distinction, the ambitious Gillespie and some of the insurer's black agents left Royal Life in 1917 to form the Public Life Insurance Company of Illinois. Two years later, Gillespie was on the move again. He resigned his position with Public Life to form what came to be known as the Liberty Life Insurance Company, which holds the distinction of being the first African American–controlled legal reserve insurance company established in the North. Ironically, when the state of Illinois awarded a charter to Liberty Life on June 30, 1919, Anthony Overton was listed as one of the insurer's ten charter members.[56]

Liberty Life, in its early quest to secure policyholders, stressed the importance of African Americans supporting black-owned enterprises. The January 3, 1920, issue of the *Chicago Defender* used Liberty Life as an example of this marketing strategy, illuminating the negative consequences of African Americans not supporting each other. Readers were told that Chicago blacks had previously "made Millionaires among every nationality known to civilization that offered them the least bit of encouragement for their patronage." Yet, at the same time, Chicago blacks had "made a PAUPER of every Negro who dared enter into competition with these people for our trade." In the end, "the results of our loyalty to the other fellow find us without any State Banks, Legal Reserve Insurance Companies, . . . necessary for the upbuilding of a Race."[57]

Such discourse reflected Anthony Overton's similar message to *Half-Century* readers under his McAdoo Baker pseudonym. Yet, curiously, although Anthony Overton was a charter member of the Liberty Life Insurance Company, no article related to the importance of insurance companies appeared with the Baker byline. Similarly, advertisements and stories related to the embryonic Liberty Life Insurance Company were markedly absent from the pages of the *Half-Century*.[58] Consequently, given Overton's apparent lack of enthusiasm for promoting Liberty Life, when the company officially commenced operations during the summer of 1921, he is not listed among the firm's officers and directors.[59] By the early 1920s, I suggest that Overton's entrepreneurial focus may have been on enterprises that he *controlled* either directly (Overton Hygienic) or covertly (*Half-Century*). This hypothesis is supported by the fact that his later involvement with the Douglass National Bank appears to have been predicated by the assurance that he would assume the presidency of this institution. It is also worth noting that, while Anthony Overton did not follow through on his initial commitment to Liberty Life, the fledgling company proceeded quite well without his involvement. In two years, by 1923, Liberty Life's insurance-in-force grew from zero to $3.5 million and the insurer had gained favorable publicity in black Chicago by investing a significant portion of its premium income back into African American community real estate.[60] (See appendix C for more details regarding Liberty Life's growth in the 1920s.)

Considering Anthony Overton's lack of background in the insurance industry, Victory Life's subsequent meteoric rise as a financial institution appeared to be a testament to his innate business instincts. Just as Overton, years earlier, made a life-altering decision when he decided to add women's face powder to the product line of the embryonic Overton Hygienic Manufacturing Company, his entrance into insurance appeared to be based on a pragmatic assessment of the marketplace. Consequently, Overton, seemingly using the banking industry as an example—where both his Douglass National Bank and the Binga State Bank had carved out comfortable economic niches—decided to start his own insurance company. Merah S. Stuart's important 1940 study of African American insurance companies, *An Economic Detour*, asserts that Overton, besides his quest for another income stream and additional entrepreneurial prestige, envisioned Victory Life as a company "which would encourage thrift, create estates, protect widows and orphans, and furnish high-type, lucrative, employment to the young men and women of his race who had trained themselves for lives of constructive service."[61] The evidence also suggests that Overton's self-assuredness about entering a new industry may have been linked to his control of the *Half-Century Magazine*. As discussed in chapter 3, *Half-Century* represented a marketing asset that his business competitors did not possess.

Another asset that Anthony Overton possessed as he formulated his plan to start an insurance company was the support of the pastor of Chicago's Mt. Olivet Baptist Church, considered to be "one of the largest Negro Baptist Churches in the world—perhaps the largest." In 1925, Rev. Dr. Lacy Kirk Williams assumed the leadership of the largest African American religious organization, the National Baptist Convention. As Stuart notes in *An Economic Detour*, "Negro business owes a debt of gratitude to the Negro church, it has received great assistance from it. In the development of all types of commercial enterprises, the doors of the church have ever been wide open . . . the voice of the ministry has been constantly raised and its influence exerted in active advocacy and defense of Negro owned and operated enterprises." Consequently, "when Anthony Overton took the initial step to organize Victory Life Insurance Company in 1923, he had no more enthusiastic supporter than Dr. L. K. Williams. Dr. Williams subscribed for a substantial block of the stock when it was first put on the market; and later was elected a member of the board of directors."[62]

Besides receiving financial assistance and encouragement from fellow Baptist Williams, Overton, a member of Chicago's Bethesda Baptist Church, also received similar support from New York City physician Phillip Maxwell Hugh Savory. Shortly after Victory Life officially commenced business on March 3, 1924, Savory, aware of Overton's growing reputation as an entrepreneur, visited Chicago to survey the fledgling insurance company as a possible investment opportunity. Although Victory Life inauspiciously began as one room in the Overton Building with three employees, Savory came away impressed with the company's potential. He subsequently bought fifty shares of company stock for $3,750 and, as is discussed later, played a major role in facilitating Victory Life's 1927 expansion into New York State.[63]

Notwithstanding having such financial backers as Rev. Williams and Dr. Savory, Overton, like Alonzo Herndon, realized that, for his proposed company to succeed, he needed someone with direct expertise in the insurance industry. Overton accomplished this goal by recruiting I. J. Joseph to serve as vice president of Victory Life. Joseph, before joining Victory Life, had managed Liberty Life's Chicago agent corps. Also, as he had done with the Douglass National Bank, Overton found places for his sons-in-law, Julian H. Lewis and Richard Hill, on Victory Life's administrative team. Lewis served as the insurer's medical examiner and Hill served as Victory Life's general counsel, and both served on the company's board of directors.[64] In addition, one of the prerequisites for Victory Life's entry into the insurance industry was to raise reserve capital of $100,000. After fulfilling this requirement through stock sales, it appears that Overton immediately invested this sum in black community real estate through another enterprise he controlled, the Great Northern Real Estate Company.[65]

Victory Life's early growth confirmed Overton's initial belief regarding the potential profits associated with the black insurance industry. At the end of 1924, Victory Life, licensed only to do business in Illinois, held insurance policies totaling $680,000. In 1925, Victory Life expanded into Texas, Missouri, Ohio, West Virginia, Kentucky, Maryland, New Jersey, and the District of Columbia. This financial maneuver caused the company's insurance in force to nearly quadruple to $2,250,000. The following year, Victory Life's insurance in force grew to $4,500,000. As a consequence, Merah S. Stuart notes that, in less than three years, the number of employees had grown from 3 to 308 in the home and branch offices as "officers, clerks, stenographers, bookkeepers, and in the field as agents, medical examiners, and inspectors."[66]

The year 1927 proved to be a truly banner year in the history of Victory Life. With the assistance of Savory, the company became the first black-owned insurer qualified to do business in the state of New York.[67] This event, among other things, represented the manifestation of one of Anthony Overton's entrepreneurial aspirations. Twelve years earlier, in August 1915, Overton had sought the assistance of Emmett J. Scott, Booker T. Washington's confidant and secretary-treasurer of Tuskegee Institute, in identifying an investor to help him expand the Overton Hygienic Manufacturing Company. Specifically, Overton informed Scott, "we have under consideration many plans for the development of the business, one of which is the establishment of a branch factory in New York City which alone would require a minimum investment of $25,000." Although this business maneuver never took place, it does indicate that the ambitious Overton had a long-standing interest in establishing a commercial presence in New York City, the nation's figurative

Anthony Overton Jr. departing Chicago for New York City in 1927 for Victory Life Insurance Company event. Frances (Overton) Hill is in the foreground; attorney Richard Hill Jr. is to her right (the woman in background and the man in the gray overcoat are unidentified). (Courtesy of Martha Harriet Bryant)

and literal capital of business activity. Moreover, after Victory Life began doing business in New York State, Overton told an interviewer in 1928, "I have in mind building a real, honest-to-goodness skyscraper in New York. That is something, however, that will have to be worked out."[68]

On February 9, 1927, "after two years of diplomacy, diligent work, and wire-pulling," the New York Department of Insurance granted Victory Life permission to conduct business in the Empire State. As Merah S. Stuart notes, "this remarkable achievement on the part of Victory Life was heralded far and wide in the press in the country; it made Victory Life a household word, and created a degree of confidence in the minds of the public that would otherwise taken years to develop." Moreover, "Victory's breaking of the ice in New York state was remarkable also because it was the only company chartered by the state of Illinois to accomplish such a feat." The following month, on March 17, 1927, "the citizens of New York and of Harlem in particular repaired to the Renaissance Casino to tender Mr. Overton and his co-workers a mammoth reception in honor of their achievement . . . it was an occasion for full dress and tuxedos for Harlem notables who are rarely seen at public functions." Among the dignitaries who came out to celebrate Victory Life's unprecedented business success was Dr. W. E. B. Du Bois.[69]

Although Victory Life's entry into New York was the company's most noteworthy accomplishment in 1927, it expanded its reach even further during that year by also qualifying to do business in Indiana, Virginia, and Michigan. As in New York, Victory Life was the first black-owned insurer granted a license to do business in Indiana. In Virginia, Victory Life was the first black insurer qualified to conduct business there since the state raised its capital reserve requirement to $200,000.[70] Moreover, having expanded into four new states in 1927, Victory Life's insurance in force nearly doubled, growing from $4.5 million to $8.5 million.[71] (See appendix D for more details regarding Victory Life's early growth.)

The 1927 Spingarn Medal

One of the immediate consequences of Victory Life's stunning 1927 business success was that it directly contributed to Overton's receipt of the NAACP's prestigious Spingarn Medal that year. Since 1915, the Spingarn Medal has annually recognized outstanding achievement by individual African Americans; Ernest E. Just was its first recipient. Anthony Overton's selection as the 1927 winner appears all the more significant when one considers Harold Cruse's important book, *Plural but Equal: A Critical Study of Blacks and Minorities and America's Plural Society*, where he states that: "at the very inception of the NAACP, the leadership split over the issue of the primacy of economic questions over civil rights questions, or vice versa." Cruse continues: "unable to resolve this conflict programmatically at the time of its founding, the NAACP dispensed with an economic program and projected a purely civil rights, or as it was then perceived, a 'civil libertarian' program."[72]

In *Plural but Equal*, Cruse refers to the NAACP's early reticence concerning the promotion of African American economic power as "non-economic liberalism." This stance, among other things, appeared to be out of touch with basic American realities. Specifically, Cruse declares "in a society where the making of money, the eager search after profits . . . the ownership of land, the perfection of technology, the expansion of industry . . . was worshipped as the highest of virtues transcending religion itself, the American Negro was being advised by white liberals to waive any program of economic advancement as a matter of priorities."[73]

Going by Cruse's observations, Anthony Overton, despite his noteworthy accomplishments, should not have received the Spingarn Medal. First, he had been a staunch friend and supporter of Booker T. Washington and the National Negro Business League. Moreover, in the *Half-Century*, Overton regularly published editorials calling for the creation of a separate black economy.[74] Thus, if the NAACP was, according to Cruse, hell-bent on trivializing African American economic development, it would have been utterly contradictory for the organization to honor Overton with the 1927 Spingarn Medal. Yet, W. E. B. Du Bois, the NAACP's most important African American official during this period, personally promoted Overton's candidacy. As discussed in chapter 1, African American business development was among the numerous causes the venerable Du Bois championed during his long career. Moreover, Du Bois attended the March 17, 1927, reception honoring Victory Life's entry into New York. Finally, to Du Bois's distinct credit, although he and Booker T. Washington had a well-publicized feud, he did not let his distaste for Washington affect his attitude toward Overton, who had been a friend and protégé of the Wizard of Tuskegee.

The nomination process for the 1927 Spingarn Medal highlighted an impressive array of African American achievers. Besides Anthony Overton, other nominees included the activist and labor leader A. Phillip Randolph; the scholar and writer Alain Locke; the noteworthy bibliophile Arthur Schomburg; and Matthew Henson, the first person to stand on the North Pole as part of Admiral Robert Peary's 1909 expedition. The records of the NAACP, as they relate to the 1927 Spingarn Medal, graphically reveal W. E. B. Du Bois's influence within the organization. On May 6, 1927, the organization issued a press release stating that "nominations for this year's award of the Spingarn Medal close on May 15." Moreover, "all names to be considered must be in on that day." Nevertheless, two days after the deadline, Du Bois submitted his letter recommending Overton for the Spingarn Medal to Bishop John Hurst, chair of the Spingarn Medal Award committee. In his submission,

Du Bois praised Overton for his work with the Overton Hygienic Manufacturing Company, the Douglass National Bank, and the Victory Life Insurance Company: "during the last year he [Overton] has succeeded in having the insurance society of which he is President, The Victory Life, . . . admitted to do business in New York. New York is admittedly the most difficult state for insurance associations to enter and the Victory is the first Negro association to achieve this distinction. The Victory Life is also the first Negro insurance company to be admitted to Indiana."[75]

The minutes of the June 2, 1927, meeting of the Spingarn Medal Committee echo Du Bois's recommendation stating that Overton would be the 1927 recipient because "of his success in a long business career and for the crowning achievement of securing the admission of the Victory Life Insurance Company as the first Negro organization permitted to do insurance business under the rigid requirements of the state of New York." Significantly, an NAACP press release issued the following day, titled "Spingarn Medal for 1927 Goes to Anthony Overton: A Pioneer in Life Insurance Organization for Negroes," includes misinformation about his pre-Chicago experiences (such as earning a law degree from the University of Kansas and serving as a municipal judge in Topeka).[76] Nevertheless, in the context of the moment, what Overton *did* or *did not do* nearly forty years earlier appeared immaterial. His well-documented *recent* accomplishments in the realm of business enterprise generated praise throughout black America.

After the NAACP announced Anthony Overton as the recipient of the 1927 Spingarn Medal, African American newspapers across the country expressed their pleasure with the decision. For instance, the *New York Amsterdam News* declared that "in awarding the Spingarn Medal a few days ago to Anthony Overton, of Chicago, the [NAACP] committee has, undoubtedly, honored the most outstanding business genius to be found in the Negro race." Similarly, the *St. Louis Argus* discussed the significance of Overton winning this award: "Mr. Overton is the first businessman to have received the Spingarn medal, the others being composers, artists, authors, educators, and a social worker." Also, "the outstanding work of the now powerful capitalist [reflects] the recent movement of Negroes for economic freedom."[77]

The *Chicago Defender*, the Windy City's most prominent African American newspaper, made a perfunctory assessment of Overton's receipt of the Spingarn Medal in a small, front-page article on June 11, 1927. On the same day that the *Chicago Defender* offered its subdued coverage of the award, Overton's *Chicago Bee* offered effusive praise for his accomplishment: "that this signal honor and distinction has been conferred upon this capable, progressive, industrious man of affairs, is evidence of the keen observation, honest desire, discernment and discriminating selection of those charged with the responsibility of picking, from a large field of eligibles, the one most worthy, a most difficult task and in this instance worthily performed." The *Bee* describes Overton as someone "engaged in constructive, practical work, a builder of industrial and financial institutions, a pioneer in the expansion of business, a courageous crusader for the rights of his people, a man of vision, a doer of dreams, a man who has capitalized his ideals, [and has] given a new value, vigor, impetus and utility to idle dollars."[78]

A "Man of the People"

After praising both the NAACP's Spingarn Medal selection committee and Anthony Overton, the *Chicago Bee* asserts that his receipt of this honor was truly special because "Mr. Overton is given to doing big things without bombast, trumpetry, display of arrogance . . . he worked quietly, honestly, steadily, and studiously toward his goal." Moreover, Overton was "a commoner beloved of the common people." Considering how Anthony Overton had previously used the *Half-Century*, it is not surprising that the *Chicago Bee* offered an extremely laudatory analysis of his receipt of the 1927 Spingarn Medal. However, an assessment of this phenomenon published by the *Pittsburgh Courier* corroborates much of the *Bee*'s reporting. A June 18, 1927, front-page article titled "'Man of [the] People' Wins Spingarn Medal" includes an illuminating subtitle: "Anthony Overton, Chicago's Millionaire Banker, Walks to His Office Every Morning—Has Never Owned an Automobile."[79]

This article, from the Chicago-based Associated Negro Press (ANP) news reporting agency, begins by asserting that "interviews among a number of leading Chicago Negroes this week, following the award of the Spingarn Medal to Anthony Overton, reveal a consensus of opinion that this year's bestowal of the prized symbol of merit and achievement is particularly noteworthy because it is made upon one of those plain men who do high thinking." The *Courier* continues: "possibly excepting George Carver of Tuskegee, Anthony Overton is more a man of the common people than any of the other thirteen remarkable Negroes who have achieved the distinction of winning the medal." To support this assertion, the June 18, 1927, *Pittsburgh Courier* article, citing its ANP source, declares that "on the street corners around here [Chicago]when the smiling old man is coming the folks who see him coming whisper that he is a millionaire, and probably he is. But one would never know it. He wears the clothes of ordinary folk, has the same feelings they have, enjoys their small talk, and believes in their God."[80]

Part of Overton's persona as a "man of the people" was the fact that he, despite his wealth, did not own an automobile. As the *Courier* reported, "each morning, except when the weather is very bad, he walks the twenty blocks from his home to his place of business, where he usually reports at half past eight. When it rains, he takes the street car or he may ride down in his son's car." Besides examining perceptions of Anthony Overton in the broader black Chicago community, this article also discusses his interaction with personnel in the Overton Building: "at the age of 62, he works right along with his employees. He not only works with them—he eats with them, eats the same kind of things, and when they play, he plays." The article concludes by asserting that Overton has "just tried to be a busy man, living simply, feeling simply and plainly, but thinking all of the time in 'high.'"[81]

This late 1920s assessment of Anthony Overton illuminates the complexity of his personality. Clearly, some of the techniques he employed to become a tycoon revealed his competitiveness. Also, it appears that Overton preferred to *lead* enterprises he was involved with (rather than *just be a member of an administrative team*). Yet, at the same time, despite his periodic engagement in hyperbole about his pre-Chicago life, Anthony Overton was a simple, unassuming, man who seemingly enjoyed *participating in commercial enterprise* more than the *perquisites* that accompany business success. Also, as Overton learned from his behind-the-scenes control of the *Half-Century Magazine*, he did not have to be in the spotlight to achieve his entrepreneurial goals.

The Mysteries of Overton's 1920s Personal Life

One of the consequences of Anthony Overton's increasingly visible ascent as an African American business icon during the 1920s was his being honored at banquets and special events. One such occasion, in December 1926, generates an interesting question about his personal life. On December 22, 1926, a gala event honoring Overton's business accomplishments took place in the Cameo Room of Chicago's Morrison Hotel and was attended by a number of African American notables from both Chicago and New York City. A *Pittsburgh Courier* article about this gathering commented on another person in attendance; "Mrs. Anthony Overton, in her quiet, sweet way, shared honors with her distinguished husband. The Overtons have three charming daughters and a son, all of whom are married."[82] Considering Clara Overton, the mother of Anthony's four children, had died in 1912, the December 1926 declaration about a living "Mrs. Anthony Overton" introduces yet another layer of mystery regarding the life of Anthony Overton.

Census data from 1920 and 1930 indicate that Anthony Overton had not remarried. In 1920, his marital status is given as "widow," and he lived with his daughter Eva and her husband (Julian Lewis). By the 1930 federal census, Overton had moved in with his other daughter, Frances, and her husband (Richard Hill). Besides confirming Overton's marital status during this period, census data confirms how simple a man he actually was. Rather than live in opulence; Anthony Overton, unlike most business tycoons, was living in a single room with two of his daughters' families.[83]

Unfortunately, details on the proceedings of the December 1926 gala for Overton do not survive. Thus, we have no way of knowing if this mystery woman was actually introduced as Mrs. Anthony Overton. Also, if the persons present did not know that the woman who accompanied Overton to this event was indeed not his wife, this suggests that, while his entrepreneurial successes were a matter of public record, his private actions were far less well known. Sheila Overton-Levi, an Overton granddaughter, confirms the fact that he did have a girlfriend (the woman introduced as Mrs. Anthony Overton in 1926). Although she cannot remember her name, Levi recalls a car ride as a child, where she accompanied her grandfather and his lady friend (in her vehicle) through Chicago's Lincoln Park.[84]

More Accolades and Visibility

After receiving the Spingarn Medal in 1927, Anthony Overton, now a national celebrity, received even more public recognition and honors. On January 13, 1928, the Harmon Foundation, associated with the Federal Council of Churches, named Overton as one of sixteen recipients of its award to honor achievement by African Americans in a variety of endeavors. As with the nominees for the NAACP's 1927 Spingarn Medal, the 1928 winners of the Harmon Award represent a virtual Who's Who of prominent African Americans. The Harmon Awards differed from the NAACP awards program in that two persons were recognized in each category. The first-place winner received a gold medal and $400 cash; the second-place winner received a bronze medal and $100 cash. Due to his accomplishments in 1927, Overton received the first place Harmon Award for Business, with second place going to William G. Pearson of Durham "for his success in organizing the only fire insurance company [Bankers Fire Insurance Company] and the only bonding company operated by his Race."[85]

While receiving the Spingarn Medal and Harmon Award no doubt contributed to Overton's positive sense of self, his election to the presidency of the National Negro Insurance Association (NNIA) in April 1929 must have been especially gratifying. A mere five years earlier, he had started Victory Life in one room with three employees. He now was recognized by his peers as the leader of one of the most important African American business organizations in the country.[86] The NNIA, organized on October 27, 1921, in Durham, North Carolina, addressed the concerns of African American insurance companies. Some of the early initiatives established by the NNIA included publishing a journal, approving funding to establish chairs of insurance in colleges, and agreeing that member companies would not employ agents dismissed by any NNIA-affiliated firm "for improper conduct."[87]

Even before becoming president of the NNIA, Overton, with the assistance of the *Pittsburgh Courier*, used the positive publicity generated from Victory Life's unprecedented business success to become a respected public spokesperson for African American economic development. Although Overton's association with the Victory Life Insurance Company enhanced his national name recognition, his first major contribution to the *Pittsburgh Courier* involved the Douglass National Bank. In a September 1927 article, he provides readers with an overview of how the federal banking system worked. Perhaps the most striking aspects of this essay are the *Courier*'s subtitles: "Race's Greatest Financial Genius Gives Practical Facts on 'Inside' of High Finance" and "Head of Douglass National Bank and Victory Life Insurance Co. Is Shining Example of What Thrift, Hard Work Can Accomplish."[88]

In a follow-up *Courier* article two weeks later, Overton declares that the Douglass National Bank, as a member of the Federal Reserve System, had the power to do business beyond the city of Chicago. He informs readers that out of 35,000 depositors, seven hundred were in cities and states outside of Illinois. Moreover, Overton suggests that, in the long run, it would make more sense for African Americans to support one strong national bank rather than several smaller black-owned financial institutions that were not "safeguarded by national government supervision."[89]

Apparently Overton's 1927 articles on the Douglass National Bank were popular with readers. The *Courier* brought Overton back in April 1928 to answer "Why the Negro Should Think More about His Economic Future." Overton responded with two articles in late April, both encouraging readers to do business with black-owned companies: "'Trade with Your Own,' Urges Anthony Overton" and "Two Billion Dollars in Insurance Carried on Lives of Negroes: 85% in White Companies."[90]

"Trade with Your Own" echoes much of what Anthony Overton had said as "McAdoo Baker" nearly a decade earlier in the *Half-Century*. The article begins with the observation that, without economic cooperation, "no race can ever acquire the strength and character necessary to enable to it to stand out as a power among the races of the world." Acknowledging the popular adage that "knowledge is power," Overton expands on this premise by asserting "in this day and time knowledge, or an education as we term it, is unattainable without funds and the power and respect given an individual, a race or a nation is predicated to a large extent upon their ability to produce and conserve wealth." Overton shares with readers his perception of reality and advises them: "the sooner we realize that every dollar spent with our group or invested in developing our own commercial enterprises is just another wedge in forcing the door of economic emancipation, the brighter will be the future of the whole group." In words that remain relevant today, Overton continues: "it does not necessitate any complicated method of analysis, nor do we have to resort to any complex system of reasoning to discover that our race is primarily a consumer." Because of this, "the house in which we live was built by and bought from another group; the food we eat is produced or made palatable by others; the money we make is deposited with and used by others in the development of their own businesses and in furnishing employment to their own group." In a preview to his April 28, 1928, *Courier* article, Overton concludes "Trade with Your Own" by sadly asserting "even in the field of insurance where we have made our greatest strides in our business life, we find from an analysis of the facts that we are pouring into the coffers of others millions of dollars which from every standpoint of reasoning should be deposited with our own institutions."[91]

Overton's next article in the *Pittsburgh Courier* provides an incisive and sobering assessment of the state of contemporary African American insurance companies. He begins by telling readers that "at the present time there are operating in this country thirty or more Negro Life insurance companies offering to our race every form of insurance—Ordinary Life with its various adaptations, Industrial, Health and Accident, and Casualty." Moreover, black insurers were "required to put up the same amount of capital, operate with highly trained management; [and] maintain the same reserves" as their white counterparts. Still, despite the fact that black insurers were governed by the same standards of operation as white insurers, Overton sadly asserts that "of the two Billion Dollars of Insurance carried on the lives of Negroes, only three hundred million is carried in Negro companies, the remaining one billion seven hundred billion is carried in white companies." He continues: "in 1927, Negroes paid into white companies fifty million dollars in premium payments, as compared to approximately ten million dollars into their own."[92]

After discussing the discrepancy between African American consumer support of black insurance companies versus white ones, Overton tells *Courier* readers that black insurers invested nearly half of their $10 million pre-

Inside the Overton Hygienic Manufacturing Company factory, ca. 1920s. (Courtesy of the Everett and Ida Overton Collection)

mium income ($4.5 million) in black community real estate loans and black business development. Conversely, "none of the fifty million which has been deposited in organizations of other groups ever returns to our race in investments that would aid in developing and strengthening our economic status." According to Overton, African Americans, as reflective of their actions in regards to insurance companies, were committing economic suicide. Thus, he urges blacks to "think seriously about our economic future," which, by necessity, must include "the acquisition and conservation of wealth."[93]

Although Overton clearly enjoyed the laurels he received as black America's "greatest business genius," the energetic businessman did not simply rest on them. His use of the Progressive Book Company to effectively promote his financial empire during the late 1920s demonstrates that he practiced what he preached (in terms of continuously working to acquire and conserve wealth). As we've already seen, Overton apparently started the publishing enterprise in 1916 as a front company, ostensibly headed by Overton Hygienic employee Beulah Haynes, to market his first book. By the late 1920s, the facade of Progressive's ownership had disappeared. Consequently, the company's 1928 pamphlet, *Songs and Spirituals of Negro Composition*, presents lyrics to pertinent songs, interlaced with Overton-related advertisements.

In yet another manifestation of Overton's business acumen, he used consumers to maximize the marketing and distribution of this pamphlet. The foreword to *Songs and Spirituals* states that "the regular selling price of this book is 50 cents, but we will send a copy free to any one who will send us the names and addresses of ten friends and fifteen cents in stamps or coin."[94]

Moreover, persons were warned that "these addresses must be complete in every detail—giving name, street number, town and state. In smaller towns where there are no street numbers, give R.F.D. and box number. General Delivery addresses cannot be accepted."[95] Essentially, Overton used *Songs and Spirituals* to establish a direct-mail campaign, partially funded by consumers, to promote a publication that, notwithstanding its advertised musical content, was replete with advertisements related to his business conglomerate.

Political Activities in the 1920s

While Anthony Overton spent most of his time during the 1920s devising ways to strengthen his business interests, from time to time he lent his name recognition and stature to promote various political causes. As a disciple of Booker T. Washington, he clearly prioritized economic development over political participation as African Americans' best path to true freedom. Yet, because he was the son of a Reconstruction-era politician and had run for political office in Oklahoma in 1892, Anthony Overton was not apolitical in the truest sense of the word.

A glimpse of Overton's political activities during the presidential election year of 1928 demonstrates how his actions in this arena were not always based on partisanship. On September 12, 1928, Overton assumed leadership of a committee sanctioned by the Republican National Committee and its Illinois branch to collect contributions for Herbert Hoover's presidential campaign among black Chicagoans. In providing his rationale for accepting this appointment, Overton notes: "I am going to support the Hoover-Curtis ticket as a business man and banker. I am convinced the economic prosperity of our country during the next four years depends upon its success." Referring to his political beliefs, Overton continues: "my adherence has always been to Republican principles which I believe are sound and should be supported by all who have the nation's welfare at heart."[96]

Although Overton appeared to be a "rock-ribbed" Republican in terms of national politics, he was far more critical of the GOP's actions in the city of Chicago. In 1927, the flamboyant William Hale "Big Bill" Thompson was reelected as the city's chief executive after having been defeated four years earlier. The Republican Thompson, long associated with gambling and other underworld activities in the Windy City, had once campaigned in the African American community with the following message: "I'll give your people jobs, and any of you want to shoot craps go ahead and do it." The moralistic Overton was appalled by the negative impact that Thompson's 1927 reelection had on black Chicago. On November 4, 1928, Overton is quoted in the *Chicago Tribune* as forcefully articulating his position on the state of local politics. Overton, along with Rev. Lacy Kirk Williams and Attorney S. A. T. Watkins, headed a grassroots effort to diminish the impact of political corruption in Chicago's black community by getting out the black vote. Overton told the *Tribune*: "our people at this election have a real opportunity to demonstrate their independence. Decent, law-abiding colored voters, I believe are going to join with those in other parts of the city next Tuesday in driving out the political element that has fostered crime and violence, particularly in our district."[97]

A primary target of the Overton-led movement to "clean up" black Chicago was Dan Jackson, who held the dubious distinction of being both a prominent undertaker and gambling kingpin. Jackson's long-standing personal and political ties to "Big Bill" Thompson allowed him to live this double life. Moreover, after Thompson's 1927 reelection, Jackson assumed a third position as ward committeeman of Chicago's all-black Second Ward. According to Harold F. Gosnell's classic study of black participation in early twentieth-century Chicago politics, ward committeemen, in the context of the era's Republican political "machine," worked with precinct captains to insure that the necessary votes were cast on election day.[98]

While working to insure that Second Ward black voters remained faithful to the Republican Party, Dan Jackson, as ward committeeman, was doing his best to insure that his gambling interests and other elements of Bronzeville's underworld operated with impunity. Apparently Jackson succeeded in this latter role because, as Anthony Overton told the *Chicago Tribune*, "Policy men and street walkers have become so bold down here that they invade our best homes and neighborhoods." He also offered the following observation as president of the Douglass National Bank and the Victory Life Insurance Company: "the gambling evils show up every day in the banking business. Hard working wage earners draw out their savings accounts, drop their life insurance, and neglect their families so they can throw their money away on policy tickets."[99]

Despite the apparent entrenchment of "Big Bill" Thompson's political machine in Bronzeville, Overton predicts in his *Chicago Tribune* interview that "there will be a lot of surprises when the black belt vote is counted Tuesday night." His prophecy proved accurate. The reformer candidate John A. Swanson (supported by the Overton-led coalition) won the crucial position of state's attorney. Consequently, the once seemingly invincible Dan Jackson died suddenly the following year while facing a variety of criminal charges.[100]

Curiously, to echo the sentiments of Christopher Reed, Gosnell's *Negro Politicians,* thought to be the definitive work on black political activity in early twentieth-century Chicago, does not discuss Anthony Overton's reform-based political actions during the 1928 elections. Even more striking, while Gosnell *does* mention Overton and Jesse Binga in *Negro Politicians* as prominent local bankers, he states that, "like Binga, Overton had neither the time nor the resources, nor the inclination to mingle in politics." As the November 4, 1928, article in the influential *Chicago Tribune* indicates, Gosnell was clearly wrong in his assessment of Overton's involvement in local politics. In fact, this article in a section titled "Leader Expects Surprises," quotes Overton's election night predictions.[101] So, to the *Tribune,* Anthony Overton was clearly the leader of this political insurgency movement. Cynics may argue that Overton spearheaded this revolt because gambling threatened the profits of his bank and insurance company. Nevertheless, as we saw in chapter 3, even before assuming the presidency of the Douglass National Bank and the Victory Life Insurance Company, Overton, as "McAdoo Baker," was forcefully expressing his disdain for gambling in the pages of the *Half-Century Magazine.*

The Embryonic *Chicago Bee*

Overton's long-standing promotion of such values as refraining from gambling, along with sobriety and thrift, were proclaimed in a new periodical, the *Chicago Bee* newspaper, beginning in April 1925. The *Bee's* early staff included some holdovers from the *Half-Century Magazine.* The most prominent was Kathryn Williams-Irvin, who served, as she had with *Half-Century,* as managing editor.[102] As discussed in chapter 6, the *Chicago Bee* later achieved enduring prominence by being a publication staffed entirely by women.

As he had with the *Half-Century,* Overton did not publicly acknowledge his ownership of the newspaper. An August 1929 *Pittsburgh Courier* article on the *Bee* reports that "Anthony Overton, manufacturer and financier, emphatically denies ownership of the Chicago Bee. He says, however, that in the interests of Negroes and because of his appreciation for the high plane on which the Bee is to be set, he has given this wonderful paper his moral and financial support." The *Courier* goes on to say that the *Bee* represented an independent corporation "in which Anthony Overton does not own one share of stock." Still, "it is true, however, that some of Mr. Overton's children own considerable interest in the *Bee*." Considering how Overton had studiously melded business and family interests during the 1920s, it is reasonable to assume that the *Chicago Bee* represented yet another instance of Overton exerting surreptitious control of a commercial enterprise.[103]

Notwithstanding Anthony Overton's pronounced interest in presiding over profitable commercial enterprises, the *Chicago Bee* provides a case study of an Overton business that prioritized principles over profits. From a purely capitalistic standpoint, Robert Abbott's *Chicago Defender* was far and away the leading black newspaper in the Windy City. The *Defender*'s employment of lurid headlines and sensationalized stories helped it to achieve commercial preeminence. Yet, in seeking *its* niche in the marketplace, the *Bee* consciously appealed to readers who wanted a more wholesome reading experience. Overton's newspaper proudly declared that it was "fit for any member of the family [to read]." Moreover, unlike the *Defender*, which regularly featured crime-related stories, "the *Bee* declared that it denied 'any man the right to become prominent by committing a crime.'"[104]

Because of its content, the *Chicago Bee* has often been characterized as a conservative publication. Yet, as a 1939 study of black Chicago newspapers indicates, notwithstanding the *Bee*'s eschewal of lurid crime and sex-related stories, it, like the *Defender*, regularly presented stories related to the economic, social, and political status of African Americans. However, the *Bee* did this without attempting to "startle, alarm, and excite that characterized the *Defender*." A later study of historic African American newspapers in Chicago confirms this assertion by contending that "the *Bee* differed from other journals more in style than substance."[105]

An early example of the *Bee*'s racial advocacy was an October 9, 1926, editorial, "The Lynching Backwash." It begins by sarcastically asserting that, "for the last two years, lynching had declined to a very low ebb. It did not seem like good old America. We were getting too good. [Thus] the tar and feather fraternity and the wielders of the rope and torch decided they would get busy and recoup the ground they had lost in lawlessness for two years." After discussing a recent rash of lynchings, the *Bee* continues: "the South was checked during the last two years by the fear that the Federal anti-lynching bill was imminent. The failure to pass such a bill emboldened the lynchocrats of Dixie. It destroyed and dissipated their fears." This editorial closes with the following less than optimistic observation; "let us hope (though it is not probable) that the Senate has sufficient statesmen to be stirred to that indignation, whereby this recent daring deviltry will be wiped out and completely extirpated by the hand of the Federal government."[106]

In 1929, Overton, seeking to both ease commercial congestion in the Overton Hygienic Manufacturing Building and to enhance his image as Chicago's—if not America's—leading black entrepreneur, financed the construction of a new home for the *Chicago Bee*. Located at 3647–55 South State Street, this three-story structure, completed in 1931, featured a striking art deco design conceived by the black architect Z. Erol Smith. Like Overton's main business structure, he envisioned the future *Chicago Bee* Building serving more than one business-related purpose. Besides featuring the offices of the *Chicago Bee* on the ground floor, the top two floors originally featured income-generating apartments. Later, as discussed in the next chapter, when the Great Depression eroded much of Overton's financial stature and prestige, he moved the Overton Hygienic Manufacturing Company into the *Chicago Bee* Building.[107]

"The Merchant Prince of His Race"

The August 10, 1929, edition of the *Pittsburgh Courier*, not only features an article on the *Chicago Bee* but includes a celebratory article on Overton titled "From Clerk in His Dad's Store to the Topmost Rung of Success." This biographical essay, like most on its subject, contains misinformation concerning Overton's early life. For instance, readers are told that Overton developed his first baking powder product because in college "he specialized in chemistry"—which he did not. Nevertheless, this article primarily focuses on Overton's well-publicized and documented business successes that earned him "the enviable name of 'Merchant Prince' of his race."[108]

One of the more interesting sections of this article proudly declares that the Overton Hygienic Manufacturing Company possessed the same financial rating as US Steel and Standard Oil as determined by the Bradstreet and R. G. Dun financial reporting agencies. As the *Courier* explains, "these two agencies give the same rating to all firms with resources above $1,000,000." This article also reveals an important family-related dynamic of Overton's cornerstone enterprise. While Anthony Overton utilized the skills of his sons-in-law Julian Lewis and Richard Hill Jr., he also nurtured and utilized the skills of his biological son, Everett. The young Overton, who *did* study chemistry in college, served as Overton Hygienic's vice president and chief

Everett V. Overton, ca. 1920s. Before becoming president of Overton Hygienic in 1946 he had served in a wide variety of capacities within the company. (Courtesy of the Everett and Ida Overton Collection)

chemist.[109] This assured that, when Overton died, Everett would have the background and experience to make a seamless administrative transition to company president.

By late 1929, Anthony Overton was exhibiting something of a Midas touch in terms of business enterprise. At the beginning of the decade, he publicly owned an increasingly profitable personal care manufacturing company and secretly owned a monthly magazine. By the end of the decade, he had become a business titan who had added a successful national bank and a nationally celebrated insurance company to his business portfolio. Yet, unbeknownst to Anthony Overton, the upcoming Great Depression would literally turn his world upside down. The so-called Merchant Prince of His Race, a man associated with business success, soon became directly associated with business failure.

5. What Goes Up Must Come Down

The Impact of the Great Depression

In late 1929, Anthony Overton was perceived by many as America's most successful black businessman. During the Roaring Twenties he evolved from a moderately successful entrepreneur into a tycoon. Overton's leadership of the Douglass National Bank and the Victory Life Insurance Company, coupled with his administration of the Overton Hygienic Manufacturing Company, made him a near legendary figure among African Americans. Yet, by the middle of the 1930s, the public's perception of Overton had shifted dramatically. Significantly, Overton's subsequent fall from grace appeared linked to both external and internal circumstances. When the Douglass National Bank commenced operations in 1922 and Victory Life began two years later, both institutions directed a significant amount of money (in the form of loans and investment capital) toward real estate in the African American community. At the time, this appeared to be a profitable strategy because the 1920s represented a boon period for the real estate market. However, when real estate values plummeted with the onset of the Great Depression, both Douglass National and Victory Life possessed dramatically depreciated assets. In all fairness to Anthony Overton, he was not the only person fooled by the 1920s real estate bubble. However, disclosure of his long-standing funneling of Victory Life Insurance Company funds into the Douglass National Bank, referred to by Merah S. Stuart as Overton's "perplexing entanglements of the affairs of the two institutions," resulted in Overton's well-publicized ouster as president of Victory Life.[1] Moreover, despite creative attempts to keep the Douglass National Bank afloat during the early 1930s, this financial institution ultimately became a casualty of the Great Depression. In the end, Anthony

Overton retained control of the Overton Hygienic Manufacturing Company and the *Chicago Bee* newspaper, but he had lost the honorific moniker the Merchant Prince of His Race.

From the Great Migration to the Great Depression

The phrase "last hired, first fired" succinctly conveys one of the economic realities of post–Civil War African American history. The twenty-year period from approximately 1915 to 1935 is especially illustrative in this regard. In fact, African American labor history, during the years spanning the Great Migration to the Great Depression, provides additional context to Anthony Overton's rise and fall as an entrepreneur.

During the World War I Great Migration, when a half million rural southern blacks migrated to northern urban areas seeking employment in war-related industries, Chicago was an especially attractive destination for persons who participated in this relocation of Black America. As Emmett J. Scott has noted, the Windy City provided these individuals "the opportunity to earn money. Coming from the South where they are accustomed to work for a few cents a day or a few dollars a week, to an industrial center where they can earn that much in an hour or a day, they have the feeling that this city is really the land overflowing with milk and honey." Furthermore, "in the occupations in which they are now employed, many of them are engaged in skilled labor, receiving the same and, in some cases, greater compensation than was paid white men in such positions prior to the outbreak of the war."[2]

As Davarian Baldwin writes, one of the psychological consequences of the Great Migration was an identifiable increase in the collective self-confidence of Chicago's African American community. "Five years before Alain Locke's famed proclamation of the Harlem Renaissance and in direct response to the race riots of 1919, word began to spread in Chicago about the rise of a New Negro." Chicago's New Negroes were animated by a desire to exert greater control over all aspects of life in their community. As Baldwin contends, "sharing a national quest to break from the chains of white economic dependence (an approach made popular by black nationalist Marcus Garvey), Chicago's black entrepreneurs, war veterans, laborers, artists, entertainers, politicians, and intellectuals attempted to build a separate economic and institutional world—and worldview—known in their time as simply 'the metropolis.'"[3]

Anthony Overton was one of the major architects of the perceived Black Metropolis that grew and prospered in the wake of the Great Migration. Yet, despite the admirable efforts of Overton and his entrepreneurial counter-parts to provide jobs to black Chicagoans, the vast majority of local African Americans derived their daily bread from employment with nonblack enterprises. Moreover, during the early days of the Depression, when such companies sought to cut their labor costs, African American laborers were the first to be dismissed. As Christopher Reed noted in his monograph on the Great Depression's impact on black Chicago, "the Chicago *Defender* in 1930 reported an increase in the number of beggars on the streets of the South Side as unemployment grew."[4]

The Binga State Bank Closes

As Chicago's New Negroes began to assess the impact of worsening economic conditions on their lives, a series of shocks involving some of the South Side's most respected individuals and institutions shook the self-confidence that had burgeoned in black Chicago during the halcyon days of the 1920s. The Chicago-based Associated Negro Press (ANP), in an August 6, 1930, wire story titled "Business Men, Laboring Classes Staggered by Closing of Binga Bank," noted that on Thursday, July 31, 1930, "a white attaché from the office of State Auditor Oscar Nelson pasted a notice on the glass of one of the doors leading into the Binga State Bank which read: 'closed for examination and adjustment.'" The ANP asserted that although "the action was quietly and methodically taken, it produced an electric effect." Consequently, throughout the rest of the day, "a steady stream of stunned persons, stockholders, and depositors, flowed to the closed little Doric temple of finance."[5]

The ANP's coverage of the bank closing conveys the mood of the persons who congregated in front of the financial institution on that fateful day. "The air was heavy and tense" because the bank's closing had a potentially devastating impact on "the washerwomen whose meager savings were tied up; the boys and girls, saving for school; [and] the young man putting dollars away for a business venture or marriage." However, according to the ANP, the "most important of the thoughts dominating the crowds which congregated in front of the institution Thursday afternoon seemed to be the effect which its closing was going to have on other Negro businessmen whose money was kept there, on the other Negro bank, the Douglass National, and on the confidence of Negroes in their own institutions."[6]

According to an unnamed Binga State Bank official interviewed by the ANP, a contributing cause of the financial institution's problems was "the unwillingness of white people to handle mortgages on property occupied by Negroes." Specifically, the bank official declared that "he culled out $200,000 of the best mortgages held by the Binga Bank on so-called colored property" and presented them to "one of the large banks in the loop which had, at other times, helped the Binga Bank dispose of them." Nevertheless, the downtown Chicago bank now claimed that "they were unable to get rid of mortgages on Negro property among white purchasers." This appeared to be the case despite the fact that the Binga State Bank sought to sell mortgages "on choice parcels of real estate on Michigan Boulevard and South Parkway."[7]

Besides liquidity problems associated with possessing less-than-attractive real estate assets, the July 31, 1930, closing of the Binga State Bank appeared directly linked to the results of an examination of the financial institution conducted by the State of Illinois earlier in the year, which revealed irregularities in its loan program. Under Illinois law, state-regulated banks could not issue loans unless they were approved by an internal bank *committee*. Jesse Binga, however, had ignored this mandate and *individually* made the bank's lending decisions. After its January 1930 examination of the Binga State Bank, the State of Illinois demanded that such a committee be formed. According to Binga biographer Carl R. Osthaus, "this group reportedly discovered loans amounting to $267,612 negotiated by [Jesse] Binga or by ventures in which he was personally interested. Also, the bank's largest block of securities were shares in the Binga Safe Deposit Box Company which, upon liquidation, were found to be worthless."[8]

Although the Binga State Bank had been operating under almost $300,000 in unreported shortfall that needed to be cleared up, several options were open to Jesse Binga that might have allowed him to keep the bank from closing. First, he approached Anthony Overton about a financial bailout. For his part, "Overton was willing to come to his rescue, but with a businessman's offer that Binga found belittling and felt obligated by pride to refuse." Another source of potential assistance, white millionaire Samuel Insull, offered Binga $200,000 to help the bank regain its solvency. Unfortunately, for Jesse Binga, an early July 1930 state examination of the Binga State Bank, conducted after the internal committee submitted its report, found additional loan irregularities totaling $379,000 (instead of $267,612), well over Insull's offered amount. Illinois state auditor Oscar Nelson, no doubt disturbed by the hike to Binga State Bank's shortfall, declared that the Binga State Bank now had to raise $430,000 in cash deposits to receive a financial clean bill of health.[9]

As Christopher Reed writes, although the monies Jesse Binga needed to keep his bank from being closed were substantial, "this sum should have been available through the city's institutional network for banking protection, the Chicago Clearing House Association, to which the Binga State Bank belonged." However, Melvin Traylor, the president of the Chicago Clearing House, who also served as the president of Chicago's First National Bank, was not sympathetic to Binga's plight. In fact, Traylor, a native of Kentucky, reportedly dismissed the Binga State Bank as an inconsequential "little nigger bank."[10]

Although the Binga State Bank may have been irrelevant to the racist Traylor, to black Chicago depositors the closing of this community institution inspired a movement to reopen the bank with needed reforms. For instance, the August 1930 ANP story about the closing of the Binga State Bank asserts that in a new, reorganized, financial institution "it can be stated authoritatively that Mr. Binga will be forced out of the bank's activities." A February 15, 1931, meeting of Binga State Bank depositors optimistically planned for the reopening of this financial institution with a new set of directors (minus Jesse Binga). One of the central figures in this reorganization effort was P. W. Chavers, the original organizer and first president of the Douglass National Bank. Also, such white financial backers as Charles R. Walgreen, the founder of Walgreens Drug Stores, and John A. Carroll, president of the Hyde Park–Kenwood National Bank, reportedly agreed to provide the needed financial backing to facilitate the Binga State Bank's reopening.[11]

Unfortunately for supporters of the closed Binga State Bank, the hoped-for reopening never took place. Instead, over the next couple of years, a public spectacle unfolded with Jesse Binga being tried for embezzling bank funds. As the ANP notes in its Binga obituary in June 1950, "subsequent court litigation which took place for three years ruined all prospects for the reorganization of the bank." Perhaps ironically, despite various allegations about Binga's profiting from "dummy loans"—funds ostensibly extended to others where Binga received the actual loan proceeds—he was initially tried for a misuse of funds associated with a plan to open a second black-owned national bank in Chicago.[12]

Seemingly linked with his ongoing competition with Anthony Overton, Binga, in early 1930, announced his intent to open up the South Park National Bank near the corner of Forty-Seventh Street and South Parkway (now King Drive). Besides hoping to use Binga State Bank funds to establish this new financial institution, Binga engaged in a stock selling campaign that generated $39,000. Yet, these monies were never accounted for in Binga State Bank records. Consequently, on July 11, 1932, Binga went on trial for embezzling these funds. In the July 16 "Jesse Binga Goes on Trial" article, the *Chicago Defender* reported that "more than two dozen witnesses testified against the banker on the first day of the actual trial." Moreover, prosecutors claimed that "the banker kept the money given to him to buy bank stock."[13]

During the course of the trial, Binga's attorney, James B. Cashin, asked the judge to issue a directed verdict of not guilty on the grounds that the State had not made its case against his client. Binga was subsequently acquitted on the technicality that the exchange of money between Binga and subscribers of the new bank was a personal matter not connected with the Binga State Bank.[14] Undaunted by this setback, the prosecution pushed forward with a new trial the following year. On November 3, 1933, after several continuances, Binga, on the strength of testimony by his secretary Inez Cantey (who turned state's evidence), was found guilty of using "dummy loans" to embezzle funds from the Binga State Bank and sentenced from one to ten years in prison.[15] The combative Binga appealed this conviction to the Illinois Supreme Court, which he lost in 1935. After Binga had served three years in prison, the Rev. Joseph F. Eckert, Binga's parish priest at St. Anselm's Catholic Church, managed to secure his parole. Binga, whose reputation had been greatly diminished, died in 1950.[16]

The Douglass National Bank

While July 31, 1930, marked the beginning of the end of Jesse Binga's banking career, Anthony Overton, in the short term, profited from the closing of the Binga State Bank. Yet, as time went along, and the activities of the Douglass National Bank and the Victory Life Insurance Company generated more public scrutiny in a worsening economy, Chicago's New Negroes witnessed the public pillorying of yet another community icon. In the end, Overton never served prison time for his alleged financial misdeeds. However, his reputation, as had Jesse Binga's, suffered.

An August 1930 ANP wire story titled "Situation Tense in Chicago as Banks Close," asserts that, despite public concern regarding the closing of the Binga State Bank and the white-controlled Bankers State Bank located in the Forty-Seventh Street and South Parkway district, the Douglass National Bank appeared to operate as usual. In fact, the ANP quotes Douglass Bank officials as stating that "new accounts have increased two hundred percent" and that "withdrawals are not undue or beyond the power of the bank to take care of." One device used by the Douglass National Bank to calm the fears of worried current and potential depositors was "a home-made sign [that] had been pasted over one of the stand-up desks used by the bank's customers reminding them that they were doing business with a 'national' bank." This distinction was indeed relevant because, unlike the Binga Bank, which could not get assistance from the Chicago Clearing House Association, the Douglass National Bank, after the Binga State Bank's closing, received $200,000 from the US Federal Reserve "to aid in paying off depositors who wished to withdraw."[17]

In the short term, the Douglass National Bank appeared to weather the storm associated with the closing of the Binga State Bank. Moreover, as a leading public advocate for African American business development, Anthony Overton had additional motivation to keep this enterprise open. Perhaps feeling the weight of the world on his shoulders, Overton knew that, if the Douglass National Bank succumbed, it would have a devastating impact on blacks' confidence in black-owned businesses.

The evidence indicates that Overton's positive reputation among Chicago blacks served the Douglass National Bank well in the months immediately following the Binga State Bank's closing. As Midian O. Bousfield, vice president of the Chicago-based Supreme Liberty Life Insurance Company, told the ANP in October 1930, "the Franklin Trust & Savings Bank is two blocks from the Binga Bank and is popularly supposed to be a Strauss bank of good strong banking. The Douglass National Bank, an Overton institution is about the same distance from the Binga Bank. The former is a white bank and today you will find very few colored people in the Franklin Bank, and the Douglass National, a colored institution, has never done as much business as it has done since the Binga Bank closed."[18]

Notwithstanding Overton's power in black Chicago, he, like everyone else (including President Herbert Hoover), could do little to stem the rising tide of unemployment and economic deprivation associated with the early 1930s across the nation. Consequently, Overton, despite being able to initially withstand the growing Great Depression, ultimately got caught in its vortex.

Commencing in 1931 and continuing into 1932, worsening economic conditions prompted Douglass National Bank depositors to dramatically increase their withdrawals from this institution. In 1929, on the eve of the Great Depression, this financial institution had deposits of $1,507,336.70. Less than three years later, when the Douglass National Bank closed its doors on May 20, 1932, its deposits had plummeted to $405,000.[19]

Along with experiencing an accelerated withdrawal of money, Overton's bank also endured financially strapped borrowers unable to pay their obligations to Douglass National, as well as a significantly depreciated real estate portfolio. Both of these problems were linked to the Douglass National Bank's investment policies during the 1920s. Similar to the Binga State Bank, the Douglass National Bank invested significant sums of money in black Chicago real estate. At the time, this appeared to be a sound financial maneuver because black community property values were appreciating. As Ingham and Feldman contend, "between 1919 and 1929, Chicago experienced a boom in its real estate market. The value of property escalated to a level of inflation that gave real estate holders a false sense of security."[20] Yet, with the onset of the Great Depression, the Douglass National Bank, similar to the Binga State Bank, discovered that its black Chicago real estate holdings had become a balance sheet wrecking burden.

Ironically, the Overton Building, which housed Overton's business triumvirate—the Overton Hygienic Manufacturing Company, the Douglass National Bank, and the Victory Life Insurance Company—became another problematic real estate holding of the Douglass National Bank. Built as a "Monument to Negro Thrift and Industry" during the prosperous days of the mid-1920s, by the early 1930s it had become a proverbial white elephant. As Abram Harris notes in his study of early twentieth-century black banks, Douglass National's ownership of the Overton Building mortgage represented an inordinately high fixed asset investment that used funds that might have been better invested in income-generating securities.[21]

The Victory Life Insurance Company

The early 1930s decline in black Chicago real estate values not only hurt the Douglass National Bank, but also had a deleterious effect on another Overton enterprise, the Victory Life Insurance Company. As already discussed, Victory Life, from the beginning, invested heavily in the same property base as Douglass National. Consequently, with the onset of the Great Depression, both Overton enterprises were hit hard. As Merah S. Stuart describes the situation, "the market value of [Victory Life's] entire mortgage holdings was far less than the amount shown on the company's books, and less than the state Insurance Department would appraise it. Repair was made all the harder because mortgages held by the company were in amounts entirely too large."[22]

Along with revealing Victory Life's shaky financial status, state examinations of the firm after the onset of the Depression revealed that Anthony Overton had initiated a number of questionable financial transactions involving Victory Life, Douglass National, and various family members (including himself). When this information entered the realm of public discourse, Overton joined Jesse Binga as a former black Chicago hero whose reputation took a beating. The evidence indicates that Overton, even before the Great Depression, funneled monies from Victory Life into Douglass National. In early 1927, Overton used $70,000 of Victory Life's cash reserves to purchase Douglass National Bank stock. Later, after Victory Life secured the right to do business in the State of New York, Overton withdrew another $60,000 from Victory Life's treasury to buy additional Douglass National Bank stock.[23] In 1931, the insurance departments in the states of Michigan, Missouri, and New York officially expressed their concerns about Overton's 1927 transactions, as well as two later Overton-initiated loans—one to his daughters ($40,000) and one to himself ($15,000)—where he used Douglass National Bank stock as collateral.[24]

Early on, Overton withstood these embarrassing revelations. Despite growing discontent among Victory Life's New York–based board members, the majority of this body—including his sons-in-law Julian Lewis and Richard Hill—remained sympathetic to Overton and deflected calls for a thorough internal investigation of his questionable financial transactions. That situation changed on January 28, 1931, when, despite the protest of Anthony Overton and his sons-in-law, Charles A. Shaw (the new company secretary) and James E. Stamps (the insurer's agency director) were elected to the Victory Life board. They immediately undertook a thorough investigation of the company. Their subsequent findings were nothing short of stunning. Published more than a year later, a *Chicago Defender* front-page article, written by Shaw, featured a photo of Overton with the following caption: "Anthony Overton, President of the Victory Life Insurance Company . . . has been openly charged of making a 'family proposition' out of the company and 'bleeding it' for self-interest."[25]

Embarrassing Revelations

Before January 1929, Overton received a salary of $4,000 a year as president. After that date, Overton demanded and received, apparently without board approval, an additional $400 a month, more than doubling his annual salary (to $8,800). According to Shaw, "in June, 1931, the deputy commissioner of the Insurance department of Michigan registered a protest against the payment of such a salary to a president who was giving very little time to the operation of the company and demanded that corrective measures be taken." Nevertheless, when Overton received word of this recommendation, he reportedly dismissed it. Another instance of Overton's alleged bleeding of Victory Life involved the *Chicago Bee* newspaper. Between 1928 and 1931, the *Bee* received a monthly advertising subsidy of $500 from Victory Life. However, protests led by Victory Life's non-Chicago board members ended this financial relationship.[26]

As noted in chapter 4, when Overton built his multiuse "Monument to Negro Thrift and Industry" on South State Street during the 1920s, one of the building's tenants was the Victory Life Insurance Company. However, as Shaw and Stamps's investigation revealed, this relationship did not benefit Victory Life: "The rent of the home office space was fixed by Overton at $500 per month for a space that could have been secured in any other location for

$250 a month." Moreover, "in spite of this already excessive rent he [Overton] demanded an additional $100 per month rent." In addition, Overton ordered that "the janitor of the building be paid $45 per month and the switchboard operator of the Overton Hygienic Manufacturing Company $11 per month out of the income of Victory Life."[27]

Another criticism of Overton's administration of Victory Life, presented by Shaw, involved the insurer's printing arrangement with the *Chicago Bee*. Calling this another way that Overton bled Victory Life for personal benefit, Shaw decried his "demand that all printing for the company [Victory Life] be done by the Bee at prices which averaged two and three times the price that could be secured in the open market." In 1931, just as internal critics of Victory Life's $500 monthly advertising subsidy to the *Chicago Bee* ended that policy, so did critics of the *Bee*'s lucrative deal to satisfy Victory Life's printing needs end that policy, as well.[28]

One of the more damaging disclosures in Shaw's March 19, 1932, *Chicago Defender* article involves Anthony Overton's alleged profiteering from selling Douglass National Bank stock to Victory Life: "Prior to the admittance of the company into the state of New York in 1926 he [Overton] purchased a block of Douglass National Bank stock at $130 or $135 per share and sold it to the Victory Life Insurance Company for $160 per share, thereby realizing a personal profit of between $20,000 and $30,000." Later, "one and one-half years after our admittance into New York he [Overton] again placed into the assets of the company [Victory Life] an additional 375 shares of Douglass National Bank stock for which he received a check dated June 11, 1928 . . . for the sum of $60,000." Even more striking, according to Shaw, was that Victory Life board meeting minutes revealed no discussion or authorization of this transaction.[29]

One of the nuances of Anthony Overton's rise as an entrepreneur was his utilization of the talents and skills of his sons-in-law. Shaw's exposé of Overton's administration of Victory Life includes the following damning evidence: "another instance of the bleeding process for the benefit of relatives is evidenced by the payment of the salary of $200 per month to Julian H. Lewis, another son-in-law, who is employed by and gives all his time to the University of Chicago." Shaw continues: "he [Lewis] bears the title of medical director of the company [Victory Life], but practically all the work of this office is done by the assistant medical director, Dr. H.C. Tolbert, who is paid an additional salary."[30]

Yet another questionable Overton maneuver, where Victory Life funds were used to bail out the Douglass National Bank, involved the building of a new Victory Life home office at 5607 South State Street. According to Shaw, "several years ago the Douglass National Bank loaned a total sum of $40,000 to the Masons for the purpose of erecting a temple on the site." Nevertheless, because of worsening financial conditions, "the loan was not paid and the bank foreclosed on the property." At the time the Douglass National Bank took control of the real estate at 5607 South State, it consisted of "a plot of ground approximately 100x160 on which had been erected a number of concrete pillars, representing the foundation for the temple."[31]

As the Douglass National Bank's financial situation worsened during early 1932, "Victory was forced to pay to the bank the $40,000 loaned to the Masons and to erect and purchase the building." Shaw and Stamps reportedly protested against this transaction and "suggested that the matter be first taken up with the insurance department of Illinois." Shaw reported that Overton responded to this suggestion by declaring that "the insurance department had nothing to do with the operation of the company and if any action were taken by them to stop this project he [Overton] would institute court proceedings against them."[32]

The final bombshell in Shaw's explosive article involves Anthony Overton and his sons-in-laws reputed demand that Victory Life pay Douglass National an assessment of $24,000 on the bank stock it owned. Considering that Victory Life had secured Douglass National Bank stock through Overton's questionable transactions, this request dripped with irony. For their part, Shaw and Stamps, similar to their reaction to Victory Life's purchase of land at 5607 South State, "protested the payment of any assessment until the matter had been referred to the insurance department." Anthony Overton's son-in-law and Victory Life's general counsel Richard Hill allowed Shaw and Stamps to bring this issue to the Illinois Department of Insurance. This agency subsequently advised Victory Life not to pay the assessment unless "it was found that the bank could be saved by its payment," thereby reinforcing Shaw's and Stamps's initial reluctance in this matter.[33] This prompted a frustrated Overton to devise a plan to rid himself of the recalcitrant—and from his perspective meddlesome—Shaw and Stamps.

On March 12, 1932, Overton hastily convened a Victory Life board meeting at which Shaw and Stamps were charged with disloyalty and noncooperation and relieved of their duties. To Overton's subsequent embarrassment, four days later circuit court judge John J. McGoorty granted an injunction in favor of Shaw and Stamps prohibiting Overton and other directors from "interfering with them [Shaw and Stamps] in the discharge of their duties as secretary and manager of agencies."[34] No doubt Overton's actions in this regard gave Shaw additional motivation to share his knowledge of Victory Life's inner workings with the *Chicago Defender*.

Overton Responds to His Critics

For Anthony Overton, Charles Shaw's public revelations about Victory Life were especially disturbing. Among other things, they conjured up memories of P. W. Chavers's earlier insinuations about Overton's business ethics. Also, Overton had worked hard to create a public persona of honesty, integrity, and positive race consciousness. Consequently, a March 30, 1932, *New York Amsterdam News* article quotes Overton's responses to Shaw's charges and allegations. Referring to Shaw and Stamps's allegations against him as "distorted, prejudiced, and biased," Overton is quoted as outlining a New York–based plot, of which Shaw and Stamps were a part of, to take control of Victory Life. As the *Amsterdam News* reports, "the veteran financier charges that his enemies plotted to take the presidency of the company away from him and make Dr. P.M. Savory of New York City the nominal president; Stamps was to become the executive vice-president and Shaw would continue in the new set-up as secretary with enlarged powers." Overton also contended that this reconfigured Victory Life leadership team planned to move the insurer's headquarters to New York City.[35]

In an effort to reestablish his integrity before the general public, Overton's response discusses the $40,000 Victory Life loan to his daughters Eva and Frances: "I transferred shares of [Douglass National] stock to my daughters to borrow $40,000 on same from the Victory Life and turned over the $40,000 to the Victory Underwriter company." Overton continues: "in this transaction neither Eva Lewis, Francis Hill or myself or any individual received one penny, but same was done solely for the interest of and for the benefit of the Victory Life Insurance Company (and the records—open to any stockholder) will verify same in every particular."[36]

In his response to Shaw's *Chicago Defender* article earlier that month, Overton admits that he had regularly engaged in transactions involving the assets of the two companies. Yet, he assures readers that all were undertaken for the benefit of Victory Life. In addition, the *Amsterdam News* article includes the following pertinent observation: "the financier also pointed out that he had invested $225,000 of his own money in the insurance company, neither Shaw or Stamps owned one share of stock prior to September, 1931, when they purchased three and one-half shares each at $35 per share."[37]

The Chief Institutional Investor

Any examination of Anthony Overton's actions as president of the Douglass National Bank and the Victory Life Insurance Company must consider the ramifications of his being the chief institutional investor in both firms. During the spring of 1922, Overton became president of the Douglass National Bank because he personally provided the funds the institution needed to commence operations. Similarly, the evidence indicates that Overton secured a controlling percentage of stock in the embryonic Victory Life insurance company.[38] Consequently, due to his significant personal investments in both Douglass National and Victory Life, Anthony Overton apparently felt justified in transferring money between the two financial institutions (as he saw fit). As discussed in chapter 4, Overton seemingly preferred to be in business situations where he was the *primary decision maker* and not part of a corporate structure requiring team-based interaction between the president or CEO and a board of directors. Also, notwithstanding Overton's limited interest in displaying his wealth, he clearly enjoyed the deal making and planning necessary to create wealth. Moreover, as Overton surveyed the business conglomerate he created during the 1920s, he may have, indeed, felt that he was—as some stated—black America's "greatest business genius."

Because of his mild-mannered personality, Overton would have been reluctant to publicly declare, as the openly belligerent Jesse Binga did, "Lots of people criticize me. They don't like my methods and they offer me suggestions. I always tell them: Jesse Binga knows what he's doing and he's doing it like Jesse Binga wants its done."[39] Nevertheless, in the context of actions speaking louder than words, Overton's likely belief that his shrewdness and hard work had singularly built the financial empire at 3619–27 South State Street may have predisposed him to conclude that no one knew better than he how it should be coordinated.

Deteriorating Relationships

Ironically, Overton's greatest business accomplishment during the 1920s, Victory Life's movement into New York State, contributed mightily to his fall from grace during the 1930s. Even before Shaw's revelations and Overton's response, Victory Life's New York board members and stockholders were becoming increasingly angry with Overton's administration of the company. Specifically, persons in the Empire State believed that, since New York customers and stockholders were responsible for a significant part of Victory Life's growth, they should have more say in company operations.

Between 1927 and 1932, $7 million of Victory Life's insurance in force came from policies sold in New York City and the surrounding Metropolitan area. This compared to $3.5 million of insurance in force generated from policies sold in Illinois and the ten other states (besides New York) where the insurer conducted business. Similarly, although Victory Life did not begin doing business in New York State until 1927, by 1929 it had sold $300,000 in policies in that state, the same amount generated by Victory Life in all the other states combined (in 1929 it was operating in twelve states).[40] Considering the prominent role of the New York territory in Victory Life's operations, Overton's actions at Victory Life's January 27, 1932, stockholders meeting in Chicago enraged the New Yorkers in attendance. At this meeting, the number of New York board members dropped from four to three (of a twenty-one-member board) when Overton reportedly orchestrated the removal of Dr. C. B. Powell. Powell's removal appeared especially controversial considering an alleged earlier agreement between Overton and the black New Yorkers who facilitated Victory Life's 1927 entry into the Empire State. According to the February 20, 1932, *Pittsburgh Courier*, "it was said that Mr. Overton told the New York stockholders in 1927 when they were trying to raise the amount required to do business in the state, that if they helped sell the stock, when vacancies occurred on the board, more New Yorkers would be elected." Yet, Powell's January 1932 removal, considering that he owned 160 shares of Victory Life stock valued at $12,500, suggested that Overton had contracted a case of amnesia. To make matters worse, from the standpoint of New York Victory Life stockholders, this meeting also featured the announcement of three new board members including the husband of Overton's daughter Mabel and two "employees of Mr. Overton's interests." In addition, of the three new Victory Life board members named, reportedly "none held more than three shares [of company stock]."[41]

At the end of this meeting, two of the three remaining New York Victory Life board members, Dr. P. M. H. Savory and his wife, Gertrude, were so angry that they refused to shake Overton's hand. Moreover, according to the *Pittsburgh Courier*, "Mrs. Savory is alleged to have told Mr. Overton she did not know he was 'such a liar' and is said to have predicted, if he continues his course, he would 'end up in jail.'" As already noted, the *Pittsburgh Courier* helped promote Anthony Overton as a well-qualified public advocate for black business development. However, its reporting of the January 1932 Victory Life stockholders meeting, which provided Overton's critics a public forum to express their discontent with his "high handed methods" and "czarist attitude," signaled a change in Overton-related press coverage. Once portrayed as a genial, nonmaterialistic businessman who focused on race advancement, Overton increasingly became presented as a control freak who could not countenance dissenting viewpoints. In its coverage of the tumult surrounding the Victory Life board of directors, the February 20, 1932, edition of the *Pittsburgh Courier* notes that "Mr. Overton even had Dr. L.K. Williams dropped from the board, it was said, because Dr. Williams opposed some of his ideas in principle."[42]

The Douglass National Bank Closes

As Overton faced a growing insurgency within the ranks of Victory Life, worsening financial conditions continued to take its toll on the Douglass National Bank. Notwithstanding allegations that he received excessive compensation from Victory Life, he and Richard Hill surrendered their salaries by 1932 to help alleviate Douglass National's growing problems. Also, to allow Overton more time to focus on maintaining control of Victory Life, on February 8 Hill assumed the presidency of the Douglass National Bank, with Overton remaining chairman of the board.[43]

By early February, the Douglass National Bank had devised a series of short-term maneuvers to remain open. For instance, there was a rule in effect "whereby the bank refused to pay depositors more than a certain percentage of their account, in most instances $10 every week or every two weeks unless a 60 day notice were given. If the 60-day notice were given, the bank was forced at the expiration of that time to pay over the entire amount due."[44] Another program instituted during Hill's presidency of Douglass National was a so-called prosperity campaign, which sought to get ten thousand people to each deposit $5.00 in the beleaguered financial institution. In order to stimulate black Chicago's interest in this initiative, the Douglass National Bank said that, after it reached its campaign goal of $50,000, new depositors would participate in a prize drawing that included an automobile. Still, this extra bit of enticement did not generate the hoped-for consumer response, and Douglass National had to seek other ways to generate assets.[45]

As Abram Harris asserts in *The Negro as Capitalist*, in addition to a growing lack of consumer confidence in the Douglass National Bank, the financial institution, in its final days, had to contend with bad loans to cash-strapped black churches and fraternal orders that used now-depreciated real estate holdings as collateral. For instance, "the Knights of Pythias, a fraternal order, had a loan of $22,800 on which only $2,300 had been paid. The Chicago African Methodist Episcopal Church Conference owed $18,000." Moreover, "these loans had not been carried as assets of the bank, but the institution's funds had been tied up in them and, as we have already noted, the bank sustained heavy losses by carrying these uncollected loans or by writing them off."[46]

Notwithstanding problems with most of Douglass National's loan portfolio, a determined Richard Hill sought to generate any and all funds he could from it. Significantly, he managed to get a $7,000 loan payment from the National Baptist Convention during April 1932.[47]

Also, in late March 1932, Hill announced that the Douglass National Bank received a loan from the Hoover administration's recently established Reconstruction Finance Corporation. In fact, as the April 2, 1932, *Chicago Defender* notes, "Douglass National is one of the first institutions in this area to secure aid from the federal government under the recent act."[48]

Despite the victories Richard Hill achieved in his quest to keep Douglass National Bank open, the enormous stress he was under manifested itself in a way that proved personally embarrassing to himself and his father-in-law. On Sunday, April 24, 1932, Hill addressed the congregation of Bethesda Baptist Church at the conclusion of its 11:00 a.m. service. Bethesda, Anthony Overton's home church, owed Douglass National Bank $7,000 on a real estate loan, and Hill sought to impress on its members the importance of paying this obligation. His comments created a firestorm: "if your doors must be closed to keep the bank open, the bank must remain open. I have no desire to foreclose on this church, but where the bank and church are concerned, I have no alternative."[49]

After upbraiding Bethesda for its slow payment of their debt to the Douglass National Bank, Hill questioned the race loyalty of its congregation: "we have over thirty-two thousand depositors and you represent 132 of that number . . . you take your money downtown and elsewhere." He continued by asserting that "it's the so-called little fellow around 29th and Dearborn and Wentworth who keep our doors open, not you. As long as I'm president I refuse to allow those people to suffer because their money has been loaned to people like you who owe an institution $7,000 and feel that it is not safe enough to deposit your own money."[50] At that point, Bethesda's pastor, Rev. E. T. Martin, asked Hill to calm down. For his part, a now thoroughly agitated Hill proceeded to blast Rev. Martin for a recent $50 loan payment from funds drawn from another bank, asking "is that fair?" Hill answered his own question by declaring "no and I'm sick and tired of it. There is no reason why you should be given any special leniency or consideration by us and in the future I am going to see to it that you receive none."[51]

Rev. Martin's response to Hill's outbursts revealed how much Anthony Overton's reputation had suffered, even in his home church. He told Hill that Bethesda's congregation "is intelligent and most of them are property owners; many of whom had bank accounts before there was a Douglass

National Bank." Consequently, "they could not be led around with a halter, buying every peddler's wares without investigating the quality thereof, and using their individual judgment for their own best interest." Also, according to the *Chicago Defender*, Martin stated that "Bethesda had during his ministry been a pulpit for consecrated worship and not an advertising agency and that he did not, at this late hour, intend that it becomes such to please anybody's whims."[52] In the end, Hill's tirade at Bethesda Baptist Church may have done more harm than good. In the final analysis, the primary cause of the Douglass National Bank's problems was not slow loan payments by black Chicago churches and fraternal organizations. Instead, the Douglass National Bank's problems were primarily caused by a worsening economic depression that hit the African American community especially hard.

Despite Hill's aggressive tactics to keep the Douglass National Bank open, this iconic financial institution closed its doors for good on Friday, May 20, 1932. Nearly two years earlier, the ANP provided in-depth coverage of the Binga State Bank's closing. Now, the ANP provided similar coverage and analysis of Douglass National's demise.

That next Monday, May 23, an ANP wire story informed readers that the Douglass National's board of directors "chose discretion as the better part of valor and ordered the famous race institution temporarily closed in the hope of being able to effect readjustments and reorganization." The ANP reported that "brown paper now covers the large front windows through which a curious public used to peer at the Douglass huge vault." Using vivid imagery, the ANP also offered a sobering current description of the once-thriving section of South State Street that separated the Binga State Bank and Douglass National: "more dreary and deserted than Goldsmith's famed Avalon is to-day the once brightly-lit and busy block which separates the old Binga Bank and the Douglass which lies in a state of coma. Behind each empty store front is a harrowing story of financial tragedy. On door after door of the favored, the gods of the depression have marked the sign of death."[53]

Besides a Depression-linked lack of public confidence in the Douglass National Bank and problems with its real estate and loan portfolios, the ANP wire story also revealed that the bank's "mainstream" investments also became problematic. As Anthony Overton told the ANP, the Douglass National Bank paid $25,000 for bonds issued by the Youngstown Steel and Tube Company that were now worth half that amount.[54]

On Saturday, May 21, a representative from the US Office of the Comptroller of the Currency posted a sign on Douglass National's door stating that it now controlled the bank's affairs. In an interview that same day, referenced in the May 23 ANP wire story, Hill told the ANP that "tonight I can go home and go to sleep for the first time in the past three months." He went on to declare that Douglass National officials and personnel "have fought a good fight" and that "federal reserve officials, bankers and officials connected with national banking have all commended us, but the odds were too great and we finally had to admit defeat."[55]

Although Richard Hill presided over the day-to-day affairs of Douglass National Bank during its final days, Anthony Overton, as chairman of the board and the longtime public face of the institution, felt obligated to compose a statement that appeared in the May 23 ANP wire story. Besides citing some of Douglass National's obvious problems, such as accelerated withdrawals coupled with the depreciation of some of its real estate and bond holdings, Overton stated that "if the bank should remain closed, it would constitute one of the worst calamities that has ever befallen the race, handicapping our racial prospects for the next 25 years." Also, when asked about "the popular charge that he and his relatives wish and have wished to make a family affair out of the institution," Overton declared that he was "willing to surrender his claims to anybody or any group which can rescue the bank from failure." Unfortunately for Overton, the closing of the Douglass National Bank raised additional troubling questions about his other financial interests. As the May 28 edition of the *Chicago Defender* noted in an article about Douglass National's apparent demise, "just how the closing of the Douglass National Bank will affect the Chicago Bee, Victory Life Insurance Company and the Overton Hygienic company is being speculated on throughout the city and country."[56]

Removal as President of Victory Life

As Richard Hill presided over the final days of the Douglass National Bank, his father-in-law presided over an increasingly combustible situation at Victory Life. Prompted by their long-standing disapproval of certain Anthony Overton transactions, the New York and New Jersey Departments of Insurance suspended Victory Life in early 1932 from doing business in their states.[57] In response, New York and New Jersey stockholders, policyholders and agents demanded that Overton tell them how he planned to react to this troubling situation. On April 14, Overton spoke on Victory Life's suspension from New York and New Jersey, as well as on the recent charges leveled at him from Charles A. Shaw and James Stamps, in the Harlem YMCA auditorium. Overton's appearance predictably generated a large crowd that overflowed into the hallway. Moreover, as the *Chicago Defender* notes, "the meeting was tense, being decidedly hostile to Mr. Overton."[58] Before Overton discussed the issue of Victory Life's suspension from New York and New Jersey, he described charges brought against him by Shaw and Stamps as "trumped up" and based on "ulterior motives."[59] He specifically focused on an allegation, related to Overton's negotiation of a possible merger between Victory Life and Chicago's Supreme Life, that did not appear in Shaw's bombshell March 19 *Chicago Defender* article. Two weeks before Overton's appearance in Harlem, the *New York Amsterdam News* published an article related to Victory Life which includes the following statement: "another underlying cause of the outbreak in Victory Life, according to Stamps and Shaw, was the negotiations conducted by Mr. Overton to merge Victory Life with the Supreme Liberty Life Insurance Company." Overton reportedly "arranged for the retention of himself and his sons-in-law, but had been willing to sacrifice all of the other officials of the company."[60]

Anthony Overton told his April 14 New York audience that he had indeed entered into negotiations with Supreme Life about a possible merger. He also declared that "both Stamps and Shaw were opposed to the proposal, and in order to prevent it they began maneuvering to get control of the company." Overton also insinuated that their opposition appeared to be based on self-interest: "Shaw knew he couldn't be secretary of the new company in the event of a merger and Stamps, though a man of ability, possessed certain characteristics that made him unfit for the merger." Overton then turned his attention to Victory Life's immediate and long-term future in New York and New Jersey. To the chagrin of persons in the audience, he did not present a concrete proposal as to how the insurer could be reinstated to do business in the two states. This prompted some Victory Life stockholders, policyholders, and agents to suggest that he should resign. For his part, Overton "refused to discuss resigning," declaring that the New York and New Jersey Departments of Insurance would not "be allowed to dictate who shall be president of the company."[61]

Not unlike Hill's provocative remarks at Chicago's Bethesda Baptist Church on April 24, 1932, Anthony Overton's provocative remarks ten days earlier in New York City widened rather than closed a deepening rift within Victory Life. Moreover, an April 20 *Amsterdam News* editorial, provocatively titled "Why Not, Mr. Overton?," represents yet another instance of increasingly critical press coverage of Overton and his business affairs. According to the *Amsterdam News*, Overton's declaration at the April 14 Victory Life–related meeting in Harlem that he would not resign "even for the greater interests of the company" exacerbated his alienation from "the stockholders here whose money made it possible for the company to operate in the states of New York and New Jersey." Moreover, Overton, "in placing his own interests above those of stockholders and policyholders . . . has given evidence to support the charge that he is no longer competent to administer the affairs of the company."[62]

Apparently ignoring the groundswell of animosity directed at him in New York City, Overton, two weeks after returning to Chicago, executed a strategy to rid himself of East Coast intransigence. The April 30 edition of the *Pittsburgh Courier* discusses Overton's machinations in a front-page story from the ANP. During an April 27 Victory Life stockholders meeting, dominated by Overton supporters, it was agreed on to voluntarily cease doing business in New York and New Jersey, rather than seek to have its suspension lifted in those states. Moreover, in an attempt to further streamline the insurer's operations, the stockholders present voted to reduce the company's capitalization from $200,000 to $160,000.[63] Overton may have viewed this maneuver as a shrewd way to write off Victory Life's troublesome East Coast territory. Yet, he soon discovered that his problems were not just limited to New York and New Jersey.

That June, after a two month investigation, the Illinois Department of Insurance suspended Victory Life from doing business in the state. No doubt, the unfavorable publicity associated with the insurer's activities in New York and New Jersey contributed to this decision.[64] Ironically, as the June 11 edition of the *Chicago Defender* notes, if the Illinois Department of Insurance demanded that Victory Life's management team be changed as a prerequisite for reinstatement, "it is reported that eastern stockholders may be in a position to refinance the company."[65] After Victory Life's crushing suspension in the state of Illinois, several Victory Life board members, who had previously supported Overton, joined forces with their East Coast counterparts to orchestrate his removal from the presidency.[66] When informed of this growing insurgency against him, the now desperate Overton had one final trick up his sleeve. On July 6, Anthony Overton, without consulting the Victory Life board, successfully petitioned to have a court-appointed receiver take over Victory Life's administration. Judge John Wilkerson subsequently appointed Archibald A. McKinley, who possessed considerable experience in the insurance industry, as Victory Life's receiver. Also, as the ANP reported on this development, "in the order appointing the receiver, the court also asked that the stockholders and directors of the company formulate a plan for the preservation and perpetuation of the company."[67]

Victory Life's late 1932 administration by a white court-appointed receiver, coupled with the recent closing of the Douglass National Bank, sent shockwaves through black Chicago. The city's African Americans looked in sheer disbelief at the crumbling of Anthony Overton's business empire. The man once regarded as the Merchant Prince of His Race now appeared to be an incompetent autocrat whose mismanagement of Douglass National and Victory Life brought down these once-proud financial institutions. But public opinion was the least of Anthony Overton's concerns in late 1932. One of the duties of the Douglass National Bank's court-appointed receiver was to sell its assets and use the proceeds to pay depositors who had a legal claim against the now-closed bank. Consequently, because the Overton Building was among Douglass National's assets scheduled for liquidation, Overton had to relocate the Overton Hygienic Manufacturing Company. Fortunately, he still owned the *Chicago Bee* Building a block away (which subsequently became Overton Hygienic's home). Nevertheless, Overton's move out of the once-touted "Monument to Negro Thrift and Industry" must have been personally humiliating as well as shocking to the neighborhood residents who witnessed this sad migration.

While Overton sought to relocate the one enterprise that he had undisputed control over, it became increasingly clear that his placement of Victory Life into receivership had only temporarily forestalled his inevitable removal as president. The proceedings of the December 5 stockholders meeting, which featured the findings of a company audit conducted by receiver Archibald A. McKinley, signaled the beginning of a transitional period. At the beginning of the meeting, Anthony Overton no doubt smiled when McKinley began by stating "your company is not in as bad condition as many have been led to believe." Yet, Overton's smile would have disappeared when McKinley revealed the company's financial problems: being $300,000 in arrears, having an unpaid loan of $78,000 from the Reconstruction Finance Corporation (RFC), losing over seven thousand policyholders and over $5 million in insurance in force (February–September 1932), having unpaid death claims of $26,000, and accounting for the issuance of 1,827 shares of unauthorized stock.[68]

Considering Victory Life's tenuous financial situation at the end of 1932, it seemed apparent that a major structural reorganization was imminent. Merah S. Stuart, in his authoritative study of early twentieth-century black insurance companies, describes what happened next: "A plan unique in its nature was evolved whereby a new stock company was to be organized, capitalized at $100,000, the new stock of which was to be paid for by the receiver with assets then on deposit with the Illinois Insurance Department, one share to be given to each of the fifteen directors and the receiver to retain the remaining 985 shares." Also, "this new company, the Victory Mutual Life Insurance Company, was then to be mutualized by retirement of the stock, after which it was to enter into a contract with the receiver of Victory Life Insurance Company, reinsuring all outstanding risks, assuming all liabilities, and taking over all assets at a value to be determined by the court." On April 5, 1933, the Victory Mutual Life Insurance Company, a firm owned by policyholders, rather than investors, emerged from the ashes of Victory Life. To Stuart, this process was important because "the company was saved for the colored race."[69]

Accompanying the transition from Victory Life to Victory Mutual was a change in the company's leadership. Because many of Victory's stakeholders perceived Overton to be arrogant, it became clear that his days as president were numbered. Federal judge Evan A. Evans, who took over jurisdiction of Victory Life's receivership case from Judge John Wilkerson, approved of Overton's administrative demise when he certified Dr. P. M. Savory's election as Victory Mutual's chairman of the board and Dr. Lacy Kirk Williams's election as president.[70]

In the immediate short term, the old Victory Life's reorganization helped the insurer regain financial stability. As a brief history of the reorganized company asserts, "after a few months of operation, when death claims to the extent of $100,000 were settled, and $78,000 was paid to the R.F.C., and $300,000 had been acquired in new business, the Company reported these accomplishments to Judge Evans at a hearing." On this occasion, a "visibly elated" Evans remarked that "we have overthrown a defective organization and established a new one, which, it seems to me, is going to make this the best and most successful colored insurance company in the United States."[71]

By the middle of 1933, Anthony Overton's world had been turned upside down. Once associated with business success, he was now associated with business failure. Moreover, the reverberations of his previous associations with the Douglass National Bank and the Victory Life Insurance Company continued.

Good News for Douglass National Bank Depositors

Fortunately for Overton, when the Douglass National Bank closed its doors on May 20, 1932, it was not insolvent. Notwithstanding problems with its real estate investments and loan portfolio, the bank technically had enough resources to meet its obligations to depositors. However, when withdrawal requests intensified during the spring of 1932, "the institution was forced to close because it was impossible to convert securities into cash fast enough to meet the demands of depositors for withdrawals."[72] In retrospect, the decision to put Douglass National in receivership that May was wise because it set the stage for the future reimbursement of depositors. This reality became verified in August 1933 when the *Chicago Defender* reported that the US Office of the Comptroller of the Currency, in response to a query by a Douglass National Bank depositor, stated that "depositors will lose very little of their savings, and payment will be made within a short time."[73] This declaration offered a sense of vindication to Overton as he struggled to overcome his recent commercial reverses.

New Legal Problems

Significantly, Overton's partial relief regarding the Douglass National Bank quickly evaporated when he later discovered that one proposed source of money to be distributed to former depositors would be the proceeds of lawsuits targeting former bank stockholders. "Overton Sued in Bank Crash" was a front-page story in the *Chicago Defender* at the end of March 1934. Readers were informed that "Anthony Overton, former president of the closed Douglass National Bank, and his son Everett Overton, were sued this week in municipal court by the receiver of the bank for money due under the stockholders liability clause of the banking act." The *Defender* continues: "under the law, in case a bank fails, all stockholders are liable for the amount of stock they own, the money to be used for the benefit of the depositors."[74] Overton was being sued for $2,000 (20 shares at $100 each) and his son, Everett, was being sued for $1,000 (10 shares at $100 each). Moreover, both men were being charged 5 percent annual interest on these amounts (commencing from November 28, 1932).[75] From Anthony Overton's perspective, perhaps an even more painful dynamic of this latest bit of bad news, was a picture of himself featured in the March 31, 1934, *Chicago Defender* with the succinct and humiliating title, "Sued."[76]

But Overton being sued for $2,000 in 1934 was relatively insignificant compared to a 1935 lawsuit brought by the Victory Mutual Life Insurance Company to have the *Chicago Bee* Building turned over to a court-appointed receiver. Considering that this structure housed the remnants of his former financial empire, the implications of this legal battle were enormous.

On April 19, 1935, Victory Mutual registered a lawsuit against the Bee Building Corporation in the Cook County Circuit Court. According to Victory Mutual, in October 1929, the Overton-controlled Bee Building Corporation secured funds from the Victory Life Insurance Company to help underwrite the *Chicago Bee* Building's construction costs. For its part, the Bee Building Corporation, to repay Victory Life, issued a number of promissory notes to the insurer. Moreover, the Bee Building Corporation initiated a trust deed listing the *Chicago Bee* Building as collateral in case of a default.[77]

One of the consequences of the collapse of Overton's financial empire was that most of these promissory notes were never paid by the Bee Building Corporation. Thus, at the time of this lawsuit's filing, the Bee Building Corporation allegedly owed Victory Mutual more than $32,000. Seeking to exercise its rights under the trust deed associated with the 1929 transaction, Victory Life asked the court to either help facilitate the sale of the *Chicago Bee* Building or to appoint a receiver who would "take charge of and to manage and control said premises with power to lease said premises subject to the said order of this court."[78] Anthony Overton's lawyers, the law firm of Ellis and Westbrooks, responded to Victory Mutual's suit by filing a motion to dismiss the case on June 3. Their chief argument was "that the complaint on its face shows that the Bee Building Corporation is not a legal entity and not subject to be sued as a corporation."[79] Indeed, Victory Mutual's April 19, 1935, lawsuit had acknowledged that fact: "the Bee Building Corporation, a corporation, was dissolved by the decree of the Superior Court of Cook County on May 2, A.D. 1931."[80]

The following day, lawyers representing the Chicago Title and Trust Company, who drew up the trust deed in question, likewise filed a motion to dismiss Victory Mutual's complaint. Their primary rationale for doing this was "as appears on the face of said complaint, the same does not set forth or state any cause of action against this defendant."[81] In fact, none of the promissory notes presented by Victory Mutual (as auxiliary evidence) in its April 19, 1935, complaint against the Bee Building Corporation cited the old Victory Life Insurance Company as their legal holder.[82] Victory Mutual's legal action against Overton and the defunct Bee Building Corporation got even shakier after his June 14, 1935, personal response to Victory Mutual's complaint, in which he contended that Victory Mutual still owed him money from an $11,000 loan he made to the insurer in December 1930. Moreover, he demanded that Victory Mutual produce or account for several specific documents that would verify his assertion.[83] Ultimately, due to problems associated with its lawsuit against Overton and the Bee Building Corporation, Victory Mutual abandoned this legal effort. On March 4, 1937, Cook County Circuit Court judge Joseph Burke filed a motion stating that the case of Victory Mutual Life Insurance Company versus the Bee Building Corporation was "dismissed for want of prosecution."[84]

The Historical Context

The favorable disposition of the Victory Mutual lawsuit, coupled with the on-going reimbursement of Douglass National depositors, contributed mightily to a gradual rehabilitation of Anthony Overton's reputation. While his previous exalted status as Merchant Prince of His Race became a distant memory, Overton, unlike many other African American entrepreneurs during the 1930s (such as Jesse Binga), was still a business owner at the end of the decade. The 1930s had been brutal not only for prominent black businesspersons such as Anthony Overton, but for a number of smaller African American entrepreneurs as well. In 1929, black America's 24,969 retail stores generated aggregate sales of $98.6 million dollars. Six years later, in 1935, the aggregate sales for black America's 22,756 retail stores had plummeted to $47.9 million. Because black-owned businesses, in the context of US apartheid, depended exclusively on black consumer support, high black unemployment rates associated with the Great Depression necessarily resulted in some African American enterprises closing their doors and lower sales and profits for those that remained.[85]

In the end, the early-to-mid-1930s represented an extremely rough period in the life and career of Anthony Overton. Due to the dynamics of the Great Depression and the consequences of his unwise melding of the business affairs of the Douglass National Bank and the Victory Life Insurance Company, Overton lost both his unprecedented business conglomerate and concurrent widespread public acclaim. Nevertheless, a chastened Overton, whose early adult life demonstrated his resiliency, still maintained control of his cornerstone enterprise, the Overton Hygienic Manufacturing Company, along with the *Chicago Bee* newspaper. Thus, with a diminished commercial and personal profile, Anthony Overton moved forward with his life.

Epilogue
Final Years and Legacy

Although Anthony Overton lost most of his business empire during the Great Depression, he maintained ownership of two significant enterprises; the Overton Hygienic Manufacturing Company and the *Chicago Bee* newspaper. In addition, Overton retained control of the *Chicago Bee* Building housing these two commercial concerns. While Overton's late 1930s commercial portfolio was now much smaller, he remained an important business leader in black Chicago. Moreover, the 1940s witnessed a continued rehabilitation of his image. Thus, at the time of his death in 1946, much of the negativity associated with the early 1930s had all but dissipated. Also, while Overton, during his later years, increasingly turned over the management of Overton Hygienic to his son, Everett, he concurrently turned over the management of his other enterprise, the *Chicago Bee*, to an all-female staff. While the *Chicago Bee* ceased operations shortly after Overton's death, the Overton Hygienic Manufacturing Company continued operating for another thirty-seven years. Everett ran the company from 1946 until his own death in 1960. Everett's son, Anthony Overton III, presided over the company from 1960 until 1983 (when Overton Hygienic closed its doors). Shortly after Overton Hygienic disappeared from the landscape of US business, a consortium of Chicagoans began a campaign to honor the legacy of the company's founder, Anthony Overton. Their efforts ultimately resulted in the physical restoration of the *Chicago Bee* Building and the Overton Hygienic Manufacturing Building (both of which had fallen into disrepair), as well as their designation as municipal landmarks. In the end, just as an Overton obituary in the July 1947 issue of the *Journal of Negro History* suggests, Anthony Overton is being remembered for his dreams and achievements and not for his failures and defeats.[1]

The Great Depression's Impact on Overton Hygienic

Although Overton maintained control of the Overton Hygienic Manufacturing Company, the evidence is that the Great Depression took an enormous toll on his cornerstone enterprise. In January 1932, R. G. Dun's *Mercantile Agency Reference Book* cited Overton Hygienic as possessing a capital rating of A ($500,000-$750,000) and a credit rating of A1 (high, the top rating in this capital category). Two years later, in 1934, the listing for Overton Hygienic did not include a financial strength or credit rating. The January 1934 *Mercantile Agency Reference Book*'s inside cover declares that "the absence of *any* rating following a name signifies circumstances which preclude forming a definite decision to financial strength or credit standing of the individual or concern named, and should suggest to the Client the advisability of reading the detailed report." Unfortunately, R. G. Dun's detailed report outlining Overton Hygienic's financial strength and credit rating in 1934 is not extant.[2] Regular reports in 1936, 1938, and 1940, published as *Reference Book of Dun & Bradstreet*, likewise, do not include a financial strength or credit rating for Overton Hygienic. Again, the in-depth reports providing this information, which were available to Dun & Bradstreet subscribers for examination in the company's offices, are not extant.[3]

The 1942 edition of *Reference Book of Dun & Bradstreet* does provide detailed financial information about Overton Hygienic's financial status and creditworthiness. The company possessed a financial strength rating of F ($10,000-$20,000) and a credit rating of 3 ½ (fair). Due to the Great Depression and other factors, Anthony Overton's cornerstone enterprise, according to Dun & Bradstreet records, lost nearly 98 percent of its net worth between 1932 and 1942. The 1944 edition of *Reference Book of Dun & Bradstreet* shows a slight improvement in Overton Hygienic's corporate financial stature. Although its capital/financial strength rating remained at F ($10,000–20,000), its credit rating improved to 3 (good).[4]

Still a Black Chicago Community Leader

Despite Anthony Overton's dramatic loss of commercial and personal wealth, he continued to be an important figure in Chicago's African American community. He was a featured speaker at the eighteenth annual convention of the Pullman Porters' Benefit Association held at the Wabash Avenue YMCA November 15–17, 1938. The November 12, 1938, edition of the *Chicago Defender* describes the Pullman Porters' Benefit Association as "one of the most outstanding organizations of its kind in the Race. It has a membership of about 5,000 and has paid as death claims approximately $3,000,000."[5]

Anthony Overton also played an important role in organizing and promoting the important American Negro Exposition, held in the Chicago Coliseum from July to September 1940. As Adam Green writes, this ambitious undertaking, perceived to be the "first Black organized World's Fair," sought to celebrate the "seventy-fifth anniversary of the end of the Civil War and Blacks' official emancipation from slavery."[6] Significantly, twenty-five years earlier, Overton had dramatically enhanced his national commercial profile at the 1915 Lincoln Jubilee held at the same venue (see chapter 2).

Perhaps the most concrete indication that the post–Great Depression Anthony Overton remained an important figure in black Chicago was his inclusion in a series of *Chicago Defender* articles on "prominent South side citizens who have been outstanding in their chosen field." Besides displaying a photo of Overton with the heading "Empire Builder," the December 26, 1942, edition featured a biographical essay on Overton that began by noting that "during the decade before the depression, the Douglass National Bank was a hub of activity. Busy people constantly streamed in and out of its ever moving revolving doors." Moreover, "on Saturday nights when the bank was busiest, a slightly stooped man [Overton] sat at a desk and smiled a friendly greeting to those who passed him."[7]

Besides presenting Anthony Overton as a community-oriented businessman during the peak of his career, the article provides a positive analysis of his reaction to the Great Depression. Although this economic downturn had a negative effect on both the Douglass National Bank and the Victory Life Insurance Company, "Overton weathered the storm better than most executives who had the same experience. During the dark days of 1929 and 1930 the papers recounted daily the suicides of men who failed and whose institutions could not be saved." Yet, the *Defender* notes that Douglass National Bank depositors ultimately "incurred a minimum of loss" and that the Victory Life Insurance Company "was able to reorganize and is now doing business as a going concern."[8]

Another dynamic of the *Defender*'s rehabilitation of Anthony Overton's image was his resurrection as a nonmaterialistic businessman: "During the years when he was perched on the dizzy heights of his vast enterprises he kept his feet on the ground. He never owned a car. He walked to work. And even now, at the age of 78, he walks from his residence at 54th and Michigan Avenue, to his office at 36th and State street every Saturday."[9] Moreover, to dispel the notion that Overton's habits were based on miserliness, the *Defender* quotes Overton: "I don't believe that a business should be milked of its assets by the owner buying big cars and flat buildings. Sound principles require that the money be kept in the business." Besides asserting that "money has never meant much to him," the *Defender* declares that, to Overton, business is "a game and he likes to play it. It's a test of his skill and his ability; it gives him a chance to match wits with competitors, to overcome complicated and perplexing problems and mould living institutions to his will." In the end, "his [Overton's] empire is smaller, but it's operating and sound. Today, as always, the zestful gleam is in his eyes. He's still eager to play the game—his game of business."[10]

Overton through the Lens of His Granddaughter

Sheila Overton-Levi, Anthony Overton's granddaughter, has vivid memories of his post–Great Depression activities, as well as her grandfather's personality. As a young child she was struck by the physical dissimilarity between her grandfather and father. Anthony was much shorter and weighed quite a bit less than his son, Everett. Also, Overton-Levi remembers her grandfather as being very reserved. She speculates that this may have been stimulated by the fact that her father had five other children besides herself. Thus, when Anthony Overton visited his son's home, he may have been "overwhelmed" by having to deal with so many grandchildren. Overton-Levi discovered that when Overton visited his other children's homes, who had fewer offspring, he apparently felt more comfortable playing the role of grandfather, including regaling his grandchildren with a variety of stories.[11]

As a teenager, Overton-Levi spent her summers working the assembly line at Overton Hygienic, placing the correct amount of High-Brown Face Powder in its packaging boxes. Although she was the president's granddaughter and the vice president's daughter, her father directed that she receive no special privileges or treatment. Also, Overton-Levi's brothers and sisters, as well as her cousins, worked in various part-time capacities for both the Overton Hygienic Manufacturing Company and the *Chicago Bee*.[12]

Especially in her grandfather's later years, Overton-Levi recalls his innate frugality. While in college, she periodically wrote a gossip column for the *Chicago Bee*. With her desk at the newspaper directly in front of his, she noticed that he would often eat only a cookie for lunch. An even more striking example of this aspect of Anthony Overton's persona occurred at Christmas. Specifically, he regularly gave his grandchildren various Overton Hygienic products as presents although, as family members, they could get these items for free.[13]

Besides providing firsthand confirmation of Anthony Overton's near-legendary frugality, his granddaughter also witnessed Anthony Overton's progressive attitudes regarding female employees. As early as 1915, Overton opened up a branch office staffed entirely by women (see chapter 2). Also, while he sought to elevate his son, Everett, and sons-in-law, Julian Lewis and Richard Hill, within his various enterprises, Overton viewed his daughter Eva as an especially trusted confidant.[14]

By the late 1930s, when Overton-Levi began working summers at the Overton Hygienic Manufacturing Company, the assembly line supervisor and the company business manager were women. Later, when she sold Overton Hygienic cosmetics at the South Center Department Store at Forty-Seventh Street and South Parkway (now King Drive), her sales manager was also a woman.[15] Along with the women who held high positions in the Overton Hygienic Manufacturing Company during the late 1930s and early 1940s, women predominated at all employment levels in Overton's other major enterprise, the *Chicago Bee* newspaper.[16] Olive Diggs's rise to editor in chief of the *Bee* is especially illustrative of this phenomenon.

Olive Diggs and the *Chicago Bee*

Before her association with the *Chicago Bee*, Diggs's background contributed to her success in the newspaper industry. Born in Mound City, Illinois, she moved at the age of three with her mother to Danville, Illinois. At the time, because few African Americans resided in this city, white negativity toward blacks was not as pronounced as it was in larger cities such as Chicago. Consequently, as a 1943 *Chicago Defender* article on Diggs notes, "Olive attended mixed schools participating in all the social activities. There were sleighing parties in the winter, hikes and lawn parties in the spring—to all these she was invited." Because of Diggs's ability to move around freely in early twentieth-century Danville, according to the *Defender*, she "never developed a 'race complex.'" Moreover, Diggs's childhood fostered her belief "that she was as good as the next American. This self-confidence is a thing that has helped her in the newspaper business. Timidity has no place in a game where people are constantly striving to be first with the best story."[17]

Significantly, Diggs's path to editor in chief of the *Chicago Bee* was circuitous, rather than direct. During the fall of 1926, Diggs began working on a degree in business at the University of Illinois. At the time, the University of Illinois Business School placed its students as interns with major corporations to help them receive real-world experience. Because of her race, Diggs had difficulty early on being placed. Ultimately, she secured an internship as an accountant with the *Chicago Bee*.[18]

Shortly after arriving in Chicago, Diggs decided to both work for the *Chicago Bee* full time and transfer to Northwestern University. During the next few years, she rose rapidly within the ranks of this Overton-owned enterprise. In 1930, she became auditor of the newspaper; the following year she became general manager. Later, because of her success in helping the company survive the worse years of the Depression, she assumed the position of editor in chief in 1934.[19]

As the *Chicago Defender* cogently notes in its 1943 profile of Olive Diggs, her transition to editor in chief of the *Chicago Bee* was not seamless. First and foremost, "work as an editor is considerably more complex than that of an accountant. Instead of dealing with set formulae for computation, she was now dealing with the swiftly moving drama of life in all its phases—politics, economics and the little daily personal tragedies which daily make the news." Thus, Diggs quickly realized that "she must understand human nature, not just mathematical figures." In the end, Diggs did what was necessary to succeed as the *Bee*'s editor in chief. As the *Defender* reveals, "she attended political meetings; she read; she visited social centers and she talked with and tried to understand the problems of all classes of people."[20]

In her new position, Diggs presided over a publication that had carved out a comfortable niche among the Windy City's African American newspapers. Published on Sundays, the *Bee*, as had its predecessor the *Half-Century Magazine*, continually sought to distinguish itself in the marketplace. For instance, prospective subscribers were told that "the Chicago Bee is a clean newspaper and does not play up crime with big headlines or resort to smut or yellow journalism in order to sell a few papers. We wholehearted assist in every way any **meritorious effort** for the advancement of our racial group." Similarly, the periodical noted that despite its Sunday publication date, "the Chicago Bee is a secular paper and is not a Sunday school publication." Nevertheless, it claimed to "[print] more church news than any other Negro newspaper."[21]

Although the *Chicago Bee* consciously portrayed itself as the Windy City's most "respectable" African American newspaper, it also portrayed itself as black Chicago's most strident advocate for African American economic development. Once again, this agenda represented a continuation of the *Half-Century*'s earlier active promotion of black business formation and development. During the early 1940s, the *Bee*, buoyed by an improving economy, became an unabashed booster of local black wealth creation. The paper proudly proclaimed that "the active, progressive **Chicago colored people**" were "the **Beacon light** for the Negroes of the world" in this regard.

These assertions were apparently linked to an Anthony Overton radio address, cited in a March 1942 edition of the *Bee*, which declared that "Negroes of Chicago own more homes than Negroes in any other city, owning most of the buildings on South Parkway (formerly known as Grand Boulevard) and Michigan Avenue—two of the finest residential thoroughfares in the world. They have also successfully developed three exclusive neighborhoods wherein their homes are palatial."[22]

Ironically, while black Chicago, according to Overton, had successfully moved beyond the Great Depression, his own Depression-related financial problems seemingly continued. Besides enduring a dramatic reduction in the net worth of Overton Hygienic, Overton also endured a financially embarrassing state of affairs related to the *Chicago Bee*. Along with most African American newspapers of the period, the *Bee* was a member of the ANP, established by Claude A. Barnett in 1919. To participate in the ANP, member newspapers had to provide both stories and payments each week. While most ANP members regularly submitted local stories that were nationally distributed by the ANP, some members were less diligent in paying the weekly fees that helped cover the ANP's operating costs.[23] The evidence indicates that Overton's *Chicago Bee*, for the last ten years of its existence (1937–47), regularly fell short of meeting its financial obligations to the Associated Negro Press.

Barnett, in an October 12, 1940, letter to Overton (seeking payment for over three years of unpaid ANP fees), informed Overton that he had been sympathetic when "you explained so eloquently the various demands upon you which have kept you from paying the long overdue account of the Bee's." Nevertheless, Barnett also declared that "our means are slender" and "we need that money." Barnett closed by telling Overton that if he brought the *Chicago Bee*'s account current by October 15, 1940, "you will save yourself worry and harassment and do us [the ANP] a tremendous favor."[24]

Two years later, Barnett again wrote Overton, this time that "the Bee is one of only three papers which remain persistently in arrears on their accounts with us." Moreover, Barnett expressed the hope that Overton would "clean up this past due amount and then establish payment on a monthly basis." Moving into the mid-1940s, the *Chicago Bee*'s delinquent ANP account remained a source of embarrassment to the newspaper. For instance, in a 1946 letter to Olive Diggs a few months after Overton's death, Barnett informed her that the *Bee*'s ANP bill "is really out of all proportions to many things, first our needs, then your ability to pay, and finally, good taste."[25]

The *Chicago Bee*'s inability to pay its ANP membership fees during the 1940s suggests that Overton was extremely cash-strapped during this period.

Unlike a generation earlier, when he successfully used the *Half-Century* to increase Overton Hygienic's profitability, a similar predominance of Overton Hygienic ads in the 1940s *Chicago Bee* apparently had a far less favorable economic impact. Given these economic realities, Olive Diggs's background as an accountant served her well as she navigated the *Chicago Bee* through troubled financial waters during the 1940s. One of the ways the Diggs-ran *Chicago Bee* proactively responded to a less than favorable economic situation was to become a semi-regional publication. Starting with its "News around Milwaukee" section and later incorporating a section titled "News . . . from Gary, East Chicago, Hammond, Indiana," the *Bee* generated additional readers and advertisers from surrounding states. While African American newspapers' self-reporting circulation numbers during this period are suspect, a display ad in a January 1944 issue of the *Chicago Bee* contends that the paper was "read by more than 4,500 Milwaukeeans."[26]

Besides featuring a predominance of Overton Hygienic Manufacturing Company ads, as well as local and regional news of interest to African Americans, the *Chicago Bee*, during the 1940s, provided periodic information about the business and personal affairs of Anthony Overton and his immediate family. For instance, the *Bee* featured a front-page story about his daughter Eva that appeared after her October 29, 1945, death. Among other things, *Chicago Bee* readers discovered that this favored daughter had "been in poor health for about fifteen years."[27] It is entirely plausible that, in addition to Overton's personal financial difficulties, Eva's long-term ill health was another source of emotional pain to the former business tycoon.

The Death of Anthony Overton

Although he had his own health problems, Anthony Overton was struck by an automobile, which undoubtedly contributed to his death at the age of eighty-one (or eighty-two) thirteen months later, on July 2, 1946. Predictably, the *Chicago Bee* paid homage to him in its July 7 and July 14 issues. This extensive recognition of his life and legacy included information about the circumstances that led to his death. The July 7 *Bee* featured several front-page references to Overton's death, including a story headlined "ANTHONY OVERTON, BEE PUBLISHER, IS DEAD." It notes that "he died Tuesday at 12:40 [p.m.] in his home at 5202 S. Wabash Ave. Direct cause of death was attributed to a cardiac condition, aggravated by his advanced age and injuries sustained when he was struck by an automobile on May 16, 1945."[28]

Although the July 7 *Chicago Bee* article begins by linking Overton's death with being struck by an automobile the previous year, it later insinuates that his death may have also been linked with a fall Overton suffered when entering the Wabash Avenue YMCA on February 8, 1946. Before that second accident, "it was felt that he was making marked improvement following the auto injuries, and he had been coming to his office for a few hours daily." However, after his February mishap at the YMCA, "he had been confined to his bed since April 5, when he was released from Wesley Memorial hospital."[29]

This article, along with other Overton memorial essays published by the *Chicago Bee* and elsewhere, includes the factually incorrect Renaissance Man narrative of his early life that Overton had carefully cultivated (see chapter 1). Yet, it also discusses Overton as a "genuine man of the masses" who "shunned any outward display of fortune or prosperity." Moreover, to situate Overton as a religious man who sought God's guidance, the July 7 *Chicago Bee* cover story shares with readers the following Overton-composed prayer, dated December 31, 1944, that was found in his personal effects: "Beloved Father: I hope you will help me to be a Christian and help me to be unselfish. Please guide me in the coming year. Please help me be fair to my fellow man. I thank you to be fair. Amen."[30] In addition, the article featured excerpts from earlier speeches given by city editor Marion M. Campbell and editor in chief Olive Diggs related to Overton.

On March 18, 1944, as part of a celebration of Anthony Overton's eightieth birthday, Campbell praised him as someone whose life "is replete with 'firsts'" (such as being "the first Negro president of a national bank"). Campbell's remarks also reveal the extent of Overton's involvement with the *Chicago Bee* before being hit by a car: "Today, at 80 he is actively engaged in publishing the Bee, rarely misses a day (unless forced to) and opens the office at 8 a.m." Two years later, on January 16, 1946, at an Overton Hygienic banquet honoring Overton, Diggs declared that, as someone "who has worked with him closely for 16 ½ years," she could honestly say that he "treats the rich and poor who come to his desk with the same air of courtesy. He [Overton] has taught us to be just rather than charitable; fair rather than self seeking, patient rather than indifferent, and has made us more sensitive to our brother's needs." Diggs concluded her heartfelt speech by declaring that "for those of us who affectionately call him 'A.O.' he stands as a bridge across a great chasm, stones of which are honesty, courage, gratitude and fair play. 'A.O.,' we are proud to call you BOSS—and friend. Thank God, for men like you."[31]

The July 14, 1946, edition of the *Chicago Bee* covers Overton's funeral extensively, which had been conducted the day before at Bethesda Baptist Church. The newspaper's front page carries the headline "NOTABLES ATTEND OVERTON RITES" along with a photograph of pallbearers carrying Overton's casket out of Bethesda after the ceremony. An accompanying article supplies details about the day's events. The *Bee* notes that "the church auditorium was crowded as business associates, leaders in civic, professional, political and religious activities, together with a cross-section of Chicago's citizens gathered to pay final tribute to a man whose business acumen, vibrant personality, and outstanding achievements had earned national recognition and acclaim." The program included Chicago Municipal Court Judge Wendell E. Green's stirring reading of Overton's printed obituary. Notwithstanding this document's distorted rendition of Overton's pre-Chicago career, one of its concluding paragraphs accurately placed his life in a larger historical context: "born at the dawn of freedom, his [Overton's] life epitomizes the road of freedom which his people have tread these 83 years. It points up the tragedies in which freedom was born, the long desperate climb with its sorrows, its struggles, its hopes and its accomplishments." One prominent Chicagoan unable to attend Overton's funeral because of a scheduled trip was Mayor Edward J. Kelly. However, in a telegram read at the service and published in the *Chicago Bee*, Kelly declared that "with the passing of Anthony Overton I lose a valued friend and Chicago a splendid leader who served his community, his people and his profession with great credit and success."[32]

Along with Judge Green's and Mayor Kelly's remarks about the deceased business legend, the *Chicago Bee*'s July 14 edition features messages of condolences from other notables. John H. Sengstacke, who succeeded his uncle Robert Abbott as the publisher of the *Chicago Defender* in 1940, declared that "Overton was a fighting courageous pioneer who inspired thousands and whose contributions to the Negro's business advancement is unequaled." Marjorie Stewart Joyner, the national supervisor of Madam C. J. Walker beauty colleges, conveyed her condolences with a personal touch. She noted that Overton "was really an inspiration to all persons in the civic and business world. He gave me my first job and for this opportunity I will ever be grateful. We all have lost a valuable friend."[33]

Besides the *Chicago Bee*'s extensive coverage and assessment of the life and death of Anthony Overton, arguably the most thoughtful Overton memorial was published in the July 1947 issue of the *Journal of Negro History*. This even-handed obituary cogently analyzes both his successes and setbacks. After discussing Overton's pre-Chicago career and his various accomplishments during the 1920s (including winning the Spingarn Medal from the NAACP in 1927), the *Journal of Negro History* observes that "things seemed prosperous for the Overton interests for a number of years, but he had undertaken too much. He had too many irons in the fire, and could not handle all the affairs requiring attention." Moreover, "the assistance at hand was not always efficient and one man could not be equal to so many tasks." In addition,

Anthony Overton Jr.'s funeral hearse, July 13, 1946. (Courtesy of the Everett and Ida Overton Collection)

Overton "stretched a limited amount of capital over a rather wide business area; and in 1929 came the crash which found the weak spot in every business enterprise not operated on a sound basis." A consequence of this economic reality was the subsequent failure of both the Douglass National Bank and the Victory Life Insurance Company.[34]

Although the Great Depression destroyed Anthony Overton's business conglomerate, the *Journal of Negro History* memorial asserts that "some of this disaster was unnecessary. Overton was a safe business man in his early career. In Chicago, however, he became ambitious. There developed a rivalry between the Overton and Jesse Binga interests. Binga had a bank, and Overton believed that he could develop a better one. Overton established a national bank and Binga set out to establish a bigger national bank." Sadly, "the rivalry continued until both lost practically everything they had, and Binga even landed in the penitentiary for corrupt business practices. Overton, although honest, was too ambitious, and he had to suffer for his unwise investments." Consequently, "his name ceased, therefore, to be the synonym of success."[35]

The destruction of Overton's business conglomerate also affected his inheritance plans. According to the same obituary, "he [Overton] had hoped to leave a prosperous banking institution to one son-in-law, a thriving insurance company to another son-in-law, and the manufacturing establishment to his own son." Nevertheless, despite the significant financial reverses he endured during the 1930s, the *Journal of Negro History* concludes that Anthony Overton "should not be condemned as a failure. He went too far to retrace his steps in time to avert disaster, but he did not descend to the zero point. He retained some assets and lived honorably until his death." In fact, Overton's life "offers many lessons to avoiding pitfalls and at the same time offers an example of painstaking effort and perseverance through trials to a measure of success. While his life shows that some achievements are not possible under certain circumstances, it demonstrates at the same time what is possible to the man of energy and enterprise."[36]

Everett Overton

One aspect of Anthony Overton's business acumen was that, early on, he began grooming his son, Everett, to someday take control of Overton Hygienic. Thus, after his father's death in 1946, Everett, who served as the company's de facto president during the 1940s, easily assumed his responsibilities as the now titular head of the company. Born in Lawrence, Kansas, in 1889, Everett Overton had spent most of his life involved with Overton Hygienic in a variety of capacities. Just before the company moved to Chicago in 1911, he served as a company salesman (see chapter 1). Shortly after arriving in Chicago, the young Overton enrolled in Chicago's Armour Institute, a precursor to today's Illinois Institute of Technology. At Armour, Everett Overton majored in chemistry. He subsequently used his skills to help Overton Hygienic diversify its product line. Arguably, Everett Overton's most significant contribution in this regard was his development of a Nut Brown shade of the company's signature High-Brown Face Powder that better complimented darker complexions.[37]

Soon after becoming president of Overton Hygienic, Everett Overton reevaluated the company's relationship with the *Chicago Bee*. Dating back three decades, the Overton Hygienic Manufacturing Company had used the *Bee* and its predecessor, the *Half-Century Magazine*, as primary marketing venues. However, by the mid-1940s, the benefits of this historic arrangement, for Overton Hygienic, became less apparent. Thus, Everett Overton decided to stop buying advertising space in the *Chicago Bee*.[38] The *Bee*'s subsequent loss of advertising revenue from Overton Hygienic proved to be an obstacle that Diggs could not overcome. Consequently, the newspaper ceased publication after its August 17, 1947, edition. Still, to Diggs's distinct credit, in the midst of the newspaper's growing economic troubles, on February 28, 1947, she submitted a $200 payment on the *Chicago Bee*'s delinquent ANP account.[39]

Considering the risk involved, Everett Overton's decision to discontinue Overton Hygienic's cornerstone marketing strategy appeared to generate no ill effects. In fact, the 1948 edition of the *Reference Book of Dun & Bradstreet* indicated that the company's financial strength ranking had more than doubled since 1944 (increasing to $35,000-$50,000 from $10,000-$20,000). Ten years later, its 1958 edition reported that Overton Hygienic's financial strength ranking had grown to the range of $50,000-$75,000. Overton Hygienic also had the highest credit rating in this capital category. Unfortunately, because company records are not extant, it is impossible to definitively determine the marketing strategy Everett Overton employed to generate this improvement.[40]

Despite limitations in assessing Overton Hygienic's marketing strategy in the years following Anthony Overton's death, an important example of Everett Overton's evolving assertiveness in this area does exist. *Scott's Blue Book Business and Service Directory*, published periodically by Vivian M. Scott, was an important community resource in mid-twentieth-century black Chicago. Curiously, in its 1950–51 edition, Overton Hygienic was not listed in the Cosmetic Manufacturers category or in *Scott's* Toilet Preparations category. Moreover, there were no company advertisements in this Bronzeville business directory. Conversely, in the 1956 edition of *Scott's Blue Book Business and Service Directory: With Inter-Racial Features*, the first page features a full-page ad for Overton Hygienic's High-Brown Face Powder. The aggressiveness of this ad placement is evident by just turning the page: the full-page ad on page 2 is from John H. Johnson's Johnson Publishing Company for its *Ebony*, *Tan*, *Jet*, and *Hue* magazines.[41] Still, despite Overton Hygienic's prominent ad placement in the 1956 edition of *Scott's Blue Book*, Everett Overton's omission from the "Who Is Who" section of this publication (featuring notable black Chicagoans) suggests that this historic company had lost some of its long-standing importance.[42]

On January 26, 1960, Everett Overton suffered a heart attack while attending a movie with his wife, Ida. Later that evening he died in Chicago's Henrotin Hospital. The January 28, 1960, *Chicago Defender* observes that Overton "had been in semi-retirement from his duties as president-treasurer of the corporation [Overton Hygienic] since September." This chronology suggests that his son, Anthony Overton III, had become de facto president before his father's death. In March, Overton Hygienic's board of directors certified Anthony Overton III's ascendancy to the company's presidency and also named Everett Overton's widow as chair of the board.[43]

Anthony Overton III

Known as Toney to family and friends, Anthony Overton III, like his siblings and cousins, grew up working part-time at Overton Hygienic. After serving in World War II, he, for a period, assisted his wife in her restaurant venture. Anthony Overton III ultimately returned to Overton Hygienic to learn all aspects of the business that his grandfather had built and his father had sustained.[44] Dun & Bradstreet reports from the 1960s suggest that Anthony Overton III's first years as president were unsettled. In 1960, as in 1958, Overton Hygienic possessed a financial strength ranking in the realm $50,000 to $75,000 and earned the top credit rating in this category. Two years later, Overton Hygienic's Dun and Bradstreet capital ranking increased to C ($75,000 to $125,000) and possessed the top credit rating in that category. Unfortunately, for Overton Hygienic, this increase in profitability was short-lived. The company's 1964 Dun & Bradstreet capital ranking dropped to D+ ($50,000 to $75,000), although Overton Hygienic maintained its excellent credit rating.[45]

The January 1966 edition of *The Dun & Bradstreet Reference Book* reveals even more disconcerting news regarding Overton Hygienic. Besides an unchanged capital strength ranking of $50,000 to $75,000, this publication reports that the company's corporate credit rating had slipped from "high" to "fair" (2½). Similar company numbers in the January 1970 edition of the *Dun & Bradstreet Reference Book* suggest that Overton Hygienic's diminished corporate stature was not a temporary condition.[46] In fact, increasing competition, from both black- and white-owned enterprises in the rapidly expanding African American personal care products industry had an accelerating negative impact on this historic black company.

In the midst of an increasingly disturbing financial situation, Anthony Overton III received a significant short-term psychological boost in 1963. On May 28, the recently built Anthony Overton Elementary School, located at 221 East Forty-Ninth Street, had an open house and official dedication ceremony. At this well-publicized event, Anthony Overton III presented a portrait of his grandfather to school officials and former *Chicago Bee* editor Olive Diggs spoke about Anthony Overton's legacy.[47]

Anthony Overton III, ca. 1950s. He assumed the presidency of the Overton Hygienic Manufacturing Company after his father's (Everett Overton) sudden death in 1960. He presided over the firm until it closed in 1983. (Courtesy of the Everett and Ida Overton Collection)

Overton Hygienic's Market Share Battle, 1960s and 1970s

Perhaps buoyed by the positive name recognition associated with the opening of the new million-dollar Anthony Overton Elementary School, Overton Hygienic undertook an advertising campaign to reinform black consumers of the company's longevity and staying power. *Scott's Blue Book Business and Service Directory 1965: Chicago's Colored Citizens with Inter-Racial Features* featured a full-page company ad, strategically placed on page 2, with the closing caption "THE OVERTON HYGIENIC MFG. CO., 1898–1965, Our 67th Year."[48] Unfortunately, Anthony Overton III's efforts to capitalize on his grandfather's positive reputation generated only limited success. Perhaps ironically, one of Anthony Overton III's local competitors, George E. Johnson, more directly reflected Anthony Overton's entrepreneurial spirit.

Johnson, who established the Johnson Products Company in 1954, subsequently developed a business empire that included Chicago's Independence Bank. Arguably, his biggest commercial coup of the 1960s was Johnson Products' development of its Afro-Sheen product line. Moreover, Johnson accentuated the profitability of this business decision by becoming the exclusive sponsor of the nationally syndicated dance show *Soul Train*. As a result of these shrewd maneuvers, in 1971 Johnson Products became the first black-owned company to be listed on the American Stock Exchange.[49]

While Johnson Products clearly profited from the ascendancy of the Afro hairstyle in the late 1960s, Overton Hygienic clearly suffered from this same phenomenon. Because of the company's tenuous financial situation, Overton Hygienic did not have the resources to develop its own Afro care products to compete with Johnson's Afro Sheen. Consequently, with a pomade-based hair care line, which seemed outdated to many African American consumers during this period, Overton Hygienic gloomily watched its market share decrease. Significantly, one of Anthony Overton's earlier business accomplishments was being the first African American personal care products manufacturer to place his products on the shelves of Woolworth's, the mainstream discount retailer.[50] Yet, decades later, his grandson saw such competitors as Johnson Products secure prime shelf space in retail establishments, while Overton Hygienic products were shunted to the periphery.

Just as the Afro hairstyle dramatically affected the African American personal care products industry during the late 1960s, the emergence of the Jheri curl during the late 1970s resulted in huge profits for some companies and increased marginalization for others. In 1964, Chicagoans Ed and Betty Gardner started Soft Sheen Products Inc. in the basement of their home. For the first fifteen years, Soft Sheen experienced limited success. However, the company's introduction of Care Free Curl in 1979 dramatically enhanced Soft Sheen's corporate profile. The Care Free Curl product line's subsequent popularity increased Soft Sheen's annual revenue from $500,000 in 1979 to $55 million in 1982.[51] Once again, because of its limited resources for product development, Overton Hygienic could not compete for market share related to the emerging popularity of the Jheri curl hairstyle.

During the late 1960s and early 1970s, Afro-Sheen secured prime shelf space in various retail outlets. Conversely, during the late 1970s and early 1980s, Curl-Free Curl had assumed this profitable position in the realm of the African American hair care industry. One thing, however, remained constant during both periods: Overton Hygienic hair products were nearly invisible to most African American consumers.

Although the Overton Hygienic Manufacturing Company produced a variety of personal care products throughout its history, its signature creation was High-Brown Face Powder. Moreover, it appears that the company, for the first decades of the twentieth century, was the preeminent manufacturer of makeup produced specifically for women of African descent. Competitors began to challenge Overton Hygienic's primacy in this area beginning in the mid-1960s. The Flori Roberts Company, established in 1965, emerged as Overton Hygienic's first major competitor in the African American female make-up market. Roberts, a white woman with an extensive background in the fashion industry, started her company because she knew black models had trouble finding facial makeup compatible with their skin tones and texture. With both financial and technical support from her physician husband, Roberts began her product line and marketed it exclusively in department stores. By the mid-1970s, the Flori Roberts Company had satisfied customers throughout the United States and in Africa.[52]

During the early 1970s, the Fashion Fair Cosmetics Company became another major presence in the African American female makeup and cosmetic industry. This company was an outgrowth of *Ebony* magazine and its popular Ebony Fashion Fair Show. The models with this traveling fashion show, along with their fashion coordinators, regularly mixed and blended various cosmetics to achieve a look that satisfied them. Moreover, after each show, women in the audience frequently inquired as to how they could duplicate the look of the models. Because of this interest, the Ebony Fashion Fair Show, using *Ebony* magazine as a test-marketing venue, offered black women samples of the same cosmetics used by its models. Black women's overwhelmingly positive response to this campaign convinced the Ebony Fashion Fair Show to accentuate its new Fashion Fair Cosmetics division. Along with an ongoing ad campaign in *Ebony*, Fashion Fair Cosmetics, by the mid-1970s, were being marketed in such upscale department stores as Bloomingdale's in New York City, Marshall Field in Chicago, and Neiman-Marcus in Dallas.[53]

Overton Hygienic Folds

By the early 1980s, because of intense competition from both black and white companies, the Overton Hygienic Manufacturing Company found itself in a seemingly hopeless situation. In a last-ditch effort to keep the company afloat, Anthony Overton III, in 1982, entered into a partnership with Eugene Peterson, a local African American entrepreneur. Peterson, the president of Impress Trading and Holding Company, likely provided Toney Overton additional working capital. In return, Anthony Overton III turned over the company presidency to Peterson. Public records from the Illinois Secretary of State verify this transaction.[54]

Notwithstanding Peterson's apparent infusion of capital into Overton Hygienic, market forces led to the company's closing in 1983. Besides representing the end of an era in black Chicago, Overton Hygienic's demise caused another unfortunate occurrence. A clearly distraught Anthony Overton III discarded company records and artifacts. While he subsequently never shared his motivation for doing this, Toney Overton later expressed his remorse for this action.[55]

The "Blake Carrington" of the Black Metropolis

Ironically, a year after the Overton Hygienic Manufacturing Company ceased operations, a March 7, 1984, proposal submitted to the Commission on Chicago Landmarks (by the Chicago Department of Planning and Development) helped stimulate a renewed interest in the life and career of Anthony Overton. The "Black Metropolis Historic District" contended that the neighborhood "centered in the general vicinity of State and 35th Streets on Chicago's Near South Side" contains some "of the most significant landmarks of African-American urban history in the United States."[56] Tim Samuelson, the author of the "Black Metropolis Historic District" proposal, had a long-standing interest in historic preservation in Chicago's Bronzeville community. For instance, Samuelson, employed by a restoration architectural firm during the 1970s, independently worked with Chicago alderman William Barnett to educate the public about the historical significance of certain South Side structures. Early on, this was a daunting task because many of these buildings were in serious disrepair.[57]

Two of the structures identified in both Samuelson's "Black Metropolis Historic District" proposal, as well as in his related lectures to various community groups, were the Overton Hygienic Building at 3619–27 South State

Street and the *Chicago Bee* Building at 3647–55 South State. Unfortunately, despite his earlier accomplishments, Anthony Overton had declined in name recognition by the early 1980s. Thus, to educate a new generation of Overton's significance, Samuelson, in public lectures, humorously referred to Overton as the "Blake Carrington" of Chicago's 1920s Black Metropolis. During the early 1980s, Blake Carrington was the patriarchal figure who presided over a financial empire in the popular soap opera *Dynasty*.[58]

One individual well aware of both Anthony Overton's historical significance, as well as the historical significance of the structures identified in Samuelson's proposal to the Commission on Chicago Landmarks, was Harold Lucas. Moreover, Lucas, a business-minded community activist, saw the revitalization of historic Bronzeville buildings as a means to simultaneously pay homage to the past as well as to spur community economic development in the present. Samuelson and Lucas subsequently melded their interests and skills to form the cornerstone of a movement that would change Bronzeville's physical landscape.[59]

One of the consequences of Samuelson's and Lucas's working relationship was the establishment of the Mid-South Planning Group (MSPG). The MSPG was a coalition of neighborhood organizations, businesses, and individuals concerned with revitalizing Bronzeville. One of the MSPG's first activities was its coordination of the renovation of the *Chicago Bee* Building into a much-needed neighborhood library. With funds from the City of Chicago, secured through the efforts of then Second Ward alderman Bobby L. Rush, this project came to a successful conclusion in the spring of 1996 when the *Chicago Sun-Times* reported that it moved from being a community eyesore into "an airy, modern $3.3 million Chicago Public Library branch-complete with computers and tributes to the late Anthony Overton, the African American businessman who built the building."[60]

After its success with the *Chicago Bee* Building renovation, the MSPG evolved into the Mid-South Planning and Development Commission and in 2000 turned its sights toward renovating the Overton Hygienic Manufacturing Building. The initial seed money for this project was a $1.43 million grant from the State of Illinois, along with $110,000 in Empowerment Zone funds from the federal government. Besides restoring what was once called a "Monument to Negro Thrift and Industry" to its former glory, the Mid-South Planning and Development Commission envisioned the renovated historic structure as a catalyst for contemporary business activity. In October 2000, the *Chicago Tribune* noted that "community leaders hope to bring the building back with stores on the first floor, and offices and business incubator space on the upper levels."[61]

Subsequent renovations to the Overton Hygienic Manufacturing Building, coordinated by the Chicago-based Davis Group LLC, included replacing three hundred terra cotta pieces and replicating 117 wooden-sash windows. Also, the Davis Group rehabilitated 1,300 square feet of street-level storefront space that had previously been boarded up. In 2009, Landmarks Illinois, associated with the Richard H. Driehaus Foundation, honored this restoration initiative: "the rehabilitation of the Overton Hygienic Building, an anchor within the community, is paving the way for future revitalization within the neighborhood."[62]

The renovated Overton Hygienic Manufacturing Building has, indeed, been serving as a venue to promote increased entrepreneurial activity in the immediate vicinity. In June 2013, First Stage Holdings Inc., a minority-led early stage venture capital firm based in Chicago, announced a wide-ranging plan to stimulate economic development in the historic Bronzeville community. This initiative's inaugural event, held at the historic Overton Building, "showcased products and services of more than 30 African American technology entrepreneurs and aspiring restaurateurs." The reporter continued: "As Elbert G. Clayton III, founder and CEO of First Stage Holdings, said, 'At First Stage Holdings, we are 100% committed to helping support the next generation of great African American business leaders in Chicago that are building innovative technology companies as well as scalable multi-location restaurant ventures. They will be the cornerstones of economic development for many years to come in historic Bronzeville.'"[63]

Clearly, the restoration and reutilization of the *Chicago Bee* Building and the Overton Hygienic Building have enhanced Anthony Overton's historical legacy. Moreover, as Timuel Black has cogently observed, these resurrected structures are powerful, *concrete* symbols of historic African American business achievement.[64] In the end, Anthony Overton's life represents an intriguing case study of the power of the human spirit. Despite his setbacks, disappointments, and human frailties, Overton's accomplishments as an entrepreneur continue to stand the test of time. Although the enterprises he established have not survived, Overton remains an important symbol of African American accomplishment in the realm of business enterprise. In this context, he may, perhaps, inspire a new generation of community-minded African American entrepreneurs in Chicago and elsewhere.

Appendix A

North Carolina Mutual Life Insurance Company

North Carolina Mutual Life Insurance Company, Selected Characteristics, 1917, 1920, 1922–24

	Admitted Assets	Insurance in Force
December 31, 1917	$358,364	$11,157,472
December 31, 1920	1,115,313	33,444,296
December 31, 1922	1,632,010	38,399,996
December 31, 1923	1,945,522	41,148,787
December 31, 1924	2,321,015	42,779,641

Source: *Best's Life Insurance Reports 1927* (New York: Alfred M. Best Company, 1927), 666.

Appendix B
Atlanta Life Insurance Company

Atlanta Life Insurance Company, Selected Characteristics, 1917–22, 1926

	Admitted Assets	Insurance in Force
December 31, 1917	$92,158	$1,235,318
December 31, 1918	136,497	2,235,124
December 31, 1919	169,536	4,523,723
December 31, 1920	201,348	7,592,816
December 31, 1921	243,814	9,464,493
December 31, 1922	405,810	9,745,978
December 31, 1926	942,034	21,441,725

Source: Alexa Benson Henderson, *Atlanta Life Insurance Company: Guardian of Black Economic Dignity* (Tuscaloosa: University of Alabama Press, 1990), 75; *Best's Life Insurance Reports 1927* (New York: Alfred M. Best Company, 1927), 71.

Appendix C
Liberty Life Insurance Company

Liberty Life Insurance Company, Selected Characteristics, 1919–20, 1922–26

	Admitted Assets	Insurance in Force
December 31, 1919	$132,808	$1,049,000
December 31, 1920	291,512	4,365,500
December 31, 1922	884,426	12,822,200
December 31, 1923	1,348,320	16,182,011
December 31, 1924	1,747,133	17,435,511
December 31, 1925	2,110,104	20,701,130
December 31, 1926	2,451,808	20,850,877

Source: *Best's Life Insurance Reports 1927* (New York: Alfred M. Best Company, 1927), 469.

Appendix D

Victory Life Insurance Company

Victory Life Insurance Company, Selected Characteristics, 1924–27

	Admitted Assets	Insurance in Force
December 31, 1924	$167,201	$687,739
December 31, 1925	170,812	2,244,495
December 31, 1926	369,603	4,541,812
December 31, 1927	438,000	8,500,000

Source: *Best's Life Insurance Reports 1927* (New York: Alfred M. Best Company, 1927), 997; Merah S. Stuart, *An Economic Detour: A History of Insurance in the Lives of American Negroes* (College Park, MD: McGrath, 1969), 95.

Notes

Introduction

1. "American Business Leaders of the Twentieth Century."

2. Tim Samuelson (cultural historian of the City of Chicago) interview, August 12, 2010. Samuelson worked with the Chicago Commission on City Landmarks during the 1980s. As one of the individuals who spearheaded the subsequent renovation of both the Overton Hygienic Manufacturing Building and the *Chicago Bee* Building, he interacted regularly with Anthony Overton III. Shortly after Overton Hygienic's closing, Overton III told Samuelson that he had discarded the company records and other related materials (including photographs). As tragic as this is from the perspective of conducting historical research, the practice of discarding records after a company closes its doors apparently is not uncommon. According to Tamar Evangelista-Dougherty, who served as the archivist for the Black Metropolis Research Consortium based at the University of Chicago, "it is not unusual for companies to destroy their own records. After all, it is the end of a life cycle and there is something emotional about the residue of memories" (Tamar Evangelista-Dougherty to the author, July 26, 2010).

3. Spear, *Black Chicago*, 113–14 fn9.

4. Bailey, "Mythmakers," 5, 14.

5. Ibid., 14.

6. "Anthony Overton," 396.

7. Peiss, *Hope in a Jar*, 58, 109.

8. Ibid., 53–54.

9. Walker, *History of Black Business*, 182–224; Butler, *Entrepreneurship and Self-Help*, 143–226.

10. Stuart, *Economic Detour*, 96.

11. *Mercantile Agency Reference Book* (R. G. Dun & Co.) 255 (January 1932), 555; *Reference Book of Dun & Bradstreet* 315 (January 1942), 642.

12. Claude A. Barnett to Anthony Overton, October 12, 1940, folder 5, box 149; Claude A. Barnett to Anthony Overton, November 18, 1942, folder 5, box 149; Claude A. Barnett to Olive Diggs, October 5, 1946, folder 6, box 149, all in Claude A. Barnett Papers, Chicago History Museum Archives.

13. For example, see Weems, *Desegregating the Dollar*, 127–29.

14. Samuelson, "Black Metropolis Historic District," 1. "The Commission on Chicago Landmarks, whose nine members are appointed by the Mayor, was established in 1968 by city ordinance. It is responsible for recommending to the City Council that individual buildings, sites, objects, or entire districts be designated as Chicago Landmarks, which protects them by law" (n.p.).

15. Lee Bey, "Rebuilding the Overton Legacy," *Chicago Sun-Times*, April 28, 1996, 8; Mickey Ciokajlo, "Bronzeville Site Stirs Pride, Hope," *Chicago Tribune*, October 20, 2000, http://articles.chicagotribune.com/2000–10–20/news/0010200259_1_housing-project-community-leaders-hope-eight-buildings.

Chapter 1. Anthony Overton's Early Life

1. Ingham and Feldman, *African-American Business Leaders*, 493. "Anthony Overton," 394; Boris, *Who's Who*, 282. "Brother Anthony Overton," 21. Deton J. Brooks Jr., "From Slave to Wealth Is Story of Overton," *Chicago Defender*, December 26, 1942, 13. US Federal Census 1870, Monroe, Ouachita, Louisiana, roll m593_526, p. 82, image 164.

2. US Federal Census 1870, Monroe, Ouachita, Louisiana, roll M593_526, p. 82, image 164. US Federal Census 1880, Topeka, Shawnee, Kansas, roll T9_396, family history film 1254396, p. 36.1000, enumeration district 3, image 0786. Williams, *Encyclopedia*, 1:34.

3. US Federal Census 1880, Topeka, Shawnee, Kansas, roll 396, family history film 1254396, p. 36A, enumeration district 3, image 0786. On January 29, 2019, Emily Bates, the great-granddaughter of Anthony Overton, shared with me the highlights of a conversation she had with Frank Overton, the grandson of Mack Wilson Overton, about Martha Deberry. Although Martha told the 1880 federal census enumerator that she was born in 1833, Frank Overton contends she was born in 1829.

4. US Federal Census 1870, Monroe, Ouachita, Louisiana, roll M593_526, p. 82A, image 167; US Federal Census 1880, Topeka, Shawnee, Kansas, roll 396, family history film 1254396, p. 36A, enumeration district 3, image 0786. The backgrounds of Martha Deberry Overton and Mack Wilson Overton become all the more mysterious when, yet, another Overton family tree–related assertion is taken into account. On February 25, 2014, Shelia Green, the great-great-granddaughter of Anthony Overton Jr., related to me an extraordinary story related to Martha Deberry and Mack Wilson Overton. Based on what she heard from an aunt, Martha Deberry, before she met Antoine Overton, had been taken by her master to New Orleans. There, she lived as a concubine to wealthy white men and had several children, the last one being Mack Wilson. Moreover, when Deberry subsequently met Antoine Overton, she asked him

to adopt Mack Wilson. Thus, according to this admittedly speculative analysis, Mack and Anthony Jr. were *half-brothers*.

5. US Federal Census 1870, Monroe, Ouachita, Louisiana, roll M593_526, p. 82A, image 167; Williams, *Encyclopedia*, 2:203.

6. Dr. James Overton's research related to the Overton family tree exemplifies the challenges associated with reconstructing genealogies associated with slavery. Over the years, this descendant of Antoine Overton's brother (Henderson) has changed his conclusions about "who was who" based on new discoveries. Early on, using circumstantial and scientific (DNA) evidence, Dr. Overton's hypothesis was that Antoine Overton's father may have been Judge John Overton, who, among other things, is the acknowledged founder of Memphis, Tennessee. Additional research suggests that Anthony Overton Sr.'s father (and Anthony Overton's grandfather) was a nephew of Judge John Overton, who lived in Louisiana during the early nineteenth century. Dr. James Overton and Robert L. Branch II intend to write a book based on their research that melds together the story of the black and the white Overtons.

7. Williams, *Encyclopedia*, 1:33–34.

8. Ibid., 33, 34.

9. Ibid., 34.

10. Williamson and Goodman, *Eastern Louisiana*, 162.

11. Williams, *Encyclopedia*, 1:35. Harvey, *Historic Ouachita Parish*, 13.

12. Foster, "Reconstruction," 4. In 1830, there were 2,838 whites in Ouachita Parish and 2,145 slaves. By 1860, there were 1,887 whites and 2,840 slaves in this area.

13. Foner, *Reconstruction*, 276; Williamson and Goodman, *Eastern Louisiana*, 165.

14. *Louisiana Intelligencer*, April 22, 1868, 2; Foster, "Reconstruction," 54.

15. Ouachita Parish Interest Group, *Images of America: Monroe and West Monroe Louisiana* (Charleston, SC: Arcadia, 2002), 48.

16. "Edict of a Political Despot," *Ouachita Telegraph*, May 21, 1870, 1.

17. "Registered Voters in Ouachita Parish," *Ouachita Telegraph*, November 5, 1870, 2; "Election News," *Ouachita Telegraph*, November 12, 1870, 2.

18. Vincent, *Black Legislators*, 114, xiii, xiv.

19. John Fowler (research librarian, Louisiana State Archives) to author, November 7, 2012. Vincent, *Black Legislators*, 120.

20. *Louisiana* 22:160, R. G. Dun & Co. Collection. Definitions of abbreviations used in the Dun reports are provided by Robert C. Kenzer, of the University of Richmond, who has extensively used the Dun Collection.

21. *Louisiana* 22:160.

22. Ibid. McKinley, "Anthony Overton," 14.

23. "The Exodus: A Talk with Mrs. Elizabeth L. Comstock about the Kansas Immigration," *Chicago Daily Inter Ocean*, May 25, 1880, 6, Louisiana State Archives Research Library, Baton Rouge. McKinley, "Anthony Overton," 14. Also, Nell Painter's classic work, *Exodusters: Black Migration to Kansas after Reconstruction*, provides a panoramic examination of this phenomenon.

24. *Weekly Kansas Herald* (later the *Herald of Kansas*), January 30, 1880, 2; March 5, 1880, 1; March 12, 1880, 1; March 19, 1880, 1; March 26, 1880, 1; April 2, 1880, 1; April 9, 1880, 1, Kansas Historical Society, microfilm roll N15.

25. "Death of a Well Known Colored Man," *Topeka Daily Commonwealth*, April 5, 1884, 8.

26. Flynn, *Negroes of Achievement*, introduction. Silverman, *Doing Business*, 55.

27. Flynn, *Negroes of Achievement*, 111.

28. Ibid., 112.

29. Kranz, *African American Business Leaders*, 210.

30. Brooks, "From Slave to Wealth." Considering the almost mythic stature that Pullman porters have in the context of African American history, it is not surprising that Overton, as a mythmaker, sought to align himself with this occupational grouping. As William H. Harris noted in his important 1977 study of the Brotherhood of Sleeping Car Porters union, a significant number of Pullman porters were black men with college degrees and professional credentials who couldn't find more commensurate employment in late nineteenth and early twentieth-century America. For instance, after a porter died in a train wreck in 1923, "authorities used his Phi Beta Kappa key to identify the body as that of Theodore Seldon, Dartmouth Class of 1922" (*Negro as Capitalist*, 23). This unfortunate reality provides context to a later erroneous assertion regarding Anthony Overton's early life. The prominent African American businessman and lay historian Dempsey J. Travis, in the prologue to a 1992 reprint of the 1936 classic *The Negro as Capitalist: A Study of Banking and Business among American Negroes*, asserted that Overton's first job after graduating from law school was working as a Pullman porter (xvi).

31. *Catalogue of the Officers and Students of Washburn College for the Academic Year 1882–3* (Topeka, KS: George W. Crane & Company, Printers and Binders, 1883), 13; *Catalogue of the Officers and Students of Washburn College for the Academic Year 1883–1884* (Topeka: Kansas Publishing House, 1883), 14.

32. *Congregational Record* 7 (March 1866): 157. Fitzgerald, *John Ritchie*, 43.

33. *Catalogue . . . 1882–3*, 26, 22–23.

34. Martha Imparato (special collections librarian, Washburn University) to author, July 27, 2009.

35. Ingham and Feldman, *African American Business Leaders*, 499, 493.

36. "Anthony Overton"; *The National Cyclopedia of American Biography* (New York: James T. White & Company, 1965), 47:256; Nicholas A. Lash, "Anthony Overton," *Encyclopedia of African American Business History* (Westport, CT: Greenwood, 1999), no pagination.

37. Brooks, "From Slave to Wealth."

38. Kansas State Census, 1885, microfilm reel 130, Kansas State Historical Society, Topeka, Kansas.

39. Cox, *Blacks in Topeka*, 201. Armitage, "Seeking a Home," 156.

40. Armitage, "Seeking a Home," 156, 159.

41. Ibid., 167; Schick, *Occupations of Blacks*, 26.

42. Schick, *Occupations of Blacks*, 26. One of Alexander Gregg's sons, John, would go on to become a prominent bishop in the African Methodist Episcopal Church.

43. Armitage, "Seeking a Home," 167; Kansas Historical Society, "John P. St. John," Kansapedia: Kansas Historical Society, last modified December 2018, http://www.kshs.org/kansapedia/john-p-st-john/17106.

44. Reagan-Kendrick, "Ninety Years of Struggle," 1. Reagan-Kendrick equivocally, identifies Selina Wilson as "probably" KU's first African American student.

45. Reagan-Kendrick, "Ninety Years of Struggle," 1–2.

46. *Lawrence City Directory for 1888*, 118.

47. Letha Johnson to author, October 12, 2009; Letha Johnson (archivist, University of Kansas) to Deborah L. Dandridge (field archivist, University of Kansas Libraries), December 12, 2011.

48. *Graduate Magazine: University of Kansas* 26 (December 1927): 26.

49. Richmond, *Requisite Learning*, 8–9.

50. Ibid., 108.

51. "Anthony Overton: Born Entrepreneur," *Issues and Views* (spring 1997): 1, www.issues-views.com/index.php/sect/1000/article/1006. "Washburn Alumni Have Left Their Marks," *Topeka Capital-Journal*, November 21, 2004, http://cjonline.com/stories/112104/ses_alumni.shtml. *Washburn College Bulletins* 4 (May 1904): 71, Washburn University Archives, Topeka.

52. "A Complete Roll of the Bar Association of the State of Kansas, 1883–1901," folder 4, box 64, Kansas Bar Association Records, 1883–1989, Ms. collection 740, Library and Archives Division, Kansas State Historical Society.

53. *Radges' Directory of the City of Topeka for 1888–1889*, 530; *Radges' Directory of the City of Topeka for 1890–1891*, 549; *Radges' Directory of the City of Topeka for 1893–1894*, 523; *Radges' Directory of the City of Topeka for 1896–1897*, 704; *Topeka Daily Capital*, April 2, 1889, 3; *Topeka Daily Capital*, November 1, 1890, 2.

54. Douglas County Kansas Marriages, 1888, KSGenWeb Digital Library, book 6, 58.

55. Littlefield and Underhill, "Black Dreams," 342.

56. Ibid.

57. Research Center, Oklahoma Historical Society, www.okhistory.org/research/library/1890/o.html; "1890 Wanamaker Census Information," submitted by Mollie Stehno, last updated August 6, 2008, www.usgennet.org/usa/ok/county/logan/census/1890/wanamaker.htm.

Although the second URL listed above situates Wanamaker in Logan County, this small black town, which disappeared by the mid-1890s, was indeed in Kingfisher County.

58. Ershkowitz, *John Wanamaker*, 22–23, 26, 39–41, 65, 69–70, 81, 119–20, 122.

59. Littlefield and Underhill, "Black Dreams," 343.

60. Dann, "From Sodom," 371.

61. Franklin, *Journey toward Hope*, 14; Littlefield and Underhill, "Black Dreams," 343.

62. Littlefield and Underhill, "Black Dreams," 343, 345.

63. Anders, *Resource Protection Planning Project*, 28.

64. *Kingfisher Panorama*, 22. Tolson, "Negro in Oklahoma Territory," 19.

65. Eunice Turner (local history archivist, Kingfisher Memorial Library, Kingfisher, Oklahoma) interview, October 19, 2009. Turner informed me of this destruction of pertinent records.

66. McKinley, "Anthony Overton," 14.

67. Ibid.

68. Anders, *Resource Protection Planning Project*, 21, 28. Franklin, *Journey toward Hope*, 255; Tolson, "Negro in Oklahoma Territory." *Chronicles of Oklahoma* 30 (1952): 101.

69. Ingham and Feldman, *African-American Business Leaders*, 493.

70. *Kingfisher Free Press*, October 13, 1892, 4.

71. Ibid., September 29, 1892, 1.

72. Ibid., November 24, 1892, 5.

73. Ingham and Feldman, *African-American Business Leaders*, 493. Book Collection, www.okhistory.org/research/directories, Oklahoma Research Center. McKinley, "Anthony Overton," 14.

74. McKinley, "Anthony Overton," 14. "Bury Anthony Overton," *Kansas City Call*, July 12, 1946, Ramos Collection, Mississippi Valley Room/Special Collections.

75. "The Dalton Gang's Last Raid, 1892," EyeWitness to History, 2001, www.eye-witnesstohistory.com; "The Dalton Gang," Gunslinger.com, www.gunslinger.com/dalton.html (dead), accessed August 10, 2014.

76. *Kansas City, Kansas, City Directory, 1895*, 96. *Kansas City, Missouri, City Directory 1897*, 524. Coulter, "*Take Up the Black Man's Burden*," 19.

77. US Federal Census 1900, Kansas City Ward 9, Jackson, Missouri, roll T623_863, p. 10B, enumeration district 103.

78. *Kansas State Gazetteer and Business Directory* (1900), 615, 1330.

79. Examples of works that discuss the 1898 founding of the Overton Hygienic Manufacturing Company include: *National Cyclopedia of American Biography*, 47:256; Brooks, "From Slave to Wealth"; Ingham and Feldman, *African-American Business Leaders*, 493.

80. Peiss, *Hope in a Jar*, 58, 109.

81. Burrows, *Necessity of Myth*, 6, 7–8.

82. Among the works that discuss the feud between Du Bois and Washington are Harlan, *Booker T. Washington: The Wizard*, 50–51; Lewis, *W. E. B. Du Bois*; Kevern Verney, *The Art of the Possible: Booker T. Washington and Black Leadership in the United States, 1881–1925* (New York: Routledge, 2001), 79–93; Raymond Wolters, *Du Bois and His Rivals* (Columbia: University of Missouri Press, 2002), 40–76; and Jacqueline Moore, *Booker T. Washington, W. E. B. Du Bois and the Struggle for Racial Uplift* (Wilmington, DE: SR Books, 2003), 61–88. Besides these secondary works, Du Bois's *Souls of Black Folk* (1903; repr., Greenwich, CT: Fawcett Books,

1961) includes an attack on Washington in the "Of Mr. Booker T. Washington and Others" chapter.

83. Walker, *History of Black Business*, 184.

84. Du Bois, *Negro in Business*, 6. Although table 1, "Negro Business Men by States," enumerated 1,906 enterprises owned by black males, the proceeding section included the following: "there are many obvious errors in these returns . . . it a probable that there are in the United States at least 5,000 Negro business men."

85. John Hope, "The Meaning of Business," in Du Bois, *Negro in Business*, 59.

86. Ibid.

87. Thornborough, "National Afro-American League"; Burrows, *Necessity of Myth*, 37.

88. Burrows, *Necessity of Myth*, 36.

89. Ibid., 40, 41, 43–44.

90. *Report of the Second Annual Convention of the National Negro Business League*, Records of the National Negro Business League, Part 1: Annual Conferences, Proceedings and Organizational Records, 1900–1919, microfilm reel 1, University Publications of America, Bethesda, MD, 9, 10.

91. Ibid., 10, 11.

92. Ibid., 54–55.

93. Ibid., 55, 56.

94. Booker T. Washington to Anthony Overton, March 3, 1904, reel 64, Booker T. Washington Papers; Gatewood, "William D. Crum," 301.

95. Washington to Overton, March 3, 1904. Anthony Overton to Booker T. Washington, March 8, 1908, reel 13, Booker T. Washington Papers.

96. Harlan, *Booker T. Washington: The Making*, ix.

97. Ibid. "To the Salesmen and Others Associated with the Overton-Hygienic Mfg. Co.," Convention Address, June 1916, personal collection of Sheila Overton-Levi (Overton's granddaughter). Overton, in 1916, hosted a convention of Overton Hygienic personnel at which his keynote remarks mentioned a letter from a New York-based supplier after the flood: "I presume from your location and the reports in the daily press that you are effected [*sic*] by the devastating floods in your section, if so, draw on me for any amount you need."

98. Jeanne C. Mithen (Special Collections librarian, Topeka Public Library) to author, November 12, 2012.

99. *Kansas City, Kansas, Directory, 1907*, 292, 231; *Kansas City, Kansas, Directory, 1910*, 292.

100. *National Negro Almanac*, 2–4, 7, 9, 11.

101. In the 1900 federal census, Overton, then living in Kansas City, Missouri, had a listed occupation as "grocer" (US Federal Census 1900, Kansas City Ward 9, Jackson, Missouri, roll T623_863, p. 10B, enumeration district 103). Yet, Overton is all but absent from some issues of the *Kansas State Gazetteer and Business Directory* (which included a complete business directory of Kansas City, Missouri): The 1900

edition did list Overton as a manufacturer's agent for "extracts" (615, 1330). However, the 1904 edition does not list Overton as a grocer or manufacturer's agent in Kansas City in either state (494, 682–86, 1358, 1464). The same was true for the 1908 edition of the *Kansas State Gazetteer and Business Directory* (567, 736, 1628).

102. Coulter, *"Take Up the Black Man's Burden,"* 342.

103. Sonny Gibson, ed. *Mecca of the New Negro* (Kansas City: Sonny Gibson, 1997), no pagination, Mississippi Valley Room/Special Collections.

Chapter 2. A Star Is Born

1. Spear, *Black Chicago*, 52, 53–54.

2. "The Overton-Hygienic Mfg. Co.," display ad, *Chicago Defender*, March 16, 1912, 5; "Deaths of the Week," *Chicago Defender*, July 27, 1912, 3.

3. "Report of the Thirteenth Annual Convention of the National Negro Business League Held at Chicago, Illinois, Wednesday, Thursday, and Friday, August 21, 22, 23, 1912," *Records of the National Negro Business League, Part 1: Annual Conference Proceedings and Organizational Records, 1900–1919*, microfilm reel 2 (Bethesda, MD: University Publications of America, 1994), 13.

4. Ibid., 13–14.

5. "Report of the Thirteenth Annual Convention," 17. Williams is identified as a Washington supporter in Spear, *Black Chicago*, 66–68.

6. "Report of the Thirteenth Annual Convention," 19.

7. Burrows, *Necessity of Myth*, 47. McKinley, "Anthony Overton," 14. Regarding Overton's 1912 comments, see Peiss, *Hope in a Jar*, 109 and 290, and Ingham and Feldman, *African American Business Leaders*, 493–94.

8. "Report of the Thirteenth Annual Convention," 96.

9. Ibid.

10. Ibid.

11. Ibid., 97.

12. Ibid., 98.

13. Ibid.

14. Ibid., 100.

15. Bundles, *On Her Own Ground*, 122, 134–36. Bundles goes on to say that, despite Washington's snub of Walker at the 1912 NNBL convention, based on her growing prominence, Washington found a place for Madam Walker at the very next annual NNBL meeting, in Philadelphia.

16. Baldwin, *Chicago's New Negroes*, 66, 262.

17. "Mrs. Overton Dead," *Chicago Defender*, July 20, 1912, 2.

18. Ibid.

19. *Kansas City, Kansas, City Directory, 1910*, 292.

20. Reed, *Knocking at the Door*, 80. See chapter 1 for detailed discussion of the misinformation associated with Anthony Overton's life before he moved to Chicago.

21. "Business League Banquets at Pullman Club," *Chicago Defender*, March 7, 1914,

4. "Standard Literary Society," *Chicago Defender*, May 17, 1913, 6. "Anthony Overton Speaks at Olivet," *Chicago Defender*, June 26, 1915, 4.

22. "Suffragettes' Convention," *Chicago Defender*, September 6, 1913, 3. "Who Is the Most Popular Girl in Chicago?" *Chicago Defender*, May 23, 1914, 4. "AKA Centennial—Regional Tributes," Alpha Kappa Alpha Sorority, www.aka1908.com/centennial/region-central.html.

23. Peiss, *Hope in a Jar*, 128–29.

24. "Overton Firm Opens New House," *Chicago Defender*, March 6, 1915, 4. "High-Brown Powder Company Gives Prizes Away Tonight," *Chicago Defender*, April 17, 1915, 4.

25. "Dunne Praises Negro Race for Vast Progress," *Chicago Tribune*, August 22, 1915, 9. L. W. Washington, "The Lincoln Celebration," *Chicago Broad Ax*, August 28, 1915, 1.

26. "Lincoln Jubilee Shows Progress of Afro-Americans," *Chicago Defender*, August 28, 1915.

27. "Lincoln Jubilee Is a Big Success," *Chicago Defender*, August 28, 1915, 1–2. "Race Shows Wonderful Progress in 50 Years," *Chicago Defender*, September 4, 1915, 3.

28. *History and Report*, 14.

29. Peiss, *Hope in a Jar*, 67. Bundles, *On Her Own Ground*, first page of images after p. 96.

30. *Poro in Pictures*, 4; "Annie Turnbo Malone," AAUW, Columbia (MO) Branch, http://columbia-mo.aauw.net/notablewomen/womenfm/annie-malone/.

31. "Annie Turnbo Malone."

32. *Poro in Pictures*, 5.

33. Ibid.; "Annie Malone," *Encyclopedia of World Biography*, www.encyclopedia.com/people/history/historians-miscellaneous-biographies/annie-turnbo-malone.

34. "Annie Malone"; *Poro in Pictures*, 5.

35. Bundles, *On Her Own Ground*, 64–65.

36. Ibid., 60, 78.

37. Ibid., 82.

38. Ibid., 82, 88–89. Charles Joseph Walker was her third husband; her previous two spouses were Moses McWilliams and John Davis.

39. *Poro in Pictures*, 5; Phillips, "Ms. Annie Malone's Poro," 6.

40. Bundles, *On Her Own Ground*, 277, 117, 189.

41. *Poro Hair and Beauty Culture* (St. Louis: Poro College, 1922), 5–6, collection of Chajuana Trawick; "Annie Malone."

42. "Annie Malone"; *Poro in Pictures*, 6.

43. "Ms. Annie Malone's Poro," 6.

44. "To the Salesmen and Others Associated with the Overton-Hygienic Mfg. Co.," June 7, 1916, 5, private collection of Sheila Overton-Levi.

45. "A Salesmen's Convention," *Half-Century Magazine*, August 1916, 10.

46. "To the Salesmen and Others," 4.

Chapter 3. The *Half-Century Magazine*

1. Rooks, *Ladies' Pages*, 68. Although Rooks states that Williams was twenty-two years old when "she assumed the reins of *Half Century Magazine*," Williams did not reach the age of twenty-two until December 31, 1916, fully four months after the appearance of the magazine. Another factual error in this otherwise fine work involves a photo of Katherine Williams on page 69. That image, taken from page 8 of the December 1916 issue of *Half-Century*, is of Associate Editor Kathryn Johnson. An earlier and more accurate assessment of Anthony Overton's relationship with *Half-Century* was Albert Lee Kreiling's 1973 "Making of Racial Identities in the Black Press," where he states that "the most important journals that distinctively mirrored the Bookerite [referring to Booker T. Washington] were those sponsored by cosmetics manufacturer Anthony Overton. In 1916 Overton started the *Half-Century,* a middle-class women's magazine, as an advertising medium for his High Brown toiletries" (257).

2. "Who Is the Most Popular Girl in Chicago?" *Chicago Defender*, May 23, 1914, 4.

3. *Half-Century*, November 1918, 16; *Half-Century*, August 1916, 3; *Half-Century*, June 1917, 3; *Chicago Bee*, July 7, 1946, 5.

4. *Half-Century*, August 1916, 11, 14.

5. *Half-Century*, September 1916, 11.

6. "Maytime in the Kitchen," Domestic Science sec., *Half-Century*, May 1918, 15.

7. *Half-Century*, March 1917, 2.

8. Ibid.

9. Weems, *Desegregating the Dollar*, 16–17.

10. "That Bleaching Proposition," *Half-Century*, April 1919, 3.

11. "Take Out the Kinks," *Half-Century*, June 1919, 3. This article doesn't include a specific source of the featured quote. Moreover, it states that "we seem to be alone in our fight to purify advertisements reflecting on Colored people." Two important contemporary sources that discuss the prevalence of racially demeaning advertisements in early twentieth-century African American newspapers are Frederick G. Detweiler, *The Negro Press in America*, and Guy B. Johnson, "Newspaper Advertisements and Negro Culture."

12. "Betrayers of the Race," *Half-Century*, February 1920, 3.

13. "Types of Racial Beauty," *Half-Century*, June 1919, 7, cited in Susannah Walker, *Style and Status: Selling Beauty to African American Women, 1920–1975* (Lexington: University Press of Kentucky, 2007), 76.

14. Walker, *Style and Status*, 76.

15. *Half-Century*, January 1920, 11.

16. *Dun & Bradstreet Reference Book* 177 (1912), part 1, 62 (Illinois listing); ibid., 187 (1915), part 1, 46 (Illinois listing).

17. *Dun & Bradstreet Reference Book* 197 (July 1917), part 1, 49 (Illinois listing); ibid., 207 (January 1920), part 1, 53 (Illinois listing); ibid., 218 (September 1922), part 1, 53 (Illinois listing).

18. "Survey of the Month," *Opportunity*, September 1928, 280. Neither the Library of Congress nor the Baker Library at the Harvard Business School hold the Dun & Bradstreet annual publications for the latter 1920s.

19. *R. G. Dun & Company Reference Book* 248, March 1930, 568.

20. Full-page advertisements for the Overton-led Douglass National Bank appear on p. 2 of each *Half-Century* issue from July–August 1917 through January–February 1925.

21. "The Douglass National Bank," *Half-Century*, July–August 1922, 6.

22. Ultimately, the new Overton Hygienic Manufacturing Building rose only four floors.

23. "A Monument to Negro Thrift and Industry," *Half-Century*, April 1922, 12–13.

24. Stuart, *Economic Detour*, 94.

25. "Victory Life Holds a Meeting," *Half-Century*, January–February 1925, 11. *Half-Century*, January–February 1925, 25.

26. "Have You a Bank Account?" editorial, *Half-Century*, October 1916, 9.

27. Ershkowitz, *John Wanamaker*, 27–29.

28. "Have You a Bank Account?"

29. McAdoo Baker, "Business and Finance," *Half-Century*, June 1917, 11.

30. Ibid.; display ad, *Half-Century*, June 1917, 11.

31. McAdoo Baker, "Making a Business Man of the Negro," *Half-Century*, September 1917, 11.

32. Ibid.

33. McAdoo Baker, "How a Colored Merchant Can Secure Credit," *Half-Century*, March 1918, 9, 9–10.

34. McAdoo Baker, "How a Colored Merchant Can Secure Credit: The Second Installment," *Half-Century*, April 1918, 9, 13.

35. McAdoo Baker, "Banks," *Half-Century*, January 1919, 9.

36. Ibid.

37. Ibid.

38. Baker, "Making a Business Man"; "The Evolution of A Negro Businessman," *Half-Century*, June 1920, 15.

39. McAdoo Baker, "Is Your Family Amply Protected?" *Half-Century*, January 1922, 6.

40. Advertisement for *How a Negro Should Conduct a Business*, *Half-Century*, August 1916, 9.

41. "Overton Hygienic Co. Opens Branch Store," *Chicago Defender*, March 13, 1915, 4.

42. *Half-Century*, August 1916, 17. *Half-Century*, September 1917, 11.

43. *Half-Century*, April 1922, 20.

44. *Songs and Spirituals of Negro Composition; Also Patriotic Songs, Songs of Colleges and College Fraternities and Sororities* (Chicago: Progressive Book Company, 1928), private collection of Tim Samuelson. In the 1980s, Samuelson, the cultural historian

of Chicago, spearheaded a movement that ultimately resulted in the renovation of two Anthony Overton–built structures and their designation as municipal landmarks.

45. "By What Name Shall the Race Be Known?" *Half-Century*, November 1919, 1.

46. Ibid., 1, 15.

47. "Are We Ashamed of Our Lineage?" *Half-Century*, January 1920, 1.

48. "General Race News," *Half-Century*, November 1919, 8; December 1919, 8; January 1920, 8; February 1920, 8; March 1920, 8; April 1920, 8; May 1920, 8; June 1920, 10; July 1920, 10; August–September 1920, 8; October 1920, 8; November 1920, 8; December 1920, 8; January 1921, 8; March–April 1921, 8; May–June 1921, 8; September 1921, 6; November 1921, 6.

49. "General Race News," *Half-Century*, May–June 1923, 9.

50. Howard J. Phelps, "In the Limelight," *Half-Century*, June 1919, 13.

51. "Chicagoans Get Degrees at Chicago University," *Chicago Defender*, June 15, 1915, 4. "J. Lewis in U.C. Faculty," *Chicago Defender*, January 22, 1916, 3. "Chicagoans Get Degrees": "Mrs. Eva Lewis, Daughter of Bee Publisher Dies; Ill 15 Yrs.," *Chicago Bee*, November 4, 1945, 1.

52. "In the Limelight," *Half-Century*, June 1919, 13, 3. Announcement, *Half-Century*, July 1919, 3. Dr. Julian H. Lewis, "The Health of the Negro," *Half-Century*, September 1919, 10.

53. "In the Limelight," *Half-Century*, July 1919, 9.

54. *Simms' Blue Book and National Negro Business and Professional Directory*, 100. "Half-Century Law Department," *Half-Century*, August 1919, 11.

55. Reed, *Rise of Chicago's Black Metropolis*, 98–99; "Chicago Bee Building," Chicago Landmarks, City of Chicago, http://webapps.cityofchicago.org/landmarksweb/web/landmarkdetails.htm?lanId=1268.

56. Kreiling, "Making of Racial Identities," 277.

Chapter 4. Business Titan

1. Some of the works that cite Overton as the organizer and founder of the Douglass National Bank include Jones, "Chicago Claims Supremacy"; Deton J. Brooks Jr., "From Slave to Wealth Is Story of Overton," *Chicago Defender*, December 26, 1942, 13; "Anthony Overton": Ingham and Feldman, *African-American Business Leaders*, 495; Walker, *Encyclopedia*.

2. Jones, "Chicago Claims Supremacy," 93. "Anthony Overton" (this obituary incorrectly cites the opening date for the Douglass National Bank; the correct year is 1922). Ingham and Feldman, *African-American Business Leaders*, 495; Walker, *Encyclopedia*.

3. Chavers-Wright, *Guarantee*, 155–78. Despite its provocative thesis, this book remains a fairly obscure work. The apparent cause for its marginality, as a truly reputable historical source, is that it combines historical narrative with historical fiction. Chavers-Wright explains: "I have used a semi-autobiographical format to present the intimate family portrait of the life and works of Pearl William Chavers, or P.W., as he was known to his family, friends, and close associates. This book is based on a true story of his life—as I knew him—and the Chicago Black Belt, as I

knew it. I have fictionalized some names, certain incidents and details, and much of the dialogue, for the purposes of drama, and at times anonymity" (xviii). Chavers-Wright's admission that she developed some of her book's incidents and dialogue for the purpose of enhancing its dramatic effect must be taken into consideration when assessing the words and actions of "Richard Owens," the apparent fictionalized name given to Anthony Overton. Also, Chavers-Wright was five years old when the Douglass National Bank commenced operations in 1922. Thus, it is highly unlikely that she could provide a credible firsthand account of this event or what preceded it. Nevertheless, while some of *Guarantee* is a manifestation of Chavers-Wright's historical imagination, to her distinct credit, this book also includes corroborating documentary evidence to support her claims regarding the establishment of the Douglass National Bank.

4. Chavers-Wright, *Guarantee*, 25, 27, 39–40.

5. Reed, *Rise of Chicago's Black Metropolis*, 88.

6. Ibid., 89. Also, in *Guarantee*, Chavers-Wright states that her father sought a federal charter for the reorganized Merchants and People's Bank because such recognition would strengthen its potential to facilitate positive black community economic development. As P. W. Chavers reportedly told his brother-in-law, "after the bank is reorganized and operating on a sound basis, it will become a mighty force on the South Side making money available for mortgages. We will be able to buy property, build factories, provide steady employment, broaden the base of a Negro entrepreneurship and help Negro families improve and maintain properties they own" (quoted in 53–54). According to Chavers-Wright, Chavers's brother-in-law cautioned him that, despite his idealistic vision about the reorganized bank's impact, he would run into opposition. Chavers-Wright described this warning to her father as follows: "As I see it, by going into the banking business you are flirting with something quite dangerous . . . the envy of others around you. . . . These Chicago people, white, black, and in-between, are jealous people. I know, I lived here many years before you came" (53). Based on Chavers-Wright's admissions regarding embellishments in *Guarantee*, it remains questionable as to whether or not the above conversations took place as depicted.

7. Chavers-Wright, *Guarantee*, 74–77. Also, the veracity of alleged dialogue below has to be taken with the proverbial grain of salt. According to Chavers-Wright, a month after Chavers proposed to name the prospective black-controlled national bank after Frederick Douglass, his wife Minnie asked him why didn't he name the institution after himself. Chavers reportedly replied I've been warned many times about fanning jealousy in Chicago. Remember what your brother George kept telling me? There is too much infighting among our people already; I don't want to incite anymore" (75).

8. "The 1st National Bank among Colored People in the United States Opens in Chicago," *Chicago Broad Ax*, April 30, 1921, 1. Notwithstanding the title of this article, an August 1925 essay in *Opportunity: Journal of Negro Life* argued that blacks in Boley, Oklahoma, received a charter for a national bank before blacks in Chicago.

See R. Edgar Iles, "Boley: An Exclusively Negro Town in Oklahoma," reprinted in the National Humanities Center Resource Toolbox, *The Making of African American Identity*, vol. 3, *1917–1968*, http://nationalhumanitiescenter.org/pds/maai3/community/text1/ilesboley.pdf.

9. "The Douglass National Bank: Will Soon Throw Its Doors Open for Business at Thirty-Second and State Streets," *Chicago Broad Ax*, May 14, 1921, 1.

10. Reed, *Rise of Chicago's Black Metropolis*, 89–90.

11. Chavers-Wright, *Guarantee*, 74. "The Douglass National Bank," *Chicago Broad Ax*, June 11, 1921, 3.

12. "The First Stockholders Meeting of the Douglass National Bank," *Chicago Broad Ax*, July 30, 1921, 2. "Big Meetings Are Being Held in the Interest of the Douglass National Bank," *Chicago Broad Ax*, September 10, 1921, 1.

13. "The Douglass National Bank, *Chicago Broad Ax*, December 3, 1921, 2.

14. "Negroes to Open Bank," *New York Times*, December 7, 1921, 19.

15. *Half-Century*, November 1921, 11.

16. Reed, *Rise of Chicago's Black Metropolis*, 90; McAdoo Baker, "Banks," *Half-Century*, January 1919, 9.

17. Reed, *Rise of Chicago's Black Metropolis*, 90–91. Chavers-Wright, *Guarantee*, 136, 141.

18. Chavers-Wright, *Guarantee*, 154, 154–55, 157–59.

19. "National Bank to Open Soon on South Side," *Chicago Defender*, July 8, 1922, 2.

20. Ibid., 158.

21. "Douglass Bank's Affairs Thrown into U.S. Court," *Chicago Defender*, November 25, 1922, 2.

22. "Bank O.K.; Court Suit Is Stopped," *Chicago Defender*, December 23, 1922, 3.

23. "The Douglass National Bank," *Half-Century*, July–August 1922, 6. "Have You Seen Them?" *Half-Century*, September–October 1922, 3.

24. "A Monument to Racial Industry," *Half-Century*, November–December 1922, 3.

25. Advertisement for the Douglass National Bank, *Half-Century*, July–August 1922, 2; ibid., September–October 1922, 2; ibid., November–December 1922, 2.

26. Chavers-Wright, *Guarantee*, 164–65, 301, 307, 355. Notwithstanding P. W. Chavers's harsh experience with the Douglass National Bank, which caused him to reflect that maybe his wife had been right in suggesting that he name the fledgling institution after himself, a later Chavers project—a campsite and resort in rural Wisconsin for blacks—represented another instance of where his strong commitment to racial uplift worked to his financial detriment. In 1926, Chavers assumed a mortgage to purchase 6,000 acres of land in Langland County, Wisconsin, which he subsequently named Camp Madrue (after his daughter). Chavers-Wright recalled her father's motivation for this project as follows: "P.W. thought of the thousands of black children playing in the dingy alleys of Chicago and how this camp, with its clean, unspoiled environment, beautiful acreage, mineral water, pure air, and plenty of sunshine, which were sorely needed by many, would provide a respite from the harsh reality of the urban

slums" (299). Regardless of Chavers's laudable intentions regarding Camp Madrue, he—as he had with his earlier efforts with the Douglass National Bank—experienced difficulty raising money to fully develop the project. The fees for the youth campers and asking prices for lots were extremely low—certainly not enough to be profitable. Chavers's actions in this regard allegedly prompted his wife to assert that "she spent as much for a single dancing lesson for one of her children as he was charging for a full week of room and board at the camp" (307).

Despite his wife's misgivings, Chavers continued in his quest to keep his lifelong promise to himself "to do something really important for colored children and to bring happiness in their lives" (301). During the economic boon period of the late 1920s, Chavers, through his contacts, was able to keep Camp Madrue financially afloat. However, the Wall Street crash of October 1929 would have a negative effect on P. W. Chavers and Camp Madrue. By June 1930, in the midst of worsening economic conditions, P.W. reluctantly accepted the fact that his vision of a "Camp for Colored Children" would not come to pass. On August 5, 1930, that realization became confirmed when the Citizens Trust and Savings Bank, which funded Chavers's land purchase in Wisconsin, closed after a run on the bank by worried depositors depleted its reserves. As Chavers-Wright noted, "with this, Daddy's equity in most of his real estate was wiped out" (355).

27. Otshaus, "Rise and Fall," 42–43. Reed, *Rise of Chicago's Black Metropolis*, 85–86.

28. Harris, *Negro as Capitalist*, xiv–xv. Travis's stated source for this information was a July 19, 1981, interview with Julian H. Lewis, Anthony Overton's son-in-law. Robert Howard, interview June 24, 2010. Howard, who has conducted research on black banks for the Chicago Black History Forum, confirmed Overton and Binga's early intent to coestablish a bank.

29. Harris, *Negro as Capitalist*, 195.

30. "The Opening of Binga State Bank: Monday, January Third, 1921, Was a History-Making Event among Colored People Residing in Chicago," *Chicago Broad Ax*, January 3, 1921, 1.

31. "A Monument to Racial Industry," *Half-Century*, November–December 1922, 3.

32. "Douglass National Bank," *Chicago Defender*, September 29, 1923, 2.

33. "Brother Anthony Overton," 23. According to this article, Overton was an honorary member of Alpha Phi Alpha through its Tau chapter (at the University of Illinois, Urbana-Champaign).

34. "Douglass National Bank." "President of Bank and Pastor in Hot Words Over Church Debt," *Chicago Defender*, April 30, 1932, 3.

35. Parks and Bradley, eds, *Alpha Phi Alpha*, 362. Reed, *Rise of Chicago's Black Metropolis*, 87.

36. Walker, *History of Black Business in America*, 182–224; Butler, *Entrepreneurship and Self-Help*, 143–226.

37. Reed, *Rise of Chicago's Black Metropolis*, 110–12.

38. "Banker Overton Talks to A.B.C.'s," *Chicago Defender*, November 24, 1923, 12.

39. Reed, *Rise of Chicago's Black Metropolis*, 111, 112.

40. Ibid., 83–84.

41. Weems, *Black Business in the Black Metropolis*, 39–40.

42. Weare, *Black Business*, 5–7; Henderson, *Atlanta Life*, 3–8.

43. Weare, *Black Business*, 12–13, 14.

44. Ibid., 29.

45. Ibid., 37–38.

46. Ibid., 32, 33. Significantly, contemporary assessments of Durham by Booker T. Washington and W. E. B. Du Bois suggest that Washington Duke indeed may have taken an interest in helping John Merrick establish an insurance company. Washington described Durham as possessing "the greatest amount of friendly feeling between the races" as well as "the sanest attitude of the white people toward the black" (Weare, *Black Business*, 38). For his part, Du Bois, was a bit more skeptical than Washington regarding the state of race relations in Durham. Nevertheless Du Bois conceded that, along with the prevalent white attitude towards blacks of "Hands off—give them a chance—don't interfere," there were some Durham whites that were "sincerely sympathetic and helpful" in terms of their attitude toward local blacks (39).

47. Weare, *Black Business*, 48, 50, 59, 63.

48. Ibid., 75, 74. By 1909, based on its steady corporate growth, North Carolina Mutual asserted on its letterhead that it was the "Greatest Negro Insurance Company in the World."

49. Henderson, *Atlanta Life*, 23, 24.

50. Ibid., 17, 19.

51. Ibid., 44–45.

52. Ibid., 46.

53. Ibid., 65–66, 79–80.

54. Ibid., 90, 83–87.

55. Weems, *Desegregating the Dollar*, 12.

56. Puth, *Supreme Life*, 14; Ingham and Feldman, *African-American Business Leaders*, 198–99.

57. "Liberty Life Insurance Company of Illinois," *Chicago Defender*, January 3, 1920, 8.

58. *Half-Century*, July 1919, 15; ibid., August 1919, 15; ibid., September 1919, 15; ibid., October 1919, 9; ibid., November 1919, 8; ibid., December 1919, 8. In the period immediately following Liberty Life's organization, this event was not included in *Half-Century's* "General Race News" section. Moreover, there were no advertisements or commentary related to the Liberty Life Insurance Company.

59. Puth, *Supreme Life*, 281.

60. Reed, *Rise of Chicago's Black Metropolis*, 94.

61. Stuart, *Economic Detour*, 94.

62. Ibid., 99, 97–98, 99.

63. Ingham and Feldman, *African-American Business Leaders*, 496; Stuart, *Economic Detour*, 94.

64. "Heralding the Victory Life," *Chicago Defender*, October 13, 1923, 3.

65. Ingham and Feldman, *African-American Business Leaders*, 496.

66. Stuart, *Economic Detour*, 94.

67. Ibid., 94–95.

68. Anthony Overton to Emmett J. Scott, letter August 5, 1915, reel 13, Booker T. Washington Papers. Floyd J. Calvin, "Calvin Has Delightful and Interesting Interview with William Anthony Overton," *Pittsburgh Courier*, March 31, 1928, A1.

69. Floyd J. Calvin, "Victory Life Justifies Faith of Anthony Overton," *Pittsburgh Courier*, March 3, 1928, 8. Stuart, *Economic Detour*, 95. Calvin, "Victory Life," 8.

70. Stuart, *Economic Detour*, 95; "Receives Virginia License," *Pittsburgh Courier*, May 21, 1927, 8.

71. Stuart, *Economic Detour*, 95.

72. "Spingarn Medal," Wikipedia, http://en.wikipedia.org/wiki/Spingarn_Medal. Cruse, *Plural but Equal*, 75.

73. Cruse, *Plural but Equal*, 76–77.

74. Ingham and Feldman, *African-American Business Leaders*, 494.

75. "Spingarn Medal 1927," box 211, series C, group 1, Records of the NAACP.

76. Ibid.

77. "Entirely Worthy," *New York Amsterdam News*, June 8, 1927, 22. "Anthony Overton Is Awarded 1927 Spingarn Medal," *St. Louis Argus*, June 10, 1927, 1.

78. "Chicago Banker Awarded Spingarn Medal," *Chicago Defender*, June 11, 1927, 1. Informed speculation suggests that the *Defender*'s "subdued" response to Overton winning the Spingarn Medal may be linked to earlier *Half-Century* editorials criticizing the demeaning personal care product advertisements published in some African American newspapers. Although Overton didn't explicitly name Robert Abbott in this regard, Abbott may have taken the *Half-Century* editorials as veiled attacks against him. "The Week's Editorial: Colored Press (From the *Chicago Bee*, June 11, 1927), "Spingarn Medal 1927," originally published as "Anthony Overton Honored," *Chicago Bee*, June 11, 1927.

79. "Chicago Banker Awarded Spingarn Medal." "'Man of People' Wins Spingarn Medal," *Pittsburgh Courier*, June 18, 1927, A1.

80. "Man of People."

81. Ibid.

82. Marian Downer, "Many Join in Ovation to Chicago 'Business Giant,' Anthony Overton," *Pittsburgh Courier*, December 25, 1926, 6.

83. U.S. Federal Census 1920, Chicago Ward 6, Cook (Chicago) Illinois, roll T625_309, p. 6B, enumeration district 315, image 742; U.S. Federal Census 1930, Chicago, Cook, Illinois, roll 422, p. 20B, enumeration district 186, image 309.0.

84. Sheila Overton-Levi to author, July 5, 2013.

85. "Sixteen Get Harmon Awards," *Chicago Defender*, January 14, 1928, 1, 3.

86. Floyd J. Calvin, "Insurance Association Heads Gather in Little Rock," *Pittsburgh Courier*, May 4, 1929, 4.

87. Stuart, *Economic Detour*, 324, 327.

88. Anthony Overton, "Anthony Overton Tells 'How to Run a National Bank,'" *Pittsburgh Courier*, September 3, 1927, 3.

89. Anthony Overton, "Overton Gives 'Inside Facts' on Douglass National Bank," *Pittsburgh Courier*, September 17, 1927, 5.

90. Anthony Overton, "'Trade with Your Own,' Urges Anthony Overton," *Pittsburgh Courier*, April 21, 1928, 2; Anthony Overton, "Two Billion Dollars in Insurance Carried on Lives of Negroes: 85% in White Companies," *Pittsburgh Courier*, April 28, 1928, A1.

91. Overton, "'Trade with Your Own.'"

92. Overton, "Two Billion Dollars."

93. Ibid.

94. Foreword, *Songs and Spirituals of Negro Composition: Also, Patriotic Songs, Songs of College Fraternities and Sororities* (Chicago: Progressive Book Company, 1928), n.p.

95. Ibid.

96. "For Hoover," *Pittsburgh Courier*, September 15, 1928, 3.

97. William Hale "Big Bill" Thompson quoted in Spear, *Black Chicago*, 187. "Colored Voters Urged to Stage Revolt at Polls," *Chicago Tribune*, November 4, 1928, 3.

98. Gosnell, *Negro Politicians*, 130–33, 137–38.

99. "Colored Voters Urged to Stage Revolt."

100. Ibid.; Gosnell, *Negro Politicians*, 133.

101. Reed, *Rise of Chicago's Black Metropolis*, 161. Gosnell, *Negro Politicians*, 107. "Colored Voters Urged to Stage Revolt."

102. *Pittsburgh Courier*, August 10, 1929, A2.

103. "The Chicago Bee Has Five Planks," *Pittsburgh Courier*, August 10, 1929, A2.

104. Kreiling, "Making of Racial Identities," 279.

105. Davis, "Negro Newspaper in Chicago," 128. Kreiling, "Making of Racial Identities," 279.

106. *Bee* editorial quoted in (no author) "A Good Neighbor Speaks," draft chapter on the national role of the Chicago black press in addressing racial and social issues, the Illinois Writers Project, folder 4, box 41, Vivian Harsh Collection.

107. Reed, *Rise of Chicago's Black Metropolis*, 98–99; "Chicago Bee Building," Chicago Landmarks, City of Chicago, http://webapps.cityofchicago.org/landmarksweb/web/landmarkdetails.htm?lanId=1268.

108. "From Clerk in His Dad's Store to the Topmost Rung of Success," *Pittsburgh Courier*, August 10, 1929, A8.

109. Ibid.

Chapter 5. What Goes Up Must Come Down

1. Stuart, *Economic Detour*, 96.

2. Emmett J. Scott quoted in Weems, *Desegregating the Dollar*, 14.

3. Baldwin, *Chicago's New Negroes*, 7.

4. Reed, *Depression Comes to the South Side*, 9.

5. "Business Men, Laboring Classes Staggered by Closing of Binga Bank," August 6, 1930, ANP wire story, folder 3, box 261, Claude A. Barnett Papers (hereafter CABP).

6. Ibid.

7. "Situation Tense in Chicago as Banks Close," August 4, 1930, ANP wire story, folder 3, box 261, CABP.

8. Osthaus, "Rise and Fall," 55.

9. "Business Men"; Reed, *Depression Comes to the South Side*, 18.

10. Reed, *Depression Comes to the South Side*, 18–19.

11. "Business Men." "To Reopen Binga Bank," *Chicago Defender*, February 14, 1931, 1.

12. Luix Virgil Overbea, "Jesse Binga Represents Vanishing Race of Self-Made Men," June 21, 1950, ANP wire story, folder 3, box 261, CABP. Harris, *The Negro as Capitalist*, 194.

13. "Jesse Binga Goes on Trial," *Chicago Defender*, July 16, 1932, 1.

14. Osthaus, "Rise and Fall," 58; "Binga Jury Disagrees," *Chicago Defender*, July 23, 1932, 1.

15. Osthaus, "Rise and Fall," 58. In his 1936 work, *The Negro as Capitalist*, Abram Harris provides the following pertinent information: "through pretended loans to the Commercial Burial Association, Henry M. Shackleford, J. Turner, J.A. Slowe, Quinlock King, N. Richardson, Fountain Thurmond, and Charles E. Worthington, Binga obtained the following amounts from the bank: $10,000; $4,700; $658; $13,000; $1,000; $9,000; $6,500; and, $8,000" (194). Also, as a November 4, 1933, article in the *Pittsburgh Courier* reveals, it is clear that Jesse Binga's lawyer, James Cashin, aggressively defended his client ("Jesse Binga Has Won Forty Continuances," 3).

16. "Binga Denied New Trial," *Chicago Defender*, March 2, 1935, 13; Overbea, "Jesse Binga,"; Osthaus, "Rise and Fall," 58. There was a discrepancy in terms of the amount of money that Jesse Binga allegedly embezzled from persons interested in investing in his proposed South Park National Bank. The *Chicago Defender*'s July 16, 1932, article states this sum as $39,000; its March 2, 1935, article gives it as $32,500. Binga was found guilty of being an embezzler, regardless of the $6,500 difference in the two published figures.

17. "Situation Tense in Chicago as Banks Close."

18. "Business Man Praises Chicago Spirit in Bank Failures," October 1, 1930, ANP wire story, folder 3, box 261, CABP.

19. Harris, *Negro as Capitalist*, 174; "Douglass Bank Closes: Chicago Southside Stunned," May 23, 1932, ANP wire story, folder 3, box 261, CABP.

20. Ingham and Feldman, *African-American Business Leaders*, 497.

21. Harris, *Negro as Capitalist*, 180.

22. Stuart, *Economic Detour*, 96.

23. Ingham and Feldman, *African-American Business Leaders*, 497.

24. Ibid. Ingham and Feldman contend that Overton used a "dummy loan," listing another individual as its recipient, to secure the $15,000 loan from Victory Life.

25. Charles A. Shaw, "Oust Victory Life Officials: Startling Charges Disclosed," *Chicago Defender*, March 19, 1932, 1, 4.

26. Ibid., 4.

27. Ibid.

28. Ibid.

29. Ibid.

30. Ibid.

31. Ibid.

32. Ibid.

33. Ibid.

34. Ibid., 1.

35. "Anthony Overton Replies to Critics," *New York Amsterdam News*, March 30, 1932, 1.

36. Ibid.

37. Ibid.

38. "The Field of Banking," p. 3, folder 2, box 261, CABP. This source insinuates that Douglass National Bank actually financed the opening of Victory Life to the tune of $150,000. It incorrectly states that Victory opened without selling stock to the public in the beginning. Merah S. Stuart's careful work on the history of black insurance companies refutes this claim. Yet, it is plausible to conclude that Overton provided $150,000 of the initial $200,000 in capitalization needed for Victory Life to commence operations.

39. Jesse Binga quoted in Osthaus, "Rise and Fall," 50.

40. "A Brief History of the Rise and Fall of Victory Life and the Birth of Victory Mutual Life Insurance Company," 1935?, folder 2, box 276, CABP.

41. "Resent Overton's Rule in Victory Life Affairs," *Pittsburgh Courier*, February 20, 1932, 4.

42. Ibid., 4, 1, 4.

43. Harris, *Negro as Capitalist*, 181; "Richard Hill Succeeds Overton as Bank President," *New York Amsterdam News*, February 10, 1932, 8.

44. "Douglass Bank Closes Doors: Chicago Southside Stunned," May 23, 1932, folder 3, box 261, CABP.

45. "Douglass National Bank Fails," *Chicago Defender*, May 28, 1932, 2.

46. Harris, *Negro as Capitalist*, 181–182.

47. "Douglass Bank Closes Doors."

48. "Federal Loan to South Side Bank Is Announced," *Chicago Defender*, April 2, 1932, 4.

49. "President of Bank and Pastor in Hot Words Over Church Debt," *Chicago Defender*, April 30, 1932, 3.

50. Ibid.

51. Ibid.

52. Ibid.

53. "Douglass Bank Closes Doors."

54. Ibid.

55. Ibid.

56. Ibid. "Douglass National Bank Fails," 2.

57. "Brief History," 3.

58. "Victory Life Stockholders of New York Hear Overton," *Chicago Defender*, April 23, 1932, 13.

59. Ibid.

60. "Anthony Overton Replies to Critics," 1.

61. "Victory Life Stockholders," 13.

62. "Why Not, Mr. Overton?" *New York Amsterdam News*, April 20, 1932, 8.

63. "Overton Defeats Opposers," *Pittsburgh Courier*, April 30, 1932, 1.

64. "Illinois Suspends Victory Life Insurance Co.," *Chicago Defender*, June 11, 1932, 1.

65. Ibid., 2.

66. "Brief History," 4.

67. "Overton Throws Victory Life into Receivership," folder 3, box 276, CABP.

68. "Probe Victory Life Report," *Chicago Defender*, December 10, 1932, 13.

69. Stuart, *Economic Detour*, 96–97.

70. Ibid., 97.

71. "Brief History," 5.

72. "Douglass Bank to Pay Depositors," *Chicago Defender*, August 26, 1933, 13.

73. Ibid.

74. "Overton Sued in Bank Crash," *Chicago Defender*, March 31, 1934, 1.

75. Ibid.

76. "Sued," *Chicago Defender*, March 31, 1934, 4.

77. "Complaint in Chancery," Victory Mutual Life Insurance Company vs. Bee Building Corporation, case 35C-6303, Circuit Court of Cook County, April 19, 1935, 3–4.

78. Ibid., 15.

79. "Motion to Dismiss Complaint," Victory Mutual Life Insurance Company vs. Bee Building Corporation, case 35C-6303, Circuit Court of Cook County, June 3, 1935, 1.

80. "Complaint in Chancery," 14.

81. "Motion to Dismiss Complaint," Victory Mutual Life Insurance Company vs. Bee Building Corporation, case 35C-6303, Circuit Court of Cook County, June 4, 1935, 1.

82. "Complaint in Chancery," appendix, exhibits D1–36.

83. "The Answer of Anthony Overton, One of the Defendants, for and on Behalf of Himself and All Other Defendants Who Have Been Properly Served and Who Desire to Join in the Defense of This Suit to the Motion of the Plaintiff for the Appointment of a Receiver," Victory Mutual Life Insurance Company vs. Bee Building

Corporation, case 35C-6303, Circuit Court of Cook County, June 11, 1935, 4; "List of Documents Requested to Be Produced by the Defendant," *Victory Mutual Life Insurance Company vs. Bee Building Corporation,* case 35C-6303, Circuit Court of Cook County, June 14, 1935, 2–3.

84. "Case Dismissal," *Victory Mutual Life Insurance Company vs. Bee Building Corporation,* case 35C-6303, Circuit Court of Cook County, March 4, 1937.

85. Walker, *History of Black Business,* 225.

Epilogue

1. "Anthony Overton." John Ingham and Lynne B. Feldman come to a similar conclusion in *African-American Business Leaders* (499).

2. R. G. Dun & Co., *Mercantile Agency Reference Book* 255 (January 1932), 555; ibid., 267 (January 1934), inside cover and 528.

3. *Reference Book of Dun & Bradstreet* 279 (January 1936), 550; ibid., 291 (January 1938), 579; ibid., 303 (January 1940), 609.

4. Ibid., 315 (January 1942), 642; ibid., 327 (January 1944), 571.

5. "Pullman Porters' Benefit at Wabash Y Set for Nov. 15–17," *Chicago Defender,* November 12, 1938, 3.

6. Green, *Selling the Race,* 19–21.

7. Deton J. Brooks Jr., "From Slave to Wealth Is Story of Overton," *Chicago Defender,* December 26, 1942, 13.

8. Ibid.

9. Ibid. At the time of this article, Overton lived with his daughter Frances and her husband, Richard Hill, at Fifty-Fourth Street and Michigan Avenue. Later, near the time of his death, Overton moved to 5202 South Wabash Avenue in an apartment across from his son, Everett, and family. Sheila Overton-Levi to author, April 26, 2014.

10. Brooks, "From Slave to Wealth."

11. Sheila Overton-Levi, interview July 7, 2010. Born in 1924, Overton-Levi provided important information about the personal side of her grandfather Anthony Overton.

12. Overton-Levi interview.

13. Ibid.

14. Ibid.

15. Ibid.

16. Grace Miller, "Negro Woman Editor Sets High Standards for Her Paper, Designed to Help Her Race," *Christian Science Monitor,* November 11, 1946. This article on Olive Diggs and the *Chicago Bee* indicates that Overton's use of female staff may have been based primarily on necessity: "for a dozen years, and until recently, it [the *Bee*'s staff] was made up entirely by girls. This was not by intention, but because qualified Negro newspaper men were hard to obtain during the depression and war." Folder 5, box 149, Claude A. Barnett Papers.

17. Deton J. Brooks Jr., "Miss Diggs Masters News Game, Becomes Editor," *Chicago Defender,* June 12, 1943, 13.

18. Ibid.

19. Ibid.

20. Ibid.

21. "To Prospective Subscribers, *Chicago Sunday Bee*," March 15, 1942, 40, folder 26, box 2, Olive Diggs Papers.

22. Ibid.

23. Hogan, *Black National News Service*, 164–65.

24. Claude A. Barnett to Anthony Overton, October 12, 1940, folder 5, box 149, Claude A. Barnett Papers.

25. Claude A. Barnett to Anthony Overton, November 18, 1942, folder 5, box 149, Claude A. Barnett Papers. Claude A. Barnett to Olive Diggs, October 5, 1946, folder 6, box 149, Claude A. Barnett Papers.

26. Unfortunately, few issues of the *Chicago Bee* have survived, as described in note 2 in the introduction. The Vivian Harsh Collection at the Carter G. Woodson Regional Library in Chicago has a microfilm collection of the *Chicago Bee* covering the period from January 3, 1943, to August 17, 1947. During this time frame, sections of the paper titled "News Around Milwaukee," "News . . . from Gary, East Chicago, Hammond, Indiana," and "News from Your 'Old Home Town'" appeared in the following issues: January 3, 1943, 22; January 2, 1944, 8, 21–22, 23; July 2, 1944, 16–17, 23; January 7, 1945, 21; July 1, 1945, 18–19, 21; January 6, 1946, 15, 16.

27. "Mrs. Eva Lewis, Daughter of Bee Publisher Dies; Ill 15 Yrs.," *Chicago Bee*, November 4, 1945, 1.

28. "Anthony Overton, Bee Publisher, Is Dead," *Chicago Bee*, July 7, 1946, 1.

29. Ibid.

30. Ibid., 5.

31. "Bee Staff Pays Tribute to 'Our A.O.,'" *Chicago Bee*, July 7, 1946, 5.

32. "Notables Attend Overton Rites," *Chicago Bee*, July 14, 1946, 1. "City Pays Tribute to Publisher," *Chicago Bee*, July 14, 1946, 1. "Text of Overton Obituary," *Chicago Bee*, July 14, 1946, 4. "Messages of Condolence Mourn Death of Bee Publisher," *Chicago Bee*, July 14, 1946, 1.

33. "Messages of Condolence," 4.

34. "Anthony Overton."

35. Ibid., 395.

36. Ibid., 395.

37. "Famed Cosmetic Dealer Dies of Heart Attack," *Chicago Defender*, January 28, 1960, A3; "Historical Sketch of Armour Institute of Technology," http://archives.iit.edu/about/news-perspectives/historical-sketch-armour-institute-technology; "Everett Overton, Head of Oldest Cosmetics Co., Dies," *Jet*, February 11, 1960, 19.

38. Within a year of Anthony Overton's death, advertising for Overton Hygienic products disappeared from the pages of the *Chicago Bee*. Overton Hygienic's absence from a special advertising section in the July 6, 1947, issue and in other parts of the newspaper indicates that Everett Overton had severed ties with the *Bee*.

39. Olive M. Diggs to Claude A. Barnett, February 28, 1947, folder 5, box 149,

Claude A. Barnett Papers. After leaving the *Chicago Bee*, Diggs entered a life of public service. In 1953, she became director of the Illinois Commission on Human Relations. Later, she served as a consultant on race relations for the National Youth Administration and worked as a Community Relations Assistant to the Chicago Land Clearance Commission. See "Olive M. Diggs: Life of Service," *Chicago Defender*, September 24, 1970, in folder 21, box 2, Olive Diggs Papers.

40. *Reference Book of Dun & Bradstreet* 351 (January 1948), 679; ibid., 411 (January 1958), 859.

41. *Scott's Blue Book Business and Service Directory, 1950–1951*, 40, 141; *Scott's Blue Book Business and Service Directory: With Inter-Racial Features* (1956), 1, 2.

42. *Scott's Blue Book* (1956), 149–78.

43. "Famed Cosmetic Dealer Dies of Heart Attack," *Chicago Daily Defender*, January 28, 1960, A3. "Anthony Overton III Heads Oldest Cosmetics Firm," *Jet*, March 17, 1960, 47.

44. Sheila Overton-Levi to author, May 27, 2014 (Anthony Overton III, now deceased, was Overton-Levi's brother). Sheila Overton-Levi to author, April 26, 2014.

45. *Reference Book of Dun & Bradstreet* 423 (January 1960), 961; ibid., 435 (January 1962), 1022; ibid., 447 (January 1964), 1018.

46. Ibid., 459 (January 1966), 1996; ibid., 483 (January 1970), 1986.

47. "Plan Dedication of New Area Schools May 28–29," *Chicago Daily Defender*, May 27, 1963, A6.

48. *Scott's Blue Book Business and Service Directory 1965: Chicago's Colored Citizens with Inter-Racial Features*, 2.

49. "Johnson Products Co.," Encyclopedia of Chicago, www.encyclopedia.chicagohistory.org/pages/2729.html; "George Johnson: Biography," HistoryMakers: The Nation's Largest African American Video Oral History Collection, www.thehistorymakers.com/biography/george-johnson-38.

50. Bundles, *On Her Own Ground*, 230.

51. "Soft Sheen Products, Inc. History," Funding Universe, www.fundinguniverse.com/company-histories/soft-sheen-products-inc-history/.

52. Weems, *Desegregating the Dollar*, 91.

53. Ibid., 92.

54. "The Overton-Hygienic Manufacturing Company," CORP/LLC-File Detail Report, https://www.ilsos.gov/corporatellc/CorporateLlcController; CORP/LLC-File Detail Report, "Impress Trading and Holding Company, Ltd.," https://www.ilsos.gov/corporatellc/CorporateLlcController.

55. Tim Samuelson, interview August 12, 2010. In 1984, Anthony Overton III expressed to Samuelson his remorse about discarding company records, which prevented the full documentation of Anthony Overton's legacy. However, Toney Overton went to his grave in 1999 without ever revealing his actual motivation for disposing of Overton Hygienic Manufacturing Company records.

56. Proposal, "Black Metropolis Historic District," submitted to the Commission

on Chicago Landmarks by the City of Chicago Department of Planning and Development, March 7, 1984, 1. See also the final note in the introduction.

57. Samuelson interview.

58. Ibid.

59. Ibid.

60. "The Dedication of the Chicago Bee Building as a Branch of the Chicago Public Library," May 4, 1996, no pagination, Research Folders Harold Lucas, interview June 16, 2012; Alf Siewers, "Bee Building at Heart of Bronzeville Rehab Talks," *Chicago Sun-Times*, February 12, 1993, 57; Lee Bey, "A Renovation for the Books: Bronzeville Bee Building Now Library," *Chicago Sun-Times*, April 28, 1996, 8 (Sunday news).

61. Mickey Ciokajlo, "Bronzeville Site Stirs Pride, Hope," *Chicago Tribune*, October 20, 2000.

62. "Award for Rehabilitation: Overton Hygienic Building," Landmarks Illinois, www.landmarks.org/preservation-programs/richard-h-driehaus-foundation-preservation-awards/2009-award-recipients/award-for-rehabilitation-2/.

63. Lisa R. Jenkins, "Business Incubator Development Plan Announced for Bronzeville," *Chicago Gazette*, June 7, 2013, http://www.gazettechicago.com/index/2013/06/business-incubator-development-plan-announced-for-bronzeville/, accessed July 13, 2019.

64. Timuel Black, interview August 6, 2010.

Selected Bibliography

Manuscript Collections

Booker T. Washington Papers, Manuscript Division, Library of Congress, Washington, DC

Claude A. Barnett Papers, Chicago History Museum Archives, Chicago, Illinois

Kansas Newspaper Collection, Kansas Historical Society, Topeka, Kansas

Mississippi Valley Room/Special Collections, Kansas City, Missouri, Public Library, Kansas City, Missouri

Oklahoma Research Center, Oklahoma Historical Society, Oklahoma City, Oklahoma

Olive Diggs Papers, DuSable Museum of African American History Archives, Chicago, Illinois

Records of the Kansas Bar Association, Kansas Historical Society, Topeka, Kansas

Records of the NAACP, Library of Congress, Washington, DC

Research Folders, Chicago Bee Branch, Chicago Public Library, Chicago, Illinois

Research Library, Louisiana State Archives, Baton Rouge, Louisiana

R. G. Dun & Co. Collection, Baker Library, Harvard University, Cambridge, Massachusetts

Topeka Room/Local History Collection, Topeka and Shawnee County Public Library, Topeka, Kansas

University Archives, Mabee Library, Washburn University, Topeka, Kansas

Vivian Harsh Collection, Carter G. Woodson Regional Library, Chicago, Illinois

Government Reports

Case 35C-6303, *Victory Mutual Life Insurance Company vs. Bee Building Corporation.* Circuit Court of Cook County, Chicago

Chronicles of Oklahoma 30 (1952)

Kansas State Census, 1885

US Federal Census 1870, Monroe, Ouachita, Louisiana
US Federal Census 1880, Topeka, Shawnee, Kansas
US Federal Census 1900, Kansas City, Jackson, Missouri
US Federal Census 1920, Chicago, Cook, Illinois
US Federal Census 1930, Chicago, Cook, Illinois

Interviews

Black, Timuel. August 6, 2010, Chicago.
Howard, Robert. June 24, 2010, Chicago.
Lucas, Harold. June 16, 2012, Chicago.
Overton, James. Phone interviews April 25, 2012, and March 16, 2019.
Overton-Levi, Sheila. July 7, 2010, Chicago.
Samuelson, Tim. August 12, 2010, Chicago.
Turner, Eunice. October 19, 2009, Kingfisher, Oklahoma.

Directories

Kansas City, Kansas, City Directory, 1895. Kansas City, MO: Hoye Directory, 1895.
Kansas City, Kansas, City Directory, 1907. Kansas City, MO: Hoye Directory Company, 1907.
Kansas City, Kansas, City Directory, 1910. Kansas City, MO: Gate City Directory, 1910.
Kansas City, Missouri, City Directory, 1897. Kansas City, MO: Hoye Directory, 1897.
Kansas State Gazetteer and Business Directory (Including a Complete Business Directory of Kansas City, Missouri). Detroit: R. L. Polk & Co., various years.
Lawrence City Directory for 1888. Lawrence, KS: P. T. Foley, 1888.
Radges' Directory for the City of Topeka for 1888–1889. Topeka, KS: Radges' City Directory, 1888.
Radges' Directory for the City of Topeka for 1890–1891. Topeka, KS: Radges' City Directory, 1890.
Radges' Directory for the City of Topeka for 1893–1894. Topeka, KS: Radges' City Directory, 1893.
Radges' Directory for the City of Topeka for 1896–1897. Topeka, KS: Radges' City Directory, 1896.
Scott's Blue Book Business and Service Directory, 1950–1951. Chicago: Vivian M. Scott, 1951.
Scott's Blue Book Business and Service Directory: With Inter-Racial Features. Chicago: Scott's Business and Directory Services, 1956.
Scott's Blue Book Business and Service Directory 1965: Chicago's Colored Citizens with Inter-Racial Features. Momence, IL: Scott's Business and Directory Services, 1965.
Simms' Blue Book and National Negro Business and Professional Directory. Chicago: James N. Simms, 1923.

Newspapers and Periodicals

Chicago Bee
Chicago Broad Ax
Chicago Defender
Chicago Sun-Times
Chicago Tribune
Dun & Bradstreet Reference Book, various issues
Half-Century Magazine
Kansas City Call
Kingfisher Free Press
Louisiana Intelligencer
The Mercantile Agency Reference Book (R. G. Dun & Co.), various issues
New York Amsterdam News
Ouachita Telegraph
Pittsburgh Courier
Reference Book of Dun & Bradstreet, Inc., various issues
R. G. Dun & Company Reference Book, various issues
St. Louis Argus
Topeka Capital-Journal
Topeka Daily Commonwealth
Weekly Kansas Herald

Other Sources

Anders, Mary A. *Resource Protection Planning Project: Settlement Patterns in the Unassigned Lands, Region 6, Oklahoma Preservation Survey.* Department of History, Oklahoma State University, 1984.

"Anthony Overton." Obituary. *Journal of Negro History* 32 (July 1947): 394–96.

"Anthony Overton: Born Entrepreneur." *Issues and Views*, spring 1997. http://www.issues-views.com/index.php/sect/1000/article/1006.

"Anthony Overton: Hygienic Manufacturing Company, 1898–1946." Great American Business Leaders of the 20th Century. Harvard Business School. www.hbs.edu/leadership/database/leaders/Anthony_Overton.html.

"Anthony Overton III Heads Oldest Cosmetics Firm." *Jet*, March 17, 1960: 47.

Armitage, Katie H. "Seeking a Home Where He Himself Is Free: African Americans Build a Community in Douglas County, Kansas." *Kansas History* 31 (fall 2008): 154–75.

Bailey, Thomas A. "The Mythmakers of American History." *Journal of American History* 55 (June 1968): 5–21.

Baldwin, Davarian L. *Chicago's New Negroes: Modernity, the Great Migration, and Black Urban Life.* Chapel Hill: University of North Carolina Press, 2007.

Best's Life Insurance Reports 1927. New York: Alfred M. Best, 1927.

Boris, Joseph J. *Who's Who in Colored America: A Biographical Dictionary of Notable Living Persons of African Descent in America 1928–1929*. New York: Who's Who in Colored America Corp., 1928.

"Brother Anthony Overton." *Sphinx* 9 (October 1923): 20–21.

Bundles, A'Lelia. *On Her Own Ground: The Life and Times of Madam C. J. Walker*. New York: Simon & Schuster, 2001.

Burrows, John H. *The Necessity of Myth: A History of the National Negro Business League*. Auburn, AL: Hickory Hills Press, 1988.

Butler, John S. *Entrepreneurship and Self-Help among Black Americans: A Reconsideration of Race and Economics*. Rev. ed. Albany: SUNY Press, 2012.

Chavers-Wright, Madrue. *The Guarantee: P. W. Chavers, Banker, Entrepreneur, Philanthropist in Chicago's Black Belt of the Twenties*. New York: Wright-Armstead Associates, 1985.

Coulter, Charles E. *"Take Up the Black Man's Burden": Kansas City's African American Communities, 1865–1939*. Columbia: University of Missouri Press, 2006.

Cox, Thomas C. *Blacks in Topeka, Kansas 1865–1915: A Social History*. Baton Rouge: Louisiana University Press, 1982.

Cruse, Harold. *Plural but Equal: A Critical Study of Blacks and Minorities and America's Plural Society*. New York: William Morrow, 1987.

Dann, Martin. "From Sodom to the Promised Land: E. P. McCabe and the Movement for Oklahoma Colonization." *Kansas Historical Quarterly* 40 (fall 1974):370–78.

Davis, Ralph N. "The Negro Newspaper in Chicago." Master's thesis, University of Chicago, 1939.

Detweiler, Frederick G. *The Negro Press in America*. Chicago: University of Chicago Press, 1922.

Du Bois, W. E. B., editor. *The Negro in Business; a report of a social study made under the direction of Atlanta university*. Atlanta, GA: [Atlanta University,] 1899.

Ershkowitz, Herbert. *John Wanamaker: Philadelphia Merchant*. Conshohocken, PA: Combined Publishing, 1999.

"Everett Overton, Head of Oldest Cosmetics Co., Dies." *Jet*, February 11, 1960, 19.

Fitzgerald, Dan, editor. *John Ritchie: Portrait of an Uncommon Man*. Topeka, KS: Shawnee County Historical Society, 1991.

Flynn, James J. *Negroes of Achievement in Modern America*. New York: Dodd, Mead, 1970.

Foner, Eric. *Reconstruction: America's Unfinished Revolution, 1863–1877*. New York: Harper & Row, 1988.

Foster, Charles Allen. "Reconstruction in Ouachita Parish, Louisiana, 1865–1877." Senior thesis, Princeton University, 1963.

Franklin, Jimmy L. *Journey toward Hope: A History of Blacks in Oklahoma*. Norman: University of Oklahoma Press, 1982.

Gatewood, Willard B. "William D. Crum: A Negro in Politics." *Journal of Negro History* 53 (October 1968):301–20.

Gosnell, Harold F. *Negro Politicians: The Rise of Negro Politics in Chicago*. Chicago: University of Chicago Press, 1969.

Green, Adam. *Selling the Race: Culture, Community, and Black Chicago, 1940–1955*. Chicago: University of Chicago Press, 2007.

Hamilton, Kenneth M., ed. *Records of the National Negro Business League, Part 1: Annual Conference Proceedings and Organizational Records, 1900–1919*. Bethesda, MD: University Publications of America, 1994.

Harlan, Louis R. *Booker T. Washington: The Making of a Black Leader, 1856–1901*. New York: Oxford University Press, 1972.

———. *Booker T. Washington: The Wizard of Tuskegee, 1901–1915*. New York: Oxford University Press, 1983.

Harris, Abram L. *The Negro as Capitalist: A Study of Banking and Business Among American Negroes*. New York: Ardent Media, 1936.

Harvey, Gordon E. *Historic Ouachita Parish: An Illustrated History*. San Antonio: Historical Publishing Network, 2007.

Henderson, Alexa B. *Atlanta Life Insurance Company: Guardian of Black Economic Dignity*. Tuscaloosa: University of Alabama Press, 1990.

History and Report of the Exhibition and Celebration to Commemorate the Fiftieth Anniversary of the Emancipation of the Negro: Held at the Coliseum, Chicago, Illinois, August 22nd to September 16th, Nineteen Hundred and Fifteen. Chicago: Fraternal Press, 1915.

Hogan, Lawrence D. *A Black National News Service: The Associated Negro Press and Claude Barnett, 1919–1945*. Rutherford, NJ: Fairleigh Dickinson University Press, 1984.

Ingham, John N., and Lynne B. Feldman, eds. *African-American Business Leaders: A Biographical Dictionary*. Westport, CT: Greenwood, 1994.

Johnson, Guy B. "Newspaper Advertisements and Negro Culture." *Journal of Social Forces* 3 (May 1925): 706–9.

Jones, Dewey R. "Chicago Claims Supremacy." *Opportunity: A Journal of Negro Life* 7 (March 1929): 92–94.

Kingfisher Panorama. Kingfisher, OK: Times Printing Co., 1957.

Kranz, Rachel. *African American Business Leaders and Entrepreneurs*. New York: Facts on File, 2004.

Kreiling, Albert L. "The Making of Racial Identities in the Black Press: A Cultural Analysis of Race Journalism in Chicago, 1878–1929." PhD diss., University of Illinois at Urbana-Champaign, 1973.

Lewis, David L. *W. E. B. Du Bois, 1868–1919: Biography of a Race*. New York: Henry Holt, 1993.

Littlefield, Daniel F., Jr., and Lonnie E. Underhill. "Black Dreams and 'Free' Homes: The Oklahoma Territory, 1891–1894." *Phylon*, fall 1973: 342–57.

McKinley, John. "Anthony Overton: A Man Who Planned for Success." *Reflexus* 1 (April 1925): 14–15, 56.

National Negro Almanac and Yearbook 1911. The Negro Almanac Co.: Kansas City, KS, 1911.

Osthaus, Carl R. "The Rise and Fall of Jesse Binga, Black Financier." *Journal of Negro History* 58 (January 1973): 39–60.

Overton, Anthony. *To the Salesmen and Others Associated with the Overton-Hygienic Manufacturing Company.* Chicago, 1916.

Painter, Nell I. *Exodusters: Black Migration to Kansas after Reconstruction.* New York: Knopf, 1977.

Parks, Gregory S., and Stefan M. Bradley, eds. *Alpha Phi Alpha: A Legacy of Greatness, the Demands of Transcendence.* Lexington: University Press of Kentucky, 2012.

Peiss, Kathy. *Hope in a Jar: The Making of America's Beauty Culture.* Philadelphia: University of Pennsylvania Press, 1998.

Phillips, Evelyn N. "Annie Malone's Poro: Addressing Whiteness and Dressing Black-Bodied Women." *Transforming Anthropology* 11, (2003):4–17.

Poro in Pictures: With a Short History of Its Development. St. Louis, MO: Poro College, 1925.

Puth, Robert C. *Supreme Life: The History of a Negro Life Insurance Company.* New York: Arno, 1976.

Reagan-Kendrick, Amber. "Ninety Years of Struggle and Success: African American History at the University of Kansas, 1870–1960." PhD diss., University of Kansas, 2004.

Reed, Christopher R. *The Depression Comes to the South Side: Protest and Politics in the Black Metropolis, 1930–1933.* Bloomington: Indiana University Press, 2011.

———. *Knocking at the Door of Opportunity: Black Migration to Chicago, 1900–1919.* Carbondale: Southern Illinois University Press, 2014.

———. *The Rise of Chicago's Black Metropolis, 1920–1929.* Urbana: University of Illinois Press, 2011.

Richmond, Robert W. *Requisite Learning and Good Moral Character: A History of the Kansas Bench and Bar.* Topeka: Kansas Bar Association, 1982.

Rooks, Noliwe M. *Ladies' Pages: African American Women's Magazines and the Culture that Made Them.* New Brunswick, NJ: Rutgers University Press, 2004.

Samuelson, Tim. "Black Metropolis Historic District." Preliminary Summary of Information Submitted to the Commission on Chicago Historical and Architectural Landmarks by the City of Chicago Department of Planning and Development. March 7, 1984.

Schick, Kathy. *Occupations of Blacks in Lawrence, 1860–1890.* Lawrence, KS: Watkins Community Museum of History Archives.

Silverman, Robert. *Doing Business in Minority Markets: Black and Korean Entrepreneurs in Chicago's Ethnic Beauty Aids Industry.* New York: Garland, 2000.

Spear, Allan H. *Black Chicago: The Making of a Negro Ghetto, 1890–1920.* Chicago: University of Chicago Press, 1967.

Stuart, Merah S. *An Economic Detour: A History of Insurance in the Lives of American Negroes.* College Park, MD: McGrath, 1969. First published 1940 by Wendel Malliet & Co. (New York).

Thornbrough, Emma L. "The National Afro-American League, 1887–1908." *The Journal of Southern History* 27 (November 1961): 494–512.

Tolson, Arthur L. "The Negro in Oklahoma Territory, 1889–1907: A Study in Racial Discrimination." PhD diss., University of Oklahoma, 1966.

Vincent, Charles. *Black Legislators in Louisiana During Reconstruction.* Baton Rouge: Louisiana State University Press, 1976.

Walker, Juliet E. K. *The History of Black Business in America: Capitalism, Race, Entrepreneurship.* New York: Twayne, 1998.

———, ed. *Encyclopedia of African American Business History.* Westport, CT: Greenwood Press, 1999. Unpaginated.

Walker, Susannah. *Style and Status: Selling Beauty to African American Women, 1920–1975.* Lexington: University Press of Kentucky, 2007.

Weare, Walter B. *Black Business in the New South: A Social History of the North Carolina Mutual Life Insurance Company.* Urbana: University of Illinois Press, 1973.

Weems, Robert E., Jr. *Desegregating the Dollar: African American Consumerism in the Twentieth Century.* New York: New York University Press, 1998.

———. *Black Business in the Black Metropolis: The Chicago Metropolitan Assurance Company, 1925–1985.* Bloomington: Indiana University Press, 1996.

Williams, E. Russ, Jr., ed. *Encyclopedia of Individuals and Founding Families of the Ouachita Valley of Louisiana from 1785 to 1850.* 2 vols. Monroe, LA: Williams Genealogical and Historical Publications, 1997.

Williamson, Frederick W., and George T. Goodman, eds. *Eastern Louisiana: A History of the Watershed of the Ouachita River and the Florida Parishes.* Vol. 1. Louisville, KY; Monroe, LA: Historical Record Association, 1939.

Index

Abbott, Mrs. Robert, 66

Abbott, Robert, 90–92, 114, 183n78

accolades for Anthony Overton, Jr. (AOJ), 102–11; Harmon Award, 107; Spingarn Medal, 1, 6–7, 102–5, 183n78

Aderhold, Wade Aaron, 96

advertising: in *Chicago Bee*, 114–15, 126, 127, 150, 154, 189n38; for Douglass National Bank, 68, 85–87; for and in Progressive Book Company, 74, 110–11; Victory Life subsidy, 126, 127; by Wanamaker, 31. See also *Half-Century Magazine*, advertising in

advertising for Overton Hygienic: in *Chicago Bee*, 150, 154, 189n38; daughters and other female employees as public face, 6, 10, 45, 53, 54; early efforts, 48; in *Half-Century Magazine*, 6, 62, 63–66; for High-Brown Face Powder, 43–44; at Lincoln Jubilee, 6, 45, 53, 54–55; in *National Negro Almanac and Yearbook*, 43–44; product demonstrations, 6, 10, 54, 55, 57; in *Scott's Blue Book Business and Service Directory*, 155, 157–58. See also Overton Hygienic Manufacturing Company

African-American Business Leaders: A Biographical Dictionary (Ingham and Feldman), 12, 24, 34, 80

African American Business Leaders and Entrepreneurs (Kranz), 21–22

African American economic power: business golden age, 90; Chavers and, 80, 81–82, 180n26; *Chicago Bee* advocates for, 148–49; Douglass National Bank and, 80–82, 83–84, 87; Du Bois and, 38–39, 39–40, 173n84; Hope and, 39; insurance companies and, 93–98; NAACP leadership split on issues, 102–3; Washington and, 5, 11, 38, 40, 46, 53. See also Great Depression, impact of

African American economic power, AOJ as advocate for: in *Chicago Bee*, 148–49; in *Half-Century Magazine*, as McAdoo Baker, 70–74, 75, 98, 108; in *Pittsburgh Courier* articles, 108–10; Republican Party and, 111–12; Spingarn medal and, 102–5; through Chicago ABC, 90–92; through Chicago NBL, 52–53, 91–92; through NNBL, 38, 41–42, 45, 46, 47–50; through NNIA, 107–8

African American fraternal organizations, 12, 89–90, 93, 132, 134

African American insurance companies, 79, 92–98, 99, 163–66; AOJ on, in *Pittsburgh Courier*, 109–10; Atlanta Life Insurance Company, 95–97, 164; Liberty Life Insurance Company, 97–98, 165, 182n58; mergers and acquisitions within, 94–95, 96; North Carolina Mutual, 93–95, 96, 163, 182n48. See also Victory Life Insurance Company

African American personal care products industry: competition within, 6, 8, 55–59, 61, 62, 156, 157–60; racially demeaning advertising, 62, 65, 66, 183n78; Turnbo-Malone and, 45, 55, 56–59, 83; Walker, Madam C. J. and, 45, 50, 55, 56–59, 83, 152, 174n15. *See also* advertising for Overton Hygienic; Overton Hygienic Manufacturing Company

African Americans, "Libranian" terminology discussions, 75–76

Afro hairstyle, 158

Afro-Sheen products, 158–59

Alpha Kappa Alpha, 53

Alpha Phi Alpha Fraternity Inc., 12, 89, 181n33

American Citizen (newspaper), 31

American Negro Exposition, 145

American Tobacco Company, 93

"Anthony Overton: A Man Who Planned for Success" (McKinley), 33, 34, 35

Anthony Overton Elementary School, 156–57

AOJ (Anthony Overton, Jr.). *See* Overton, Anthony, Jr.

Arden, Elizabeth, 54

"Are We Ashamed of Our Lineage?" (*Half-Century Magazine* editorial), 76

Associated Business Clubs (ABC), 90–92

Associated Negro Press (ANP), 8, 105, 120, 122, 137; *Chicago Bee* as member, 149–50; on Douglass National Bank, 123, 134–35

Atlanta Baptist College/Morehouse College, 39

Atlanta Benevolent Protective Association, 95

Atlanta Life Insurance Company, 95–97, 164

Atlanta Mutual Insurance Association, 95

Bailey, Thomas A., 2, 3

Baker, John Quincy Wesley, 12, 15, 16

Baker, McAdoo (AOJ pseudonym), 78, 83, 113; advocates for African American economic power, 70–74, 75, 98, 108

baking powder, 5, 36, 37, 48, 49, 115; advertising for, 64

Baldwin, Davarian, 50, 119

barbershops, 93, 95

Barnett, Claude A., 149

Barnett, Ferdinand L., 52

Barnett, William, 160

Bee Building Corporation, 141

Bentley, Charles E., 52

Bester, William S., 60

Bethesda Baptist Church, 99, 133–34, 151–52

Binga, Jesse, 53, 80, 87, 88, 90–92, 130; embezzlement trial, 122–23, 185n12, 185nn15–16; individual lending decisions by, 121; *Journal of Negro History* on, 153; politics of, 113

Binga State Bank, 80, 87–90; closing of, 120–23, 124

Black, Timuel, 162

black business ownership. *See* African American economic power

Black Chicago: The Making of a Negro Ghetto, 1890–1920 (Spear), 1

Black Metropolis Historic District, 160

Blacks in Topeka, Kansas 1865–1915 (Cox), 20

Bousfield, Midian O., 124

Bowen, J. W. E., 54

Branch, Robert L., II, 169n6

Breedlove, Hettie Martin, 57

Breedlove, Sarah (Madam C. J. Walker), 45, 50, 55, 56–59, 83, 152, 174n15

Bronzeville district, 160–62

Brown, Nathan, 70

Browne, William Washington, 93

Bundles, A'Lelia, 50, 57

Burke, Joseph, 141

Burrows, John H., 40, 47–48

Butler, John Sibley, 6, 90

Campbell, Marion M., 151

Camp Madrue, 180n26

Cantey, Inez, 123

Care Free Curl product line, 158–59

Carroll, John A., 122

Cashin, James B., 122–23, 185n15

census data: AOJ's marital status, 107; birthdate clarification, 12; children of AOJ, 36; family lineage, 12, 13–14, 15; judge myth, 24

Chavers, Pearl William (P. W.), 80–85, 129, 178n3, 179nn6–7, 180n26; Binga State Bank reopening plans and, 122; removal from Douglass National Bank presidency, 80, 84, 87; suit against Douglass National Bank, 85, 87. *See also* Douglass National Bank

Chavers-Wright, Madrue, 80–81, 84–85, 178n3, 179nn6–7, 180n26

Chicago, Illinois: African American population (Great Migration), 5, 9, 46, 47, 97, 119; African American real estate development in, 149; AOJ moves to, 5, 44, 45;

Associated Business Clubs of, 90–92; Bronzeville district, 160–62; Negro Business League of, 45, 52–53, 91–92

Chicago Bee (newspaper), 1, 79, 113–15; advertising in, 114–15, 126, 127, 150, 154, 189n38; AOJ maintains control of, through Great Depression, 8, 119, 142, 143; AOJ secretly owns, 113–14; on AOJ's receiving the Spingarn Medal, 104–5; circulation of, 150; Diggs as editor, 3, 147–50, 151, 155, 188n16; on life and death of AOJ, 150–52; moral principles of, 114, 148; Overton, Everett severs ties, 154–55, 189n38; Overton Hygienic advertised in, 150, 154, 189n38; replaces *Half-Century Magazine,* 78, 113; surviving issues of, 189n26; Victory Life advertising subsidy, 126, 127; women-only editorial staff, 10, 113, 143, 147, 188n16

Chicago Bee Building, 7, 79; Overton Hygienic moves to, 115, 138, 143; restoration and designation as municipal landmark, 9, 143, 160–62; Victory Mutual lawsuit against, 140–42. *See also* Overton Building

Chicago Broad Ax (newspaper), 54, 81–82, 88

Chicago Chamber of Commerce, 52

Chicago Clearing House Association, 123

Chicago Defender (newspaper), 46; Abbott as editor, 90–92, 114, 183n78; on AOJ's financial fall, 126–29, 135–36, 140; on AOJ's receiving the Spingarn Medal, 104, 183n78; on Binga's embezzlement trial, 122, 185n16; biographical essay on AOJ in, 12, 22, 24, 145–46; on Diggs, 147, 148; on Douglass National Bank, 84, 85, 89, 127, 133–35, 140, 145; on Great Depression, 120; *Half-Century Magazine* as competition, 91; on Lewis, 76–77; on Liberty Life, 98; on Negro Business League, 46, 52; Overton, Clara Gregg's obituary in, 50–52; on Overton, Everett, 155; on Overton Hygienic, 54–55, 74, 155; on Pullman Porters' Benefit Association, 144–45; Sengstacke as editor, 152; sensationalized stories in, 114; on Victory Life, 126, 128, 129, 135–36, 137, 145; "Who Is the Most Popular Girl in Chicago?" contest, 53, 63

Chicago Negro Business League, 45, 52–53, 91–92. *See also* National Negro Business League (NNBL)

Chicago Public Library, 161

Chicago Sun-Times, 161

Chicago Tribune, 112, 113, 161

church support and involvement: Bethesda Baptist Church, 99, 133–34, 151–52; Olivet Baptist Church, 52–53, 99

Civil War, 15–16

Clayton, Elbert G., III, 162

College, Washburn, 30

Colored Laborers' and Business Men's Industrial Convention, 38

Commission on Chicago Landmarks, 8–9, 160

Cook-Turnbo, Isabella, 56

Cook-Turnbo, Robert, 56

Coulter, Charles E., 36, 44

Cox, Thomas C., 20

Crum, William D., 42

Cruse, Harold, 102–3

Dalton Gang, 35–36

Davis Group LLC, 162

Dawkins, Pinkney W., 93

death of AOJ, 3–4, 24, 36, 80, 143, 150–54

desegregation in Chicago, 5, 46

Diggs, Olive, 1, 3, 147–50, 151, 155, 188n16; post-*Bee* career, 189–90n39; speaks at elementary school opening, 156

Doing Business in Minority Markets: Black and Korean Entrepreneurs in Chicago's Ethnic Beauty Aids Industry (Silverman), 21

Douglass, Frederick, 81, 82

Douglass National Bank, 1, 79–92; AOJ becomes president, 6, 7, 83–85, 88; AOJ on, in *Pittsburgh Courier,* 108–9; Binga State Bank and, 87–90; charter secured, 84, 85, 179n6; Chavers files suit against, 85, 87; Chavers removed from presidency, 80, 84, 87; *Chicago Defender* on, 84, 85, 89, 127, 133–35, 140, 145; D&B rating, 68; deposits and revenue, 88–89, 124; funding for, 81–83; *Half-Century Magazine* and, 68, 73, 85–87; money put into circulation, 86–87; naming, 81, 179n7, 180n26; officers of, 81; in Overton Building, 7, 79, 87, 89, 125; sons-in-law at, 78, 90, 132, 133–35

Douglass National Bank, Great Depression and, 123–30, 145, 153; ANP on, 123, 134–35; bad loans, 132–34; closing of, 7, 8, 124, 132–35; depositors reimbursed, 139–40, 142; federal aid, 123–24, 133; lawsuits, 140; Overton Building sold as asset, 138; real estate investments, 118, 124–25; Victory Life financial entanglement and, 7–8, 118, 125–26, 127–28, 129–30, 186n38; withdrawals accelerate, 124, 139–40, 142. *See also* Great Depression, impact of

Du Bois, W. E. B., 38–40, 102, 173n84, 182n46; promotes AOJ's candidacy for Spingarn Medal, 103–4; Washington feud, 38, 103, 172n82

Duke, Washington, 93–94, 95, 182n46

Dun, R. G., 144

Dun & Bradstreet ratings, 72–73; *Half-Century Magazine*, 66; Overton, Antoine, 18–20; Overton Hygienic, 5, 66–68, 115, 144, 155, 156; Victory Life, 68

Dynasty (soap opera), 161

Eagleson, W. L., 31, 32

Ebony Fashion Fair Show, 159

Ebony magazine, 159

Eckert, Joseph F., 123

Economic Detour, An (Stuart), 99

economic development and emancipation for African Americans, 82

education, 17, 52; of AOJ's family, 51, 76–77; of Diggs, 147–48

education of AOJ, 2; at University of Kansas, 22, 23–24, 26–30; at Washburn College, 22–23, 30

Ellis and Westbrooks law firm, 141

Encyclopedia of African American Business History (Walker), 24, 80

Evans, Evan A., 139

"Evolution of a Negro Merchant, The" (Baker article), 73

Exoduster movement, 4, 9, 20

family of AOJ: lineage of, 12–15, 169n6; Overton, Anthony, III (grandson), 1, 8, 143, 156–60, 167n2, 190n55; Overton, Mack Wilson (brother), 4, 13–14, 19–20, 25, 168n4; Overton, Martha Deberry (mother), 12–15, 168n3; Overton-Levi, Sheila (granddaughter), 107, 146–47; uncertain records, 12–15, 168n4, 169n6. *See also* Hill, Frances Overton (daughter); Hill, Richard, Jr. (son-in-law); Lewis, Eva Overton (daughter); Lewis, Julian H. (son-in-law); Overton, Anthony, Sr. (Antoine); Overton, Clara M. Gregg (wife); Overton, Everett (son); Overton, Mabel

(daughter); Overton Hygienic Manufacturing Company, family employed at

Fashion Fair Cosmetics Company, 159

Feldman, Lynne B., 11–12, 23–24, 34, 35, 80, 124

Fifteenth Amendment, 17

financial fall of AOJ, 142; AOJ removed from Victory Life presidency, 7, 8, 118, 129, 135–39; *Chicago Defender* on, 126–29, 135–36, 140; Douglass National Bank and Victory Life financial entanglement, 8, 118, 125–26, 127–28, 129–30, 186n38; Douglass National Bank closes, 118, 124; Shaw and Stamps investigation, 126–29, 130, 135–36. *See also* Douglass National Bank, Great Depression and; Great Depression; reputation of AOJ, financial fall harms; Victory Life Insurance Company, Great Depression and

First Stage Holdings Inc., 162

Flori Roberts Company, 159

Flynn, James J., 21, 23

Fourteenth Amendment, 17

Franklin, Jimmie Lewis, 32, 33

fraternal organizations, 12, 89–90, 93, 132, 134

frugality of AOJ, 3–4, 105, 106, 145–47

Gales, William, 60

gambling, 72, 112–13

Gardner, Ed and Betty, 158

Georgia Insurance Act (1912), 96

Gillespie, Frank, 97

Goodman, George T., 16

Gosnell, Harold F., 112, 113

Great Depression, impact of, 7–8, 115, 117, 120–42; on African American labor force, 120, 142; on Binga State Bank, 120–23, 124; on *Chicago Bee*, 8, 119, 142, 143; *Chicago Defender* on, 120; on Overton Building, 125; on Overton Hygienic, 8, 118–19, 142, 143, 144; on Victory Life, 118, 125–28, 129–32, 135–39, 140–42, 145, 153. *See also* Douglass National Bank, Great Depression and; financial fall of AOJ; Victory Life Insurance Company, Great Depression and

Great Migration, 9, 97, 119–20

Great Northern Real Estate Company, 100

Green, Adam, 145

Green, James Woods, 29–30

Green, Wendell E., 152

Gregg, Alexander, 26
Gregg, Clara. *See* Overton, Clara M. Gregg (wife)
Guarantee, The (Chavers-Wright), 80–81, 84–85, 178n3, 179nn6–7, 180n26

Half-Century Magazine, 1, 62–78; AOJ secretly owns, 62, 63, 113; Baker (AOJ pseudonym) articles in, 70–74, 75, 78, 83, 98, 108, 113; *Chicago Defender* as competition, 91; D&B rating, 66; founding of, 42, 61, 62, 63, 67; Liberty Life Insurance Company and, 98, 182n58; Lincoln Jubilee and, 63; locations of, 63, 79; Overton Building construction and, 68–69, 87, 89; replaced by *Chicago Bee,* 78, 113; sons-in-law at, 62, 76, 77–78; women on staff, 42, 62, 63; as women-oriented, 6, 42, 62, 64, 78, 176n1
Half-Century Magazine, advertising in: for Douglass National Bank, 68, 85–87; for Overton Hygienic, 6, 62, 63–66; for Progressive Book Publishers, 74; for Victory Life, 69, 99. *See also* advertising
Hall, George C., 47
Harding, Warrren G., 84
Harlan, Louis R., 42
Harmon Foundation Awards, 107
Harris, Abram, 88, 125, 132, 185n12, 185n15
Harrison, Benjamin, 31
Haynes, Beulah, 74, 111
Henderson, Alexa B., 95, 96
Henson, Matthew, 103
Herndon, Alonzo B., 95–97
High-Brown Face Powder, 48, 146, 154, 155, 159; advertising for, 43–44; product launched, 5, 37. *See also* Overton Hygienic Manufacturing Company
Hill, Frances Overton (daughter), 6, 36, 37, 53, 101; AOJ lives with, 107, 188n9; education of, 51; marries Hill, 77
Hill, Richard, Jr. (son-in-law), 101, 147; AOJ lives with, 107, 188n9; at Douglass National Bank, 78, 90, 132, 133–35; at *Half-Century Magazine,* 62, 76, 77–78; at Overton Hygienic, 90, 115; at Victory Life, 78, 100, 126, 128. *See also* Lewis, Julian H. (son-in-law)
Hoover, Herbert, 111
Hope, John, 39
How a Negro Should Conduct a Business (Overton, published anonymously), 74

Howard, C. E., 60
Hurst, John, 103
Hygienic Pet Baking Powder, 48, 64

Illinois Supreme Court, 123
Impress Trading and Holding Company, 160
Independence Bank, 158
Ingham, John N., 11–12, 23–24, 34, 35, 80, 124
Insull, Samuel, 121
insurance companies. *See* African American insurance companies

Jackson, Dan, 112, 113
Jackson, Robert R., 81
Jheri curl, 158
Johnson, Edward A., 93
Johnson, George E., 158
Johnson, John H., 155
Johnson Products Company, 158
Jordan, A. E., 60
Joseph, I. J., 100
Journal of Negro History (periodical), 12, 24, 152–54
Journey toward Hope: A History of Blacks in Oklahoma (Franklin), 33, 34
Joyner, Marjorie Stewart, 152
Just, Ernest E., 102

Kansas Bar Association, 28–29
Kansas City Call (newspaper), 36
Kelly, Edward J., 152
Kingfisher Free Press (newspaper), 34–35
Knox, George, 49–50
Kranz, Rachel, 21–22
Kreiling, Albert Lee, 78

Ladies' Pages: African American Women's Magazines and the Culture That Made Them (Rooks), 63, 78, 176n1
Lawrence, Kansas: African-American population, 24–26
Lewis, Eva Overton (daughter), 6, 36, 37, 43, 53, 147; AOJ lives with, 107; death, 150; education of, 51; feature in *Chicago Bee,* 150; marries Lewis, 77
Lewis, Julian H. (son-in-law), 147; AOJ lives with, 107; at Douglass National Bank, 90; at *Half-Century Magazine,* 62, 76–77, 78; at Overton Hygienic, 90, 115; at Victory Life, 100, 126, 127. *See also* Hill, Richard, Jr. (son-in-law)
Liberia, 75

Liberty Life Insurance Company, 97–98, 165, 182n58
"Librarians" (terminology for African Americans), 75–76
Library of Congress records, 5
life and career myths initiated by AOJ, 1–4; judge, 2, 11, 23–24, 30, 52; at NNBL convention, 47–48; Overton Hygienic location, 43; Pullman porter, 2, 22, 170n30; Renaissance man, 2, 11, 52, 151
life and career myths perpetuated by media: birthdate uncertainty, 11–12, 15; in *Chicago Bee*, 151; in Flynn, 21, 23; in Ingham and Feldman, 11–12, 23–24, 34, 35; in Kranz, 21–22; on moves to Kansas, 21–22, 23–24, 36, 170n30; on move to Oklahoma, 33–34, 35; in obituary, 12, 24, 36, 80, 152; personal life, in 1920s, 106–7; in *Pittsburgh Courier,* 115–17; in Spingarn Medal press release, 104
Lincoln College (aka Lincoln Monumental College, Washburn College), 22
Lincoln Jubilee, 6, 45, 53, 54–55, 63, 145
Locke, Alain, 103, 119
Louisiana State House of Representatives, Antoine in, 18
Lucas, Harold, 161
Lucas, J. Gray, 80
lynching, 114–15

Madam Walker's Hair Culturists' Union, 58
"Making a Business Man of the Negro" (Baker article), 71, 73
Malone, Aaron Eugene, 58–59
"man of the people," media persona of AOJ, 105–6
marketing. *See* advertising
Martin, E. T., 133–34
Mason, Bettie (Williams-Irvin pseudonym), 78
McAdoo Baker (AOJ pseudonym). *See* Baker, McAdoo (AOJ pseudonym)
McCabe, Edward Preston, 31–32
McGoorty, John J., 128
McKinley, Archibald A., 137, 138
Mercantile Agency Reference Book (Dun), 144. *See also* Dun & Bradstreet ratings
Merchants and People's Bank, 80, 179n6
mergers and acquisitions, 94–95, 96, 136
Merrick, John, 93–95, 96, 182n46
Metropolitan Life of New York, 92–93

Mid-South Planning and Development Commission, 161
Mid-South Planning Group (MSPG), 161
Miller, Edward S., 81
misinformation. *See* life and career myths
Moore, Aaron M., 93, 94
Morehouse College, 39
mortgage holdings. *See* real estate investments
Morton, Oliver P., 17
Mt. Olivet Baptist Church, 52–53, 99
"Mythmakers of American History, The" (Bailey's presidential address), 2

National Afro-American Council (NAAC), 39–40
National Association for the Advancement of Colored People (NAACP): awards Spingarn Medal to Overton, 1, 6–7, 102–5, 183n78
National Baptist Convention, 99
National Conference of Colored Men, 38
National Cyclopedia of American Biography, The, 24
National Negro Almanac and Yearbook, 43–44
National Negro Business League (NNBL), 11, 38–42, 46–50, 103; AOJ's involvement with, 4, 38, 41–42, 45, 46, 47–50; Chicago Negro Business League, 45, 52–53, 91–92; Thirteenth Annual Convention, 45, 46, 47–50
National Negro Insurance Association (NNIA), 107–8
National Urban League, 68
Negro as Capitalist, The (Harris), 88, 132
Negroes of Achievement in Modern America (Flynn), 21
Negro Politicians (Gosnell), 113
Nelson, Oscar, 120, 121
New Negroes, 119–20
New York Amsterdam News, 104, 129, 136
New York City, New York, 100–101
New York State, Victory Life licensed to operate in, 6, 79, 100–102, 104, 130–31; suspension from, 135–36
New York Times, 82
NNBL. *See* National Negro Business League (NNBL)
North Carolina Mutual Life Insurance Company, 93–95, 96, 163, 182n48

obituary of Overton, 3–4, 24, 36, 80, 143, 152–54

Oklahoma Historic Preservation Survey, 34

Oklahoma Immigration Association (OIA), 31

Oklahoma Land Rush (1889), 9, 30–35

Olivet Baptist Church, 52–53, 99

Opportunity: A Journal of Negro Life (National Urban League magazine), 68, 79–80, 179n8

Organization of American Historians, 2

Osthaus, Carl R., 121

Ouachita Parish politics, 12, 15–16, 17

Overton, Anthony, III (Toney) (grandson), 1, 8, 143, 156–60, 167n2, 190n55

Overton, Anthony, Jr.: birthdate uncertainty, 11–12, 15; death and obituary, 3–4, 24, 36, 80, 143, 150–54; marries Clara Gregg, 30–31; moves to Chicago, 5, 44, 45; moves to Kansas, 20, 36; moves to Oklahoma, 31, 32–33. *See also specific topics*

Overton, Anthony, Sr. (Antoine) (father), 4, 13–20; birthdate uncertainty, 12; business ownership, 18–20; during Civil War, 15–16; death and obituary, 20; moves to Kansas, 20, 22; in politics, 16–20; relationship with Martha, 13–15

Overton, Clara M. Gregg (wife), 5, 24, 26, 28, 34, 106; children of, 36, 37; death, 45, 46, 50–52; marries AOJ, 30–31; obituary, 50–52; at Overton Hygienic, 10, 43, 51–52

Overton, Everett (son), 6, 8, 31, 36, 37, 147; daughter Sheila, 146; death, 143, 155–56; education of, 51; lawsuits against, 140; manages Overton Hygienic, 8, 115–16, 143, 154–56; at Overton Hygienic, 8, 43, 115–16, 143, 154–56; severs ties with *Chicago Bee,* 154–55, 189n38

Overton, Henderson (uncle), 169n6

Overton, Ida (daughter-in-law), 155, 156

Overton, James (distant relative), 169n6

Overton, John (distant relative), 169n6

Overton, Mabel (daughter), 6, 36, 37, 43, 53, 131; education of, 51

Overton, Mack Wilson (brother), 4, 13–14, 19–20, 25, 168n4

Overton, Martha Deberry (mother), 12–15, 168n3

Overton Building: construction of, 68–69, 87, 89; Douglass National Bank in, 7, 79,

87, 89, 125; Great Depression and, 125; liquidation, 138; Overton Hygienic in, 7, 79, 125, 138; restoration and designation as municipal landmark, 9, 143, 160–62; Victory Life Insurance in, 7, 79, 125, 126–27. *See also Chicago Bee* Building

Overton Building Corporation, 69

Overton High-Brown Beauty College, 83

Overton House (boardinghouse), 20

Overton Hygienic Manufacturing Company, 110; baking powder production, 5, 36, 37, 48, 49, 64, 115; in *Chicago Bee* Building, 115, 138, 143; *Chicago Defender* on, 54–55, 74, 155; closing of, 1, 8, 143, 160; competition for, 6, 8, 55–59, 61, 62, 156, 157–60; Convention, 1916, 60–61; D&B rating, 5, 66–68, 115, 144, 155, 156; employs African Americans exclusively, 48; expansion of, 42–43, 100–101; flooding destroys facilities, 43; founding of, 35–37; Great Depression and, 8, 118–19, 142, 143, 144; High-Brown Face Powder, 5, 37, 43–44, 48, 146, 154, 155, 159; locations of, 43, 53–54, 68–69, 87, 115; male traveling sales corps, 60–61; in Overton Building, 7, 79, 125, 138; Peterson becomes president, 160; records destroyed, 1, 48, 155, 160, 167n2, 190n55; revenue, 66–67, 72, 89, 115, 144, 155, 156; Victory Life funds for operations, 127; women-only staffed branch, 6, 10, 45, 53, 54–55, 74, 146, 147. *See also* advertising for Overton Hygienic; African American personal care products industry

Overton Hygienic Manufacturing Company, family employed at: daughters, 6, 10, 45, 53, 54–55, 74; granddaughter, 146–47; grandson, 8, 143, 156–60, 167n2, 190n55; son, 8, 115–16, 143, 154–56; sons-in-law, 90, 115; wife, 10, 43, 51–52

Overton-Levi, Sheila (granddaughter), 107, 146–47

Palmer, Potter, 32

Pearson, William G., 93, 107

Peary, Robert, 103

Peiss, Kathy, 54

Peterson, Eugene, 160

philanthropy, 58, 59

Pittsburgh Courier, 105, 106, 108–11, 113–14, 115–17; on AOJ's financial fall, 131–32, 137

Plural but Equal: A Critical Study of Blacks and Minorities and America's Plural Society (Cruse), 102–3
political activities: of AOJ, 34–35, 111–13; of Binga, 113; of McCabe, 32; of Overton, Antoine, 16–20; Republican Party, 34–35, 111–12
Poro College, 59
Powell, C. B., 131
product demonstrations, 6, 10, 54, 55, 57. *See also* advertising
Progressive Book Company, 110–11
Progressive Book Publishers, 74–75
Prudential Insurance Company of Newark, 92–93
Public Life Insurance Company of Illinois, 97
Pullman Porters' Benefit Association, 144–45

racial solidarity philosophy. *See* African American economic power
Randolph, A. Phillip, 103
real estate investments, 7, 120–21; by Douglass National Bank, 118, 124–25; by Overton, Antoine, 18, 19; by Victory Life, 118, 125
Reconstruction, 9, 16–18, 38
Reconstruction Act (1867), 17
Reconstruction Finance Corporation (RFC), 133, 138
Reed, Christopher, 81, 90, 113, 121
Reference Book of Dun & Bradstreet, 144, 155
Reflexus magazine, 20, 22
Republican Party, 34–35, 111–12
reputation of AOJ, financial fall harms, 118, 123, 125, 130–31, 133–34, 138; rehabilitation after, 3, 8, 142, 143, 145. *See also* financial fall of AOJ
reputation of AOJ, positive, 6–7, 92, 102, 108, 124, 158
R. G. Dun & Company, 18–20. *See also* Dun & Bradstreet ratings
Richard H. Driehaus Foundation, 162
Roane, Ted, 89–90
Roane, Warren, 60
Robinson, John W., 81, 83, 88
Rooks, Noliwe, 63, 78, 176n1
Roosevelt, Theodore, 42
Royal Life Insurance Company, 97
Rozol Complexion Clarifier, 64

Rubenstein, Helena, 54
Rush, Bobby L., 161
R. W. Woodford Bank, 80

Samuelson, Tim, 160–61, 167n2
Savory, Gertrude, 131
Savory, Phillip Maxwell Hugh, 99–100, 131, 139
Scholtz, Edmund L., 57–58
Schomburg, Arthur, 103
Scott, Emmett J., 100, 119
Scott, Vivian M., 155
Scott's Blue Book Business and Service Directory, 155
Scott's Blue Book Business and Service Directory 1965: Chicago's Colored Citizens with Inter-Racial Features, 157–58
segregation: desegregation in Chicago, 5, 46
self-help philosophy. *See* African American economic power
Sengstacke, John H., 152
Shaw, Charles A., 126–29, 130, 135–36
Shepard, James E., 93
Sheridan, Phil, 17
Silverman, Robert M., 21
slavery, 17, 26; AOJ's parents in, 12, 15, 169n6
Smith, O. F., 81
Smith., Z. Erol, 115
Soft Sheen Products Inc., 158
Songs and Spirituals of Negro Composition; Also Patriotic Songs, Songs of Colleges and College Fraternities and Sororities (pamphlet containing Overton business promotion), 75, 111
Soul Train (television show), 158
South Park National Bank, 122
Spaulding, Charles Clinton, 94, 96
Spear, Allan H., 1, 46
Sphinx (Alpha Phi Alpha Fraternity publication), 12, 89–90
Spingarn Medal (NAACP), AOJ receives, 1, 6–7, 102–5, 183n78
Stamps, James E., 126–29, 130, 135–36
Stephenson, John D., 15–16
St. John, John P., 26
St. Louis Argus (newspaper), 104
stock holdings: in Atlanta Mutual, 96–97; in Douglass National Bank, purchased with Victory Life funds, 125, 127–28; in Johnson Products, 158; in Victory Life, 131

Stuart, Merah S., 99, 100, 102, 118, 125, 138–39
Supreme Liberty Life Insurance Company, 124
Swanson, John A., 113

"Take Up the Black Man's Burden": Kansas City's African American Communities, 1865–1939 (Coulter), 44
Thompson, William Hale "Big Bill," 112, 113
Tolbert, H. C., 127
Tolson, Arthur L., 34
"Trade with Your Own" (Overton article in *Pittsburgh Courier*), 108–9
Travis, Dempsey J., 87
Traylor, Melvin, 121–22
True Reformers (fraternal organization), 93
trusts, 49
Tucker, Bruce K., 60
Turnbo-Malone, Annie, 45, 55, 56–59, 83

Union Mutual Relief Association, 96
University of Chicago, 127
University of Illinois, 147–48
University of Kansas, AOJ at, 22, 23–24, 26–30

Victory Life Insurance Company, 1, 98–104, 166; AOJ's renown through association, 6–7, 92, 102–4, 108; becomes Victory Mutual, 139; D&B rating, 68; expansion of, 99–102, 131; financing of, 99–100, 186n38; in *Half-Century Magazine*, 69, 99; locations, 7, 79, 125, 126–27, 127–28; New York operations licensing, 6, 79, 100–102, 104, 130–31; in Overton Building, 7, 79, 125, 126–27; in *Pittsburgh Courier*, 108; sons-in-law at, 78, 100, 126, 127, 128. *See also* African American insurance companies
Victory Life Insurance Company, Great Depression and, 125–32, 153; AOJ removed from presidency, 7, 8, 118, 129, 135–39; AOJ's reputation suffers, 8, 118, 123, 130–31, 138; *Chicago Bee* Building lawsuit and, 140–42; in *Chicago Defender*, 126, 128, 129, 135–36, 137, 145; Douglass National Bank financial entanglement, 7–8, 118, 125–26, 127–28, 129–30, 186n38; in *Pittsburgh Courier*, 132; real estate investments, 7, 118, 125; Shaw and Stamps investigation,

126–29, 130, 135–36; structural reorganization, 138–39, 145; suspension in Illinois, 137; suspension in New York and New Jersey, 135–36. *See also* Great Depression, impact of
Vincent, Charles, 18
voting rights, 17

Walgreen, Charles R., 122
Walker, Charles J., 58
Walker, Juliet E. K., 6, 80, 90
Walker, Madam C. J. (Sarah Breedlove), 45, 50, 55, 56–59, 83, 152, 174n15
Walker, Susannah, 66
Wall Street crash (1929), 7. *See also* Great Depression, impact of
Wanamaker, John, 4, 31, 33, 70
Wanamaker settlement, 27, 31, 171n57
Washburn, Ichabod, 22
Washburn College, AOJ at, 22–23, 30
Washington, Booker T., 46, 52, 70, 82, 182n46; AOJ friendship, 4, 41–42, 43, 50, 75, 103; Du Bois feud, 38, 103, 172n82; NNBL and, 11, 38–42, 47, 50; Walker, Madam C. J. and, 50, 174n15
Watkins, S. A. T., 112
Watson, Dock, 93
Weare, Walter B., 93, 94, 95
Wells-Barnett, Ida B., 53, 66
"Who Is the Most Popular Girl in Chicago?" (*Chicago Defender* contest), 53, 63
"Who Is the Prettiest Colored Girl in the United States?" (*Half-Century Magazine* contest), 66
Who's Who in Colored America (periodical), 12
Wilkerson, John, 137, 139
Wilkins, Roy E., 21
Williams, Lacy Kirk, 99, 112, 132, 139
Williams, S. Laing, 47
Williams-Irvin, Katherine E., 63, 74, 78, 113, 176n1
Williamson, Frederick W., 16
Wilson, Arthur Jewell, 89–90
Wilson, Selina, 26
women: AOJ's progressive attitude toward, 9–10, 147; *Chicago Bee* editorial staff, 10, 113, 143, 147, 188n16; daughters of AOJ on Overton Hygienic staff, 6, 10, 45, 53, 54–55, 74; granddaughter of AOJ on Overton Hygienic staff, 146; *Half-Century*

Magazine oriented to, 6, 42, 62, 64, 78, 176n1; *Half-Century Magazine* staff, 42, 62, 63; Overton Hygienic staff, 6, 10, 45, 53, 54–55, 74, 146, 147; Washington's attitude toward, 50

women, African American beauty products, 5, 37, 44, 48, 159; racially demeaning advertising, 62, 65, 66, 183n78; Turnbo-Malone and, 45, 55, 56–59, 83; Walker, Madam C. J. and, 45, 50, 55, 56–59, 83, 152, 174n15

Wonderful Hair Grower, 56

Woolworth's (retailer), 158

World's Fair (1904, St. Louis), 57

Youngstown Steel and Tube Company, 134

Robert E. Weems Jr. is the Willard W. Garvey Distinguished Professor of Business History at Wichita State University. His books include *Business in Black and White: American Presidents and Black Entrepreneurs in the Twentieth Century* and *Building the Black Metropolis: African American Entrepreneurship in Chicago.*

The University of Illinois Press
is a founding member of the
Association of University Presses.

———————————————

Composed in 10.5/13 Adobe Minion Pro
with Univers display
by Jim Proefrock
at the University of Illinois Press
Cover designed by Jennifer Fisher
Cover images: Anthony Overton Jr., ca. 1920s.
(Courtesy of the Everett and Ida Overton
Collection); Overton Hygienic Building
drawing from Half-Century Magazine, ca. 1920s.
Manufactured by Sheridan Books, Inc.

University of Illinois Press
1325 South Oak Street
Champaign, IL 61820-6903
www.press.uillinois.edu